More GRAMMAR PLUS
A Communicative Course

More Grammar Plus

A Communicative Course

STUDENT BOOK

DAPHNE MACKEY ▪ ANITA SÖKMEN
UNIVERSITY OF WASHINGTON

Sharon Hilles, Grammar Consultant

Longman

More Grammar Plus: A Communicative Course

Copyright © 1996 by Addison Wesley Longman, Inc.
All rights reserved.
No part of this publication may be reproduced, stored in a retrieval system, or transmitted in any form or by any means, electronic, mechanical, photocopying, recording, or otherwise, without the permission of the publisher.

Addison Wesley Longman, 10 Bank Street, White Plains, N.Y. 10606

Editorial Director: Joanne Dresner
Acquisitions Editor: Allen Ascher
Development Editors: Kathy Sands-Boehmer, Françoise Leffler
Production Editor: Thea Mohr
Text Design: Marshall Henrichs
Cover Design: Curt Belshe
Text Art: Curt Belshe, Lloyd P. Birmingham, Len Shalansky, Meryl Treatner

Grateful acknowledgment is given to the following for granting permission to reproduce photos:
page 16, The Smithsonian Institution, Washington, D.C.; page 17, American Philosophical Society; page 25, top and bottom left, Laima Druskis/Jeroboam; top right, © Frank Siteman MCMLXXXI/Jeroboam; page 41, Image of Elvis used by permission, the Estate of Elvis Presley; page 43, European/FPG International; page 47, AP (Imperial Household Agency); page 87, Associated Press Photos; page 104, left, Gerard Fritz/Jeroboam; right, Rose Skytta/Jeroboam; page 155, Motorola; page 166, UPI Bettmann; page 192, left, Smugglers Notch Resort; center, Mark Richards; right, Nevada Commission on Tourism; page 206, both photos from 1000 Islands International Council, Inc.; page 207, Courtesy of David and Elizabeth Black; page 227, McDonald's Corporation; page 232, UPI Bettmann; page 252, FPG International; page 277, left, Keystone View Co./FPG International; right, David R. Frazier; page 309, © Joel Gordon

Mackey, Daphne.
  More grammar plus : student book / Daphne Mackey, Anita Sökmen;
  Sharon Hilles, grammar consultant.
    p. cm.
  Includes index.
  ISBN 0-201-87675-2
  1. English language—Textbooks for foreign speakers. 2. English
    language—Grammar—Problems, excercises, etc. I. Sökmen, Anita.
    II. Title.
  PE1128.M276   1995
  428.2'4—dc20   95-24396
                                                                   CIP

ISBN 0-201-87675-2

    4 5 6 7 8 9 10—CRS—00

To George and Caroline, Süheyl and Joseph

CONTENTS

Unit	Grammar	Context	
1	**Present and Past**	**Students**	**2**
	1 Present Continuous		2
	2 Simple Present		4
	3 Non-Continuous Verbs		9
	4 More Non-Continuous Verbs		12
	5 Simple Past		15
	6 Past Continuous		21
	7 Verb Agreement		24
	8 *Trouble Spots: Comparatives and Superlatives*		26
	9 *Prepositions*		27
	10 *Phrasal Verbs with Into*		28
2	**Present and Past Perfect**	**Turning Points**	**32**
	1 Present Perfect		32
	2 Present Perfect Continuous		36
	3 Past Perfect		40
	4 Past Perfect Continuous		45
	5 *Trouble Spots: Most, Almost, Other, Another*		49
	6 *Phrasal Verbs with On*		50
3	**Future and Future Perfect**	**My Future, Our Future**	**54**
	1 Future		54
	2 Present Tenses for the Future		59
	3 Future Continuous		62
	4 Future Perfect and Future Perfect Continuous		64
	5 Future in the Past		68
	6 *Trouble Spots: Non-Count Nouns*		71
	7 *Trouble Spots: Articles*		73
	8 *Prepositions and Phrasal Verbs*		74
4	**Modals and Related Structures: Advice, Obligation, Expectation**	**Parents and Children**	**78**
	1 Advice and Opinion		78
	2 Advice and Opinion Referring to the Past		81
	3 Obligation and Necessity		84
	4 Absence of Necessity		86
	5 Expectation		90
	6 Expectation in the Past		92
	7 *Trouble Spots: Word Choice; Articles*		96
	8 *Prepositions and Phrasal Verbs*		97

Unit	Grammar	Context	
5	**Modals and Related Structures: Suggestion, Invitation, Possibility**	**Socializing**	**102**
	1 Suggestion		102
	2 Invitation		105
	3 Possibility and Probability in the Present or Future		107
	4 Possibility and Probability in the Past		110
	5 *Trouble Spots:* Articles		114
	6 *Prepositions and Phrasal Verbs*		116
6	**Modals and Related Structures: Requests, Preference, Ability**	**Living Together**	**120**
	1 Imperatives and Requests		120
	2 Permission		123
	3 Preference		124
	4 Ability		128
	5 Unfulfulled Potential or Possibility		130
	6 Past Habit		132
	7 *Trouble Spots:* Used to versus Be / Get Used to; Articles; More Non-Count Nouns		133
	8 *Prepositions and Phrasal Verbs*		136
7	**Passives**	**Technology**	**140**
	1 Active Voice versus Passive Voice		140
	2 Forms of the Passive		142
	3 More about Passives		148
	4 Active and Passive Participial Adjectives		150
	5 *Trouble Spots:* Numerical Relationships; More Non-Count Nouns; Articles		153
	6 *Phrasal Verbs with Up*		157
8	**Review**	**Work**	**160**
	1 Review of Verb Tenses		160
	2 Review of the Passive		165
	3 Modals and Related Structures		168
	4 *Trouble Spots:* Do versus Make; Articles		177
	5 *Prepositions and Phrasal Verbs*		178

Unit	Grammar	Context	
9	**Infinitives**	**Travel**	**182**
	1 Infinitives and Gerunds		182
	2 Verb + Infinitive		184
	3 Verb + Noun Phrase + Infinitive		187
	4 Causatives and Verbs of Perception		189
	5 Infinitives as Subjects		190
	6 Forms of Infinitives		193
	7 Infinitives with *Too* or *Enough*		197
	8 *Trouble Spots: Word Choice; Articles*		198
	9 *Prepositions and Phrasal Expressions*		200
10	**Gerunds**	**Recreation**	**204**
	1 Verb + Gerund		204
	2 Verbs That Take Infinitives or Gerunds		207
	3 Verbs That Take Infinitives or Gerunds but Change in Meaning		209
	4 Gerunds as Nouns		212
	5 Modifying Gerunds		215
	6 Forms of Gerunds		216
	7 *Trouble Spots: Word Choice; Parallelism; Articles*		218
	8 *Prepositions and Phrasal Verbs*		220
11	**Adjective Clauses**	**Eating**	**224**
	1 Replacing the Subject in an Adjective Clause		224
	2 Replacing the Object in an Adjective Clause		226
	3 Replacing the Object of the Preposition in an Adjective Clause		229
	4 Possession in an Adjective Clause		231
	5 Adjective Clauses with Relative Adverbs		233
	6 Adjective Clauses That Give Additional Information		235
	7 Expressions of Quantity in Adjective Clauses		238
	8 Reductions		240
	9 *Trouble Spots: Word Choice*		242
	10 *Prepositions and Phrasal Expressions*		243

Unit	Grammar	Context	
12	**Noun Clauses and Indirect Speech**	**In the News**	**248**
	1 Noun Clauses		248
	2 *That* Noun Clauses		249
	3 *Whether / If* Noun Clauses		251
	4 *Wh-* Noun Clauses		254
	5 *-ever* Words to Introduce Clauses		258
	6 Reported Speech		261
	7 Noun Clauses with Expressions of Urgency		264
	8 *Trouble Spots: Word Choice*		267
	9 *Prepositions and Phrasal Verbs*		269
13	**Adverb Clauses and Related Connectors**	**Courtship, Marriage, and Divorce**	**274**
	1 Sequential Time		274
	2 Other Ways to Express Sequential Time		276
	3 Simultaneous Time		278
	4 Place		281
	5 Contrast		285
	6 Cause and Result		289
	7 Reduced Adverb Clauses		295
	8 *Trouble Spots: Word Choice*		297
	9 *Prepositions and Phrasal Verbs*		298
14	**Conditionals**	**Alternatives**	**302**
	1 Real Conditions		302
	2 Unreal Conditions: Present and Future		305
	3 Unreal Conditions: Past		308
	4 Conditions and Consequence Expressions		312
	5 Mixed Past and Present Conditions		315
	6 Modals in Conditional Clauses		318
	7 Reduced and Implied Conditional Clauses		321
	8 *As If / As Though*		323
	9 *Trouble Spots: Wishes and Hopes*		325
	10 *Prepositions and Phrasal Verbs*		328
Appendix A	Non-Continuous Verbs		A-1
Appendix B	Spelling Rules for Verbs		A-2
Appendix C	Irregular Verbs		A-4
Appendix D	Phrasal Verbs		A-6
Appendix E	Verbs with Gerunds or Infinitives		A-11
Appendix F	Connecting Words		A-16
Appendix G	Files		A-21
Index			I-1

More Grammar Plus
A Communicative Course

UNIT 1

Present and Past

Students

1 PRESENT CONTINUOUS

	past — now ~~~ future	
USE	Use the **present continuous** for: • an action which is happening now, is continuous, or is a temporary action • an action which is happening not at the exact moment but in the general time period	(a) Wei **is studying** hard for the TOEFL tomorrow. (b) **Are** they **preparing** for the class project? (c) Roberto **is learning** English from a native speaker this quarter. (d) I'm not **taking** classes this quarter.
FORM	Use the present tense of **be** + **present participle** of the verb. (See Appendix B for spelling rules with this tense.)	I **am studying** We **are studying** You **are studying** You **are studying** He/She **is** studying They **are studying** (e) Lucha's still **studying** French. (f) I **am doing** my homework. (g) They **are taking** a test.
	For questions, use: **be** + subject + **present participle** For negative sentences, use: **be** + negation + **present participle**	(h) **Are** you **studying**? (i) We **are** not **studying**.

TIME WORDS	right now, at this moment, at present, currently, today, these days, this month	(j) **At this moment,** he's **preparing** for the test. (k) He's **trying** to telephone his parents **today** but the lines are all busy. (l) **At present** we **are studying** the verb tenses.
	When **always** is used with this tense, it can express anger or annoyance. It goes between **be** and the **present participle**.	(m) He's **always skipping** classes! I'm tired of it.

A.

B.

C.

D.

1.1 Get in Motion: Present Continuous

Use the present continuous to describe the people in the classroom scenes above.

In picture A, the professor is sitting . . .
He is wearing . . .

UNIT 1 Present and Past

1.2 Present Continuous

Choose the verb which best fits the sentence. Put it in the present continuous.
Use each verb once.

| argue | get | study | discuss | teach | make | learn | take | put | lecture |

1. The students _____ verb tenses today.
2. The teacher _____ n't _____ like teachers in my country.
3. Why _____ n't the teacher _____ to the class?
4. Why _____ n't the students _____ notes?
5. The teacher _____ the students in groups of three.
6. The students _____ possible answers to the exercises in their groups.
7. One student _____ strongly about his answer.
8. The students _____ a lot of noise during this activity.
9. _____ they really _____ during this kind of group work?
10. At least they _____ a lot of speaking practice.

2 SIMPLE PRESENT

past   now   future

USE	Use the **simple present** to express:	
	• a present condition, habit, or custom	(a) He **goes** to school five days a week.
		(b) The teacher always **corrects** your mistakes.
		(c) Japanese elementary school children **memorize** 1,000 Chinese characters.
	• a general fact or truth, including definitions. These are sentences which are not time-bound	(d) Good elementary education **is** important.
		(e) "Elementary" **means** basic.
		(f) Two plus two **is** four.

FORM	Use the **base form** of the verb for all persons, except the third person singular (**-s / -ies** ending).	I **study** You **study** He/She **studies**	We **study** You **study** They **study**
		(g) They **study** at a good university. (h) I **go** to school every day. (i) He **goes** to school eight hours a day. (j) She **talks** to friends after class.	
	Be has a completely irregular simple present.	(k) I **am** an international student. (l) She **is** a very tough teacher. (m) They **are** hard-working students.	
	With negatives and questions, use *do* or *does*,	(n) **Do** they **go** to school in the summer? (o) **Doesn't** he **have** an 8:30 class? (p) What **do** they **think** about that course? I **don't know**.	
	except with the verb *be*.	(q) **Are** you in English 101 this quarter?	
	Use the third person singular verb with *who, what,* or *which* as subjects in questions.	(r) Who **makes** the decision about classes? (s) What **influences** their choices? (t) Which **is** the best choice?	

TIME WORDS	**Adverbs of Frequency**
	0%- 100%
	never *seldom,* *once a* *occasionally* *often,* *usually* *always,*
	         rarely *week /* *sometimes* *every*
	                   day / year *time*		

	We usually place these adverbs before the verb: *never, rarely, seldom, occasionally, usually, often, always.* The adverb follows *be* or an auxiliary verb. The longer adverbs may also go in initial or final position. If a sentence or clause begins with a negative adverb such as *rarely, seldom,* or *never,* change the word order to **verb + subject**. This emphasizes the negative word.	(u) He **never asks** questions in class because he is shy. (v) I **rarely see** him in class. (w) She **is** *rarely* late. (x) I **don't** *usually* say very much in class. (y) *Sometimes* we **study** together. (z) They **study** together *once a week*. (aa) *Rarely* **do I see** him in class. (bb) *Seldom* **does she** ask me a question.	

UNIT 1 Present and Past

2.1 Get in Motion: Tense Contract

Look at the drawings. How are these scenes similar or different from university classes in your country?

In picture A, the professor is wearing . . .
This is different from classes in . . .
In (country), professors never / usually . . .

A.

B.    C.    D.

2.2 Adverbs of Frequency

A. Read these statements about class behavior. Say what is true in your country. Use adverbs of frequency: *always, often, sometimes, occasionally, usually, all the time, once a day / week / year, rarely, seldom, never.*

EXAMPLE
Teachers correct students' mistakes.
Teachers usually correct students' mistakes.

1. Teachers lecture and students take notes.
2. Students take part in teaching by giving ideas and answers, and by making presentations.
3. Students work on projects in small groups or in pairs.
4. The teacher asks students to read aloud in class.
5. Students memorize a lot of information and have big tests at the end of the year, rather than unit tests.
6. If students have problems, they go to the teacher's office for help.
7. If students have problems, they go to the teacher's home for help.
8. If students make a mistake in class, the teacher corrects them.
9. Teachers assign a lot of homework.
10. Students who do not do their homework receive punishments.
11. Students disagree with the teacher.
12. Students express their disagreement with the teacher.

B. If you have used *never, seldom,* or *rarely* in any of the sentences above, try putting them in initial position for emphasis. Don't forget to invert the word order.

EXAMPLE
Seldom do students work on projects in small groups or in pairs.

2.3 Tense Contrast

Complete the sentence with the correct form of the verb in parentheses. Use the simple present or the present continuous. Circle the time clues.

1. School children in China _____ (have) 45 hours a week of Chinese language, math, and a foreign language. Pei Ling _____ (study) English this year.

2. Schools in Russia usually _____ (offer) English, German, French, and Spanish as foreign languages in 5th–10th grades. Vadim _____ (take) French now.

3. Currently Maria _____ (study) home economics and Jose _____ (get) manual training in their secondary schools in Mexico City.

4. Secondary school students in the People's Republic of China _____ (attend) classes for 29 hours a week. They also _____ (have) work training as part of their program.

5. Saudi children _____ (spend) 66 periods each week in religious studies and 57 in Arabic studies. Right now Mahmoud _____ (work) on his Arabic homework.

6. After middle school many Mexican students _____ (choose) general studies, vocational and technical training, or teacher education. For example, at present Francisca _____ (train) to be a secondary school teacher.

7. Keiko _____ (be) a first-year high school student in Japan. At this time, she _____ (attend) a *juku* or private class after school to prepare for exams.

8. How much homework _____ teachers usually _____ (assign) in your country? Our teacher _____ (give) us too much grammar homework this quarter.

9. In some cultures, the schools _____ (not, allow) students to disagree with the teachers in class. At this moment, Lisa _____ (argue) with the teacher about her answer on an exam.

10. Ali _____ (not, have) his homework to hand in today. Now the teacher _____ (punish) him in front of the other students.

UNIT 1 Present and Past

2.4 Editing Practice

Correct the error in each sentence. There is only one error in each sentence.

1. In the United States, teachers not always tell you when you need to come in for extra help. This is a student's responsibility.
2. Sometimes teachers ask me about my personal life and makes me uncomfortable.
3. In my country, teachers address me as Mr. Kim, but here they are call me by my first name.
4. In American schools teachers are often dividing students into small groups to solve problems or do projects.
5. What does happen to students who do not do their homework?
6. We do only speak if the teacher calls on us.
7. When students are coming to class late, they apologize to the teacher before they enter the class, but in the United States, they just quietly take a seat.
8. There are usually 60 students in a class, so the teacher rarely get to know them as individuals.
9. We think the teachers are always having the right answers.
10. In your country, does a teacher spends time with students outside of school time?

2.5 Making Questions and Negatives

A. With a partner, make questions with the words in parentheses.

EXAMPLE

I'm trying to register for an economics course. (What course)
What course are you trying to register for?

1. We're not offering Urban Economics this term. (Why)
2. People always take 201 after they take 200. (When)
3. I need that course to graduate. (Why)
4. This term Professor Miller is away. (Who)
5. That course usually meets off campus. (Where)
6. The term lasts for ten weeks. (How long)
7. They don't offer Industrial Organization and Price Analysis in the fall. (Why)
8. The department chairperson makes that decision. (Who)

```
ECON 200  Intro to Microeconomics
ECON 201  Intro to Macroeconomics
ECON 311  Intro to Economic
          Statistics
ECON 316  Urban Economics
ECON 404  Industrial Organization
          and Price Analysis
```

B. Make the following sentences negative.

EXAMPLE

We're offering that course this term.
We're not offering that course this term.

1. You need to get the instructor's permission.
2. That's a graduate level course.
3. I have to get into that course.
4. We're offering it next quarter.
5. Are you registering for that course?

6. They always offer Introduction to Microeconomics.
7. It's always possible to take the course in the fall.
8. He's planning to graduate in the spring.

2.6 Optional Writing

Write a two- or three-paragraph composition answering one of these questions. Use adverbs of frequency when appropriate.

1. From your experience, how are teachers and teaching styles different in different cultures?
2. Describe the educational system in your country. For example, at what age do children begin school? How many years are they in elementary school?

3 NON-CONTINUOUS VERBS

Non-continuous verbs are verbs that state perceptions, conditions / possession, and attitudes. Since they are **not actions**, we cannot use them in continuous tenses.*

Verbs of Perception or Physical Sensation	(a) I **notice** you don't stand when the teacher comes into the classroom. (b) He **sees** the need to study. (c) That **sounds** like a good class to take. (d) That is a strange sensation. It **feels** like I'm falling down, but I'm not!
Verbs of Mental Perception	(e) I **feel** it's time to stop talking. (f) I **don't know** the answer. (g) "Disruptive behavior" **means** actions which disturb others. (h) I **understand** you now. (i) She **seems** OK to me.
Verbs of Condition or Possession	(j) He **is** a university student. (k) It **costs** a lot to study abroad. (l) I **have** some homework for you.
Verbs of Attitudes and Emotions	(m) I **agree** with the research. (n) I **doubt** the results of their study. (o) We **hope** the school is a good one. (p) **Do** girls **need** more attention from the teacher? (q) They **want** to go away for a weekend. (r) They **like** their school a lot.

*Many of these verbs have other meanings that indicate actions. See Box 4 and Appendix A for more non-continuous verbs and exceptions to the rules.

3.1 Get in Motion: Tense Contrast

Complete the sentences with the correct form of the verb in parentheses. Use the simple present or the present continuous. Circle the time clues.

(1) Frank Thomas _____ (be) the principal at a high school. (2) Today he _____ (observe) a science class. (3) He _____ (look) at the class very carefully today because he just finished reading a report on "gender inequity" in education. (4) Gender inequity _____ (mean) treating boys differently from girls in classrooms. (5) Researchers _____ (agree) that teachers spend more time helping boys in class than girls and they _____ (feel) it is time for a change. (6) Today Frank Thomas _____ (see) that the research _____ (be) true. (7) He _____ (notice) that the boys in the class _____ (be) very active, but the teacher _____ (ignore) their behavior. (8) On the other hand, she _____ (want) the girls to behave. (9) During his observation, Frank can see that the girls _____ (listen) and _____ (watch) much more than the boys. (10) Frank _____ (observe) that the boys _____ (feel) that they need to be actively involved in the project. (11) They _____ (want) a hands-on experience to understand how this principle of science works.

3.2 Tense Contrast

Complete the sentences with the correct form of the verb in parentheses. Use the simple present or the present continuous. Remember: If it is a non-continuous verb, you must use the simple present. Circle the time clues.

1. It _____ (appear) that public schools in the United States _____ currently _____ (spend) more money on male sports than on female sports.

2. In general, when students _____ (need) help, teachers _____ (give) girls answers but _____ (make) boys find the answers.

3. The observer _____ (see) that the teacher _____ (now, ask) a boy to do a more difficult and abstract question than the girls in this class.

4. The teacher _____ (know) girls _____ (need) the same amount of help as boys. Therefore, she always _____ (try) to make as much eye contact with girls as with boys in her class.

5. The teacher _____ (see) all of the children each day. She _____ (know) that Sally _____ (have) amazing math skills.

6. He usually _____ (try) to be equitable but it is clear that he _____ (want) the girls to be quieter than the boys.

7. Researchers _____ (notice) that teachers always _____ (call on) boys to do the more complex math problems.

8. Making classrooms gender equitable _____ (sound) easy. But it _____ (mean) changing social customs.

9. It _____ (cost) a lot for the university to provide equal money for women's sports.

10. Reactions to the report _____ (be) different. In general, people _____ (hope) schools will offer a more equal education to both sexes, but they _____ (doubt) that change will happen overnight.

11. Some _____ (argue) that boys usually _____ (not, have) male teachers as role models in elementary school. In addition, female teachers _____ (not, understand) a boy's energy level or the pressures on boys to compete.

12. _____ you _____ (feel) that girls belong at home rather than at school? _____ they usually _____ (learn) all they _____ (need) from their mothers?

13. The Smiths _____ (consider) putting their daughter Susan in an all-girl school because they _____ (feel) boys get more attention in a co-ed class. Susan _____ (want) to stay in a co-ed class.

14. They _____ (study) a lot every day. They _____ (understand) the importance of a college degree.

(Continued on the next page)

UNIT 1 Present and Past 11

15. She usually _____ (do) well in math. She always _____ (have) good grades.

16. Her parents _____ (not, want) her to study abroad. They _____ (feel) she will change too much.

4 MORE NON-CONTINUOUS VERBS

Verbs of Perception or Physical Sensation	(a) I **hear** they are putting her in a girls' school. (b) You **smell** wonderful. What is that perfume? (c) It **tastes** good to me.
Verbs of Mental Perception	(d) What **do** you **think**? (e) **Do** you **believe** the report? (f) I **find** it hard to believe. (g) This report **proves** it. (h) **Do** you **suppose** it is true? (i) I **remember** when it happened.
Verbs of Condition or Possession	(j) It **doesn't** really **matter**. (k) **Does** it **belong** to you? (l) They **require** 580 on the TOEFL now. (m) The report **includes** a lot of statistics.
Verbs of Attitudes and Emotions	(n) It **appears** to be correct. (o) I just **don't trust** him.

See Box 3 and Appendix A for more non-continuous verbs and their exceptions.

4.1 Get in Motion: Present or Present Continuous

Complete the sentences with the correct form of the verb in parentheses. Use the simple present or the present continuous.

(1) It's 10 a.m. An older visitor _____ (walk) down the hall in the high school.

(2) Something _____ (smell) wonderful, but he _____ (not, know) what the smell could be — garlic? onions? in a high school?

(3) He _____ (look) in the doorway of the classroom.

(4) It _____ (appear) to be a cooking class.

UNIT 1 Students

(5) He _____ (ask) himself, "What _____ (be) the name of this class? (6) I _____ (forget). (7) It's that class that girls always _____ (take). (8) They _____ (learn) about how to take care of the house, I _____ (think). (9) Oh — I _____ (remember)! (10) Home economics is the name of the class, but this class _____ (include) boys. (11) I _____ (find) it hard to believe that boys _____ (study) home economics! (12) Well, I _____ (suppose) boys _____ (need) to learn to cook more now than when I was a boy. (13) I wonder if high schools _____ (require) this class for boys and girls. I'm glad I'm not in the class. 10 a.m. is a little early for me. (14) I _____ (not, want) to eat garlic and onions this early in the morning!"

4.2 Listening: A Tough Decision

A. Match the words and their opposites.

_____ 1. intelligent   a. wrong

_____ 2. private   b. stupid

_____ 3. co-educational   c. public

_____ 4. pretend   d. all one sex

_____ 5. correct   e. not play a role

B. Sally's parents are discussing her performance in school. Listen and circle the <u>subject</u> of each sentence:

1. The father   _____ (consider) sending Sally to a girls' school.
   The mother

2. The teacher   _____ (not, believe) Sally _____
   The mother   (work) hard in her class.

3. Sally   _____ (want) boys to like her.
   The teacher

4. The mother   _____ (pretend) she _____
   Sally   (not, know) the answers.

5. Sally   _____ (observe) class when she _____
   The mother   (help) the teacher.

(Continued on the next page)

6. Sally _____ (hear) the wrong answer.
   The teacher

7. The mother _____ (give) Sally a lower grade.
   The teacher

8. The mother _____ (believe) it's important for Sally to go to a
   The father   good university.

9. The mother _____ (not, think) it's important for Sally to go to a
   The father   good university.

C. Now go back and write the correct form of the verb. Is it active or non-continuous?

4.3 Talk It Over and Optional Writing

A. What's your opinion? Make affirmative or negative sentences. Discuss them with your classmates.

1. Girls _____ (need) an education as much as boys do.

2. Girls _____ (try) to please their teachers by being quiet, helpful, and working hard.

3. Teachers _____ (require) boys to do more difficult and abstract problems than the girls.

4. Teachers _____ (allow) boys to be more disruptive in class than girls.

5. It _____ (matter) if more money is spent on sports for boys than for girls.

6. Girls _____ (learn) just as well in co-educational classes as they do in all-girls classes.

7. Girls _____ (get) a better education in a girls' school.

8. Young girls and boys _____ (have) the same opportunities in co-educational classes. Teenage boys and girls _____ (need) different classes.

B. Choose one of these topics and write your opinion about it.

1. Do you feel teachers or schools treat girls differently than boys?
2. Do you think it is better to go to a co-ed school or a same-sex school?
3. Are there some classes where expectations of boys and girls should be different?
4. Should schools spend as much money on girls' sports as on boys' sports?

5 SIMPLE PAST

past — now — future

USE	We use the **simple past** for: • an action that was finished in the past • a repeated action or one that lasted a long time	(a) I **graduated** from college last year. (b) **Did** you **find** a job? (c) **Did** you **visit** your grandmother each week? (d) I **studied** at a large university.
FORM	Regular verbs: add *-(e)d* (For irregular verbs and spelling rules, see Appendix B.) *Be* has two forms in the simple past: *was* (singular) and *were* (plural).	I **studied** We **studied** You **studied** You **studied** He/She **studied** They **studied** (e) We **walked** and then **biked** for four hours. (f) I **ran** to the phone, but it **stopped** ringing before I **got** to it. (g) She **spoke** to him yesterday. (h) They **were** there yesterday, but I **wasn't**.
	Use *did* in questions and negatives. When *who* or *what* is the subject of the question, do not use *did*.	(i) **Did** you **read** about the accident? (j) No, I **didn't**. (k) **Who called**? (l) **What happened**?
TIME WORDS	yesterday, last night/week/month/year, in . . . , . . . ago, from . . . to . . .	(m) We **saw** them *last week*. (n) **Did** you **live** there *in the 1980s*? (o) I **finished** my degree *two years ago*. (p) My dad **was** a soldier *from 1942 to 1945*.

5.1 Get in Motion: Interview

Follow these steps to interview a classmate.

1. Draw a time line on a piece of paper. At one end, write the date of your birth. At the other end, write today's date.
2. Choose five important events in your life and write them on the time line.
3. Talk with a partner about the events on your time lines. Were these events turning points in your life?
4. Tell the class one or two things you learned about your partner.

5.2 Pronunciation of Past Tense Endings

A. The regular past tense ends in *-ed*, but the ending has three different sounds: / t /, / d /, and / id /, depending on the sound of the letter before the ending. Listen and put a check under which past tense sounds you hear.

Thomas Edison with his favorite invention, the phonograph

Thomas Edison, a famous American inventor, was born in Ohio in 1847.

/ t / / d / / id /

___ ___ ___ 1. Surprisingly, he only <u>attended</u> school for three months at the age of seven.

___ ___ ___ 2. His mother <u>tutored</u> him and he <u>educated</u> himself by reading.

___ ___ ___ 3. In 1859, as a 12-year-old, he <u>worked</u> on the railroad as a train-boy.

___ ___ ___ 4. He used his money to buy books because he <u>loved</u> to learn.

___ ___ ___ 5. He also <u>needed</u> money for items for a chemistry lab.

___ ___ ___ 6. At that time, he <u>learned</u> telegraph code from a station manager.

___ ___ ___ 7. By the age of 15, he <u>managed</u> a telegraph office.

___ ___ ___ 8. Because of his experience, he <u>invented</u> the transmitter and receiver for the automatic telegraph.

___ ___ ___ 9. He <u>produced</u> his first major invention when he was 21: a stock printer.

___ ___ ___ 10. Because he <u>received</u> $40,000 for this invention, he <u>established</u> his first manufacturing shop and laboratory.

___ ___ ___ 11. In 1877 he <u>invented</u> the phonograph.

___ ___ ___ 12. The next year he <u>developed</u> the electric light bulb.

___ ___ ___ 13. In 1882 he <u>installed</u> the first large central power station in New York City.

___ ___ ___ 14. Based on his success, he <u>founded</u> Edison Electric Company, which later became the General Electric company.

___ ___ ___ 15. The maker of over 1,000 inventions, he <u>died</u> in 1931.

16   UNIT 1 *Students*

B. What sounds do these past endings follow?

/ t / _____

/ d / _____

/ id / _____

C. The following chart provides information about four famous historical figures. Some of the information is missing. Work with a partner to find out the missing information about these people. Make questions using the cues on the left. Partner 1, look at this page. Partner 2, look at File 1 in Appendix G.

EXAMPLE
Who was Caruso?   *When did he live?*
He was an opera singer. *He lived in the . . . century.*

Cue Words	Enrico Caruso	Auguste Rodin	Sir Isaac Newton	Sir Winston Churchill
who / be	opera singer		scientist	
when / live		19th century	17th century	
where / work	Italy		England	England
what problem / experience / in school	"had no voice" (his teacher)	failed to get into art school three times		hated school; failed the 6th grade

5.3 Listening: Benjamin Franklin

A. Practice the pronunciation of these words.

candlemaking	printer	retired
scientist	lightning	electricity
slavery	Philadelphia	Revolutionary War

Benjamin Franklin

UNIT 1 Present and Past

B. The dates below were important for Benjamin Franklin. Listen and write the events that happened at these times.

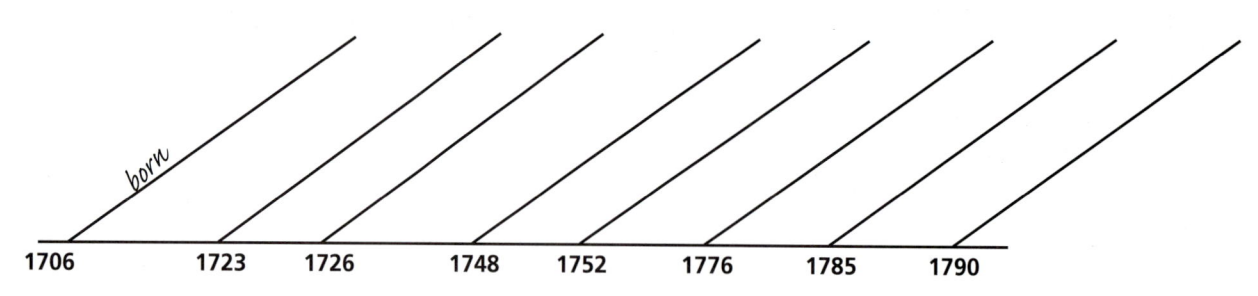

```
        born
     /      /      /      /      /      /      /      /
  1706   1723   1726   1748   1752   1776   1785   1790
```

C. Ask each other questions about Benjamin Franklin's life to check your answers.

What happened in . . . ?
When did / was . . . ?

5.4 Simple Past

Complete the sentence with the correct form of the verb in parentheses.

1. Benjamin Franklin _____ (live) in the American colony of Pennsylvania in the early 1700s.

2. He _____ (become) famous as a printer, writer, philosopher, scientist, inventor, public servant, and diplomat.

3. Surprisingly, his formal education _____ (last) less than two years.

4. He _____ (like) to read and _____ (educate) himself while he _____ (work) in a printing shop. However, he _____ (be) a terrible speller and poor at math.

5. He _____ (remain) a printer for many years. He also _____ (operate) a bookshop and _____ (own) a newspaper.

6. In 1740 he _____ (invent) the Franklin Stove, an alternative to a fireplace.

7. Twelve years later he successfully _____ (show) the relationship between lightning and electricity.

8. He also _____ (design) ships, _____ (track) storms, and _____ (create) bifocal glasses.

9. Along with his scientific career, he _____ (serve) for 40 years in public life.

10. At age 70, he _____ (join) the revolutionary movement to fight against British rule.

5.5 Optional Writing

Write about a famous person's life or someone who you admire in your own life.

5.6 Tense Contrast

With a partner, give the correct form of the verb in parentheses. Use the simple present or the simple past tense. Then guess who the famous person in history is. Answers are in File 2 in Appendix G. Considering his success in life, each man has some surprising news about his student life.

A. Many people (1) _____ (feel) this man is the greatest Russian novelist of all time. He (2) _____ (be) born in 1828 and nine years later (3) _____ (become) an orphan. Two aunts (4) _____ (raise) him. He eventually (5) _____ (go) to a university, but he (6) _____ (flunk) out and (7) _____ (join) the military. His teachers said he (8) _____ (be) "both unable and unwilling to learn." Many of his works (9) _____ (show) the influence of his childhood and his years in the military. He (10) _____ (write) *War and Peace,* a novel about several families during the Napoleonic Wars. It (11) _____ (show) his strong dislike of wars.

His name is _____

B. This scientist (1) _____ (be) born in 1822 in France.

He (2) _____ (discover) the relationship between germs and diseases.

This discovery (3) _____ (result) in the creation of the field of microbiology.

The milk we (4) _____ (drink) today (5) _____ (carry) his name. How (6) _____ (do) this famous chemist do in school?

He (7) _____ (not, do) well as a university student. In fact, his chemistry grades (8) _____ (put) him 15th in a class of 22!

His name is _____.

(Continued on the next page)

UNIT 1 *Present and Past* 19

C. Most history books (1) _____ (call) this man the greatest military leader in history. As commander of the French revolutionary armies, he (2) _____ (control) most of Europe in the late 18th and early 19th centuries. However, this successful military leader (3) _____ (graduate) 42 out of 58 in his military class! In 1804 he (4) _____ (make) himself Emperor of France. Eventually he (5) _____ (give) up his throne and (6) _____ (live) as an exile on an island off the west coast of Africa.

His name is _____.

D. This man (1) _____ (be) born in the late 18th century in Germany and (2) _____ (live) most of his life in Vienna. We (3) _____ (look) to him as one of the greatest musical composers of classical music. But his music teacher (4) _____ (believe) he was a hopeless composer. He (5) _____ (write) many symphonies, such as his famous Ninth. The last half of his life he (6) _____ (suffer) greatly from deafness and the loss of his nephew.

His name is _____.

E. This German-American scientist (1) _____ (make) the greatest contributions to physics in the 20th century. He (2) _____ (develop) the theory of relativity. His failures as a student (3) _____ (be) very surprising to us today. He (4) _____ (hate) school and (5) _____ (fail) math. One teacher (6) _____ (describe) him as "mentally slow." One school even (7) _____ (expel) him! He (8) _____ (die) in 1955.

His name is _____.

20   UNIT 1 *Students*

6 PAST CONTINUOUS

```
  past      now      future
~~~~~~~~|~~~~~~~~~|~~~~~~~~~~
```

USE	Use the **past continuous** for: • an action which was continuous at a specific time in the past • an action in the past which was interrupted by another action or which took place at the same time as another action	(a) I **was preparing** for the college entrance exams that summer. (b) When my roommate came home from the party, I **was** still **studying.** (c) I **was studying** while my roommate **was watching** TV.
	The past continuous may not be used with non-continuous verbs. *(See Appendix A for a list of non-continuous verbs.)*	(d) It **seemed** like a good idea at the time. (e) The book **belonged** to my friend.
FORM	Use *was / were* + **present participle** of the verb	I **was** studying We **were** studying You **were** studying You **were** studying He/She **was** studying They **were** studying (f) I **was studying** at the university at that time.
	For questions, use: *was / were* + subject + **present participle** For negative sentences, use: *was / were* + negation (+ **present participle**)	(g) **Were** you **going** to high school when Elvis was popular? (h) No, I **wasn't.** (i) I **wasn't** even **going** to grade school then!
TIME WORDS	*while, as*	(j) **While** Prince Charles **was speaking**, a man tried to shoot him. (k) **As** I **was waiting** for the bus, I met a very interesting person.

UNIT 1 *Present and Past*

A hurricane or typhoon    *A tornado*

An earthquake    *A flood*    *A volcanic eruption*

6.1 Get in Motion: Interview

Interview a classmate.

Were you ever . . .   in an accident?
　　　　　　　　　　in a hurricane or a typhoon?
　　　　　　　　　　in a tornado?
　　　　　　　　　　in an earthquake?
　　　　　　　　　　in a flood?
　　　　　　　　　　near a volcanic eruption?

What were you doing when it happened? What was happening around you?

6.2 Past Continuous: Pair Work

Famous people are often the targets of attacks or personal intrusions. Work with a partner to find out the missing information about these incidents. Partner 1, look at the example on this page and at the chart on the facing page. Partner 2, look at File 3 in Appendix G.

EXAMPLE
What was President Kennedy doing when . . . ?
He was . . . when someone . . .

22   UNIT 1 Students

Who	Where	What	What
President Kennedy	Dallas	?	shoot
Monica Seles	?	play / a tennis tournament	stab
Queen Elizabeth	?	sleep	break into her room
John Lennon	New York	?	?
Prince Charles	New Zealand	give / a speech	spray / deodorant at him

6.3 Past Continuous and Simple Past

Complete the sentence with the correct form of the verb in parentheses. Use the past continuous or the simple past.

1. While John F. Kennedy _____ (attend) Harvard University, he _____ (write) his first book, *Why England Slept*.

2. During World War II, John F. Kennedy _____ (command) a patrol boat that was hit. He _____ (rescue) many of the men while the boat _____ (sink).

3. When Queen Elizabeth _____ (be) a child, she _____ (not, attend) school. Her father and grandmother _____ (teach) her to become a queen.

4. As long as Monica Seles _____ (compete) in tennis tournaments, her attacker _____ (be) unhappy. He _____ (want) Steffi Graf to be the number one female tennis player.

5. While Charles _____ (study) at Cambridge, he _____ (receive) the title of Prince of Wales.

6. Prince Charles _____ (receive) his education outside of the royal palace. He _____ (be) the first British royal to do this.

7 VERB AGREEMENT

Subjects and verbs must agree in number.

Use a singular noun and the third person singular verb form with **each** and **every**.	(a) **Each** student **studies** hard in this class. (b) **Every** student **deserves** a good education.
Use a plural noun but the third person singular verb form with **each of the** and **none of the**. Pronouns following these words will be singular also. (Note: In informal speaking and writing, a plural verb is often used after *none of the* + a plural noun.)	(c) **Each of the** students **has** an opportunity to learn. (d) **None of the** students **feels** very confident about **his** or **her** English, but this will change.
Use the third person singular verb form with **the number of,** but the plural verb form with **a number of**. **A number of** means "quite a few."	(e) **The number of** immigrants **has increased** dramatically. (subject = *the number*) (f) **A number of** immigrants **have moved** into that school district. (subject = *immigrants*)

7.1 Practice with Verb Agreement

Underline the best choice to complete each sentence.

1. Every teacher (hope / hopes) each (children / child) will succeed.
2. The number of ESL programs (has increased / have increased) rapidly in the past ten years.
3. None of the newly arrived students (have studied / has studied) English before. It makes it hard to start school.
4. (Each of / None of) the students failed. Everyone passed the class.
5. Each of the boys (is / are) responsible for (his / their) own work.
6. A number of problems (has / have) come up because of the number of foreign-language speakers in the class.
7. Every teacher (faces / face) challenges in teaching diverse groups of students.
8. The number of bilingual teachers (is / are) growing.

7.2 Speaking Practice

School administrators are looking for a teacher for this class:

```
30 students
    9 from Mexico
    5 from China
    1 from Japan
    1 from Haiti
    2 from Ethiopia
   12 from the United States
```

Compare the teachers. Who is best for a job with the class listed? Why? Use these words to discuss them.

1. each of the / each / every
2. none of the
3. a number of / the number of

TOM JENKINS
Experience: 10 years of teaching ESL in the United States
Education: B.A. degree in Education + teaching certificate
Language(s): 2 years of college Spanish

BRIAN LEATHER
Experience: 5 years teaching ESL as a teacher assistant
              while in graduate school
              no overseas experience
Education: Ph.D. in Chinese
Language(s): Chinese; some knowledge of Japanese

PAT O'DONNELL
Experience: 2 years of teaching English in Thailand
              1 year of teaching English in Japan
Education: M.A. degree in French
              3 courses in teaching
Language(s): French; Thai (conversation, not writing)

UNIT 1 Present and Past

8 TROUBLE SPOTS: COMPARATIVES AND SUPERLATIVES

	Comparative	Superlative	
One-syllable adjective or adverb	*er . . . than*	*the . . . -est*	(a) This book is **longer than** the first one. (b) His grade was **the highest** in the class.
Two-syllable adjective or adverb which ends in *-y*	drop the *-y*, then add *-ier . . . than*	drop the *-y*, then add *the . . . -iest*	(c) It looks **easier than** it is. (d) It's not **the easiest** test I have ever taken.
Adjective or adverb with two or more syllables, or any noun	*more . . . than*	*the most*	(e) That's **more expensive than** ours. (f) Is this **the most difficult** part for you? (g) He has been there **more times than** anyone. (h) We always have **the most fun** with them.
to show the opposite of *more* with nouns: non-count	*less . . . than*	*the least*	(i) That book costs **less than** the others. (j) Carl had **the least** difficulty.
count	*fewer . . . than*	*the fewest*	(k) I have **fewer** problems **than** he does. (l) His exam has **the fewest** mistakes.
irregular forms *good / well,* *bad / badly,* *far*	*better,* *worse,* *farther*	*the best,* *the worst,* *the farthest*	(m) He's doing much **better** than he did last year. In fact, he's **the best** student in the class. (n) Did you do **better** or **worse** than you did on the last test? (o) This text was **the worst!** (p) Franny lives **farther** away than Michaela, but Nancy lives **the farthest** away.
	the more, the -er		(q) **The more** I study, **the easier** it gets!

26 UNIT 1 Students

8.1 Comparatives and Superlatives

Look at the backgrounds of the three teachers in Exercise 7.2. Write sentences about them using these comparative and superlative forms.

EXAMPLE

the . . . -est
Brian has **the highest** level of education.

1. more . . . than
2. -er . . . than
3. the most
4. the least
5. less . . . than
6. the . . . -est
7. fewer . . . than
8. the best

9 PREPOSITIONS

Prepositions of Location		in	on	at
in (to)	location in a place or area	in a city, in a state, in a room, in a country, in a house, in a dorm, in an apartment, in a college, in the mountains, in a desert, in a book, in a magazine, in a car, in a taxi, in a corner *(inside a room or object)*		
on	along or touching	on an avenue, on a street, on a river, on a bay, on a lake, on a beach, on an ocean, on a ship, on a plane, on a bus, on a subway, on the right / left, on a corner *(outside)*		
	(idiomatic) for trips / vacations	on a vacation, on a trip, on a holiday, on a safari		
	for some types of communication	on TV, on the radio		
at	point or target	at 24th Avenue and Second Street, at home, at work, at school, at church, at the airport, at a university; at 16 *(years of age)*		

9.1 Practice with Prepositions

A. Complete the sentences with the correct preposition. Use *in(to)*, *on*, or *at*.

1. He is living _____ a dorm _____ 45th Street but he wants to move _____ a house.

2. You arrive _____ the airport and you go _____ a subway to the international concourse.

(Continued on the next page)

UNIT 1 Present and Past

3. I live _____ an apartment which is within walking distance to campus.

4. We were _____ that room all day. Finally, we got _____ a bus and went somewhere.

5. They are _____ vacation, so someone is house-sitting for them.

6. They have a cabin _____ the mountains _____ a river that has salmon _____ it.

7. He's _____ high school normally, but he is not _____ school this week. He is visiting his older sister _____ the university.

8. They are at church while we are _____ home reading what is new _____ the newspaper.

B. Fill in the prepositions in this description.

(1) _____ my country, I usually live with my parents _____ a house _____ a residential area _____ the northern part of Bogotá, Colombia. (2) My room is _____ the second floor of the house. (3) The house is _____ an avenue we call Avenida de Chile. (4) It is actually _____ the corner of Avenida de Chile and 70th. (5) It is _____ the right side of the street.

C. Now write a description of where you live. Put blanks for the prepositions. Test a classmate to see if she or he can guess the missing prepositions.

10 PHRASAL VERBS WITH *IN(TO)*

In(to) is used with verbs. Often these phrases have special meanings. Phrasal verbs are very common in conversation.

(a) I don't want to **break in on** their meeting, but there is an important call. (*interrupt*)
(b) I always **give in** and let him watch TV before doing his homework. (*concede*)
(c) She **comes into** the office at 8:30 every day. (*arrive at*)
(d) The teacher **is dividing** the students **into** small groups. (*partition*)
(e) **Fill in** the correct form of the verb in parentheses. (*complete*)
(f) If you **get in(to)** those classes, you can graduate in one year. (*be accepted*)
(g) She's really **into** studying English right now. (*be interested in, like*)
(h) Has he been **handing in** his homework on time lately? (*submit*)
(i) **Let** her **in**! It's cold outside. (*allow in; admit someone*)
(j) **Look into** taking that course. It's very interesting! (*investigate; do informal research*)
(k) We have **put in** a lot of hours on this project. (*contribute, spend*)
(l) I always **run into** her in the library. (*meet accidentally*)
(m) He **has taken part** in several school plays. (*participate in*)
(n) Don't **stay in** all day studying! (*remain inside*)

For definitions of other phrasal verbs, see Appendix D.

10.1 Practice with Phrasal Verbs

Match the definition with the two-word verb.

_____ 1. I'm just not **into** spectator sports. I don't enjoy watching football games on TV.

_____ 2. Don't **give in**! Stand firm with your opinion.

_____ 3. If you **come into** class late, quickly take a seat by the door. Don't **break in on** the teacher's lecture.

_____ 4. Let's **divide** the work **into** three parts. Then everyone will **put in** the same amount of work.

_____ 5. All you need to do is **fill in** the blanks with the correct preposition.

_____ 6. I'm **looking into** getting into her class. She's a good teacher.

_____ 7. Don't forget to **hand in** your homework before you leave.

_____ 8. If you **run into** any trouble, call me.

_____ 9. You must **take part in** class discussions. It's part of your grade in this class.

_____ 10. It's very nice today. Unfortunately, I have to **stay in** and get some work done.

_____ 11. Keep the door closed! Don't **let** the cold air **in**.

_____ 12. They wouldn't **let** him **into** the class. It filled up early during registration.

a. admit into
b. complete
c. meet by accident
d. like
e. contribute
f. surrender
g. remain inside
h. arrive
i. separate
j. participate
k. interrupt
l. allow to enter
m. submit
n. investigate

UNIT 1 Present and Past

LISTENING TEST

Listen and circle the letter of the best restatement or answer.

1. a. You called me.
   b. You didn't call me.
   c. You need to call me now.

2. a. They usually study in Mexico.
   b. They are studying in Mexico right now.
   c. They sometimes study in Mexico.

3. a. I studied it last year.
   b. I'm studying it right now.
   c. I often have trouble.

4. a. I stopped my homework.
   b. I interrupted his homework.
   c. He stopped his homework before I arrived.

5. a. They went shopping first.
   b. They didn't have lunch.
   c. They ate lunch first.

6. a. The speaker used to live at home.
   b. The speaker lives at home.
   c. The speaker is no longer going to school.

7. a. He needs to take one course in the future.
   b. He needs to take three courses in the future.
   c. He needs to take four courses in the future.

8. a. This person rarely has homework.
   b. This person often has homework.
   c. This person never has homework.

9. a. They drove home as quickly as possible.
   b. They went to work.
   c. They were driving to work.

10. a. I generally get there at 8:00.
    b. I got there at 8:00 today, but I don't always.
    c. I am never in the office before 9:00.

QUIZ YOURSELF

Circle the letter of the best answer to complete each sentence.

1. Bill and Mary usually _____ classes 30 hours a week.
    a. attend
    b. are attending
    c. attends

2. I _____ the teacher's permission before.
    a. don't need
    b. am not needing
    c. didn't need

3. _____ you _____ that guy in the back of our math class yesterday?
    a. Did . . . notice
    b. Do . . . notice
    c. Are . . . noticing

4. That _____ what you think.
    a. doesn't mean
    b. isn't meaning
    c. don't meant

5. I am tired of being a student. This quarter, I _____ as much as I need to.
    a. am not studying
    b. didn't study
    c. studied

6. Who _____ the test schedule each quarter?
    a. decides
    b. is deciding
    c. does decides

7. Seldom _____ into her on campus.
    a. runs
    b. I run
    c. do I run

8. In the 1980s thousands of immigrants _____ this program.
    a. entered
    b. are entering
    c. enter

9. He _____ his assignment when I walked in.
    a. wasn't finishing
    b. didn't finish
    c. isn't finishing

10. My phone was busy because I _____ to call you.
    a. try
    b. was trying
    c. am trying

UNIT 1 *Present and Past*

UNIT 2

Present and Past Perfect

Turning Points

1 PRESENT PERFECT

past → now   future

USE	Use the **present perfect** for: • an action which began in the past and is still happening now • an action which is just finished or is important to the present • an action which happened at an unspecified time • a repeated action in the past which happened at an unspecified time • an action which the speaker views as incomplete	(a) I've **studied** English for two years. (*I am still studying it.*) (b) He **has** just **heard** from the school. (c) He's **taken** several engineering courses. (d) He's **seen** her several times in the last year. (e) NOT: He's **seen** her last month. (f) **Has** she **received** her letter yet? (g) I **haven't applied** yet.
FORM	Use the present tense of *have* + **past participle** of the verb.	I **have worked** We **have worked** You **have worked** You **have worked** He/She/It **has worked** They **have worked** (h) I **have not finished** my required courses yet. (i) He **has taken** a foreign language class.
	For questions, use: *have* + subject + **past participle** For negative sentences, use: *have* + negation + **past participle**	(j) **Have** you **worked** there? (k) We **haven't been** there.

TIME WORDS	Use *for* for a period of time. Use *since* from a point in time.	(l) I **have studied** here *for* three years. (m) She **has studied** here *since* 1994.
	already, yet	(n) I've *already* **seen** my advisor. (o) **Have** you **taken** the TOEFL *yet*?
	so far, up until now, lately, recently, in recent years, in the past week	(p) *So far* I **have taken** six courses. (q) I've **been** busy *recently*.

1.1 Get in Motion: Present Perfect

A. Stand up and walk around your classroom. Talk to as many classmates as possible. Follow these steps.

1. Ask your classmates questions in the present perfect. *Have you ever . . . ?*

EXAMPLE
study English
Have you ever studied English?
Yes, I have. / No, I haven't.

2. Write down the name of the first classmate who says "yes." You may want to ask for more information!

Name	Activity
_____	win a prize
_____	visit or live in another country
_____	eat an unusual type of food
_____	be on television
_____	meet a famous person
_____	take the TOEFL
_____	participate in a marathon, "dance-a-thon," or any other endurance contest

B. Now share your answers.

EXAMPLE
Who has won a prize? (Name)

UNIT 2 *Present and Past Perfect* 33

1.2 Listening: Interviews for a Scholarship

A. Read the notice below and complete the sentences.

Studying in Canada

Are you interested in studying in Canada? The Canadian Scholarship Committee is offering to pay tuition for a year of college in Canada. You need to get accepted at a college or university in Canada and provide $4,000 for room and board. For more information, write to the Canadian Scholarship Committee in Toronto.

---

1. This scholarship is to study in _____.
2. It pays for _____.
3. The student needs to pay _____.
4. The student also needs to _____.

B. Listen to the interviews with two students who are applying for this scholarship to study in Canada. Check off what each candidate has done on this list.

Monica		Francesca
_____	finish one year of college	_____
_____	finish three years of college	_____
_____	study English	_____
_____	study French	_____
_____	decide to major in political science	_____
_____	decide to major in English	_____
_____	have pen pals in Canada	_____
_____	save $4,000	_____
_____	apply to a university in Canada	_____
_____	get into a university in Canada	_____

C. Check your answers with a classmate. What has Monica done? What has Francesca done?

D. You are one of the members of the scholarship committee. Who do you think you should give the scholarship to? Why?

Erik in his interview

34 UNIT 2 *Turning Points*

1.3 Present Perfect

A. Read what is happening in Erik's scholarship interview. Complete the sentences using a verb from the list in the present perfect tense and, if necessary, *not*. Each verb should be used only once.

| make | ask | show | arrive | be | question |

1. Erik is arriving late to the interview because he didn't try to get to the building before the interview day.
   He _____ on time and that will make a bad impression.

2. Erik is looking at his hands while the interviewer is talking.
   He _____ eye contact with the interviewer yet.

3. Erik is taking out a pack of cigarettes.
   He _____ if it's okay to smoke yet.

4. Erik is placing his hand in front of his mouth when he talks.
   The interviewer _____ able to understand him so far.

5. Erik is telling him how much he needs the scholarship money.
   The interviewer _____ him about his financial need yet. Right now, he is asking about his academic goals.

6. Erik is leaving without saying, "Thank you for the interview."
   He _____ good manners in this interview.

B. Are these interview manners different from ones in your culture?

1.4 Admissions Role Play

Work in groups of three or four. You will take the roles of admissions director and students applying to the Berkelee College of Music. This school is famous for its graduates who have gone on to be famous musicians.

1. You will each learn some information about your role. Student #1 (admissions director), look at File 4 in Appendix G. Student #2, look at File 6. Student #3, look at File 8. Student #4, look at File 13. Read the instructions in the file and discuss your role with other students with the same number / identity as you have.

2. The admissions director will interview the students together.

3. The admissions director can only accept one student. Explain which student you want to accept and why.

UNIT 2 Present and Past Perfect

2. PRESENT PERFECT CONTINUOUS

past — now — future

USE	The **present perfect continuous** emphasizes that an action began in the past and is still happening now. The speaker may view the action as temporary.	(a) I've **been studying** English for six months.
	With some verbs, it has the same meaning as the present perfect. However, the speaker may want to emphasize how long an action has been happening.	(b) I've **taught** English for 20 years. (c) I've **been teaching** English for 20 years.
	Use the **present perfect**, not the present perfect continuous, with non-continuous verbs, adverbs of frequency, or a specific number of times.	(d) **Have** you **heard** of that restaurant? (e) I've always **lived** here. (f) He's **moved** twice in the last year.
	Verbs that indicate the beginning or end of an action may not make sense in the continuous.	(g) I **haven't started** my homework yet. (h) NOT: I **haven't been starting** my homework yet.
FORM	Use *has / have* + *been* + present participle of the verb.	I have been working We have been working You have been working You have been working He/She/It has been working They have been working (i) We've **been working** on this for days.
	For questions, use: *has / have* + subject + *been* + present participle For negative sentences, use: *has / have* + negation + *been* + present participle	(j) **Has** he **been studying** English long? (k) **Have** you **been having** problems with these verb tenses? (l) They **haven't been studying** English for very long.
TIME WORDS	Since *just* emphasizes time close to now, it often indicates this tense.	(m) I've *just* **been talking** to my advisor about next quarter's classes.
	Same time clues as present perfect tense: *so far, up until now, lately, recently, in recent years, in the past week*	(n) What **have** you **been doing** *lately*?

UNIT 2 Turning Points

2.1 Get in Motion: Present Perfect Continuous

A. These people are all newcomers to the United States. They have been busy trying to manage their lives in their new country. How will they answer this question?

What have you been doing lately?

1. Arturo / look for a bigger apartment

2. Beatrice / try to find a job

3. Rayna / stay at home, not feel very well

4. Yuri / work at Domino's Pizza

5. Tran / study English

6. Jill / not look for a job, take care of her three young children

B. How about you? What have you been doing recently?

UNIT 2 Present and Past Perfect   37

C. Now contrast the present perfect continuous and the present perfect. Make sentences with these cues.

1. Arturo / look for a bigger apartment. He / look / at three today.
2. Beatrice / try to find a job. She / have / six interviews / so far.
3. Rayna / stay at home / because / she / not feel / well. She / see / the doctor / already.
4. Yuri / work at Domino's Pizza. He / work / there / for three months.
5. Tran / study English. He / take / two courses / so far.

2.2 Present Tenses in Contrast

Underline the best choice to complete each sentence. If you see any time expressions that help you know which verb tense is correct, circle these time clues.

(1) Canada and Germany (is / are) two countries with a large number of immigrants. (2) Since 1951, more than five million immigrants (have moved / have been moving) to Canada. (3) The largest increase in recent years (is / has been) from Asia. (4) Because Canada (has been attracting / attracts) immigrants for years, its government continually encourages schools to value different cultures and protect human rights. (5) Canadian schools (provide / have been providing) instruction in English and French since the 1970s when Canada made both languages official. (6) According to the government, there (are / have been) two official languages, but Canada (has had / has) no "official culture." (7) Perhaps this (has made / is making) it easier for immigrants to maintain their own cultural identities over the years.

(8) In the past decade the government (has been starting / has started) to eliminate discrimination against foreigners in the schools. (9) The government (has been trying / has tried) repeatedly to provide an equal education to all minority children. (10) Every year the government (trains / is training) teachers to work with culturally diverse classes.

(11) Germany (is experiencing / has been experiencing) a large increase in immigrants in recent years. (12) Some of the newcomers (arrive / have arrived) from Russia and Eastern Europe, but their ancestors were originally German. (13) These "ethnic German" newcomers (have "resettled" / "resettle") in Germany, the home of their ancestors. (14) Many of these immigrants already (speak / have spoken) German. (15) Another immigrant group for the last couple of decades (has been / is) guest workers from Greece, Turkey, and Yugoslavia. (16) These immigrants (are bringing / have brought) different cultural and religious customs to Germany. (17) They (make / have made) Germany a more diverse country.

(18) As a result, the German education system (has had / is having) to consider how to integrate these workers' children into the school system. (19) Educators (have not wanted / are not wanting) to destroy the newcomers' cultural identity. (20) The government (begins / has begun) a number of joint commissions with Greece, Turkey, and Yugoslavia. (21) These days, the commissions (deal / are dealing) with issues of educating foreign children.

(22) For centuries Christian religious instruction in school (has always been / is always) part of a German child's education. (23) How (is / has) the German government currently (providing / provided) religious instruction for the large number of Muslim, Turkish, and Yugoslavian children? (24) (Have / Are) these children (been becoming / becoming) a part of German culture without losing their cultural and religious identity? (25) These (are / are being) very difficult questions for Germany and for other countries with similar situations.

2.3 Tense Review

Complete the sentences with the correct form of the verb in parentheses. Use the simple present, the present continuous, the simple past, the present perfect, or the present perfect continuous.

(1) The experience of moving to another country _____ (be) always _____ difficult. (2) Soo-Hyun is an immigrant. She _____ (choose) to move to another country. (3) Dong is a refugee. He _____ (not, want) to leave his country, but he and his family _____ (leave) because of war.

(4) When Dong first _____ (come) to the United States, he _____ (have) a difficult time. (5) Now, things _____ (go) a little better for Dong and his family. (6) When Dong first _____ (arrive), he _____ (find) a job easily, but it _____ (not, pay) well. (7) For the past three years, Dong _____ (go) to school at night. (8) He _____ (study) in a technical college. (9) Dong _____ (want) to find a higher-paying job when he finishes his courses. (10) He is looking forward to finishing his courses. While he _____ (study) at night and _____ (work) in the daytime, he _____ (not, see) very much of his family. (11) This _____ (be) difficult for all of them.

(Continued on the next page)

(12) In general, how _____ immigrant or refugee families _____ (adjust) to their new culture? (13) This _____ (vary) from person to person. (14) Some immigrants _____ (try) to assimilate into the new culture. (15) For example, Soo-Hyun and her mother _____ (live) in Canada for several years now. (16) Soo-Hyun _____ (associate) with Canadians since arriving, but her mother _____ (stay) with Korean people as much as possible. (17) Today, Soo-Hyun _____ (feel) she _____ (not, belong) to either culture. (18) However, she _____ (gain) a strong sense of self-esteem because she _____ (learn) another language and _____ (make) a successful life for herself in Canada.

2.4 Talk It Over and Optional Writing

In small groups, discuss these questions. Choose one of these topics and write a composition about it.

1. What have you been doing to improve your English?

2. Do you know any newcomers to your city / country? What have they been doing to establish themselves here? What difficulties have they faced?

3. How has learning another language or living in another country been a turning point in your life?

3 PAST PERFECT

past 1 2 now future

USE	Use the **past perfect** for: • the first of two actions that were completed in the past	(a) When he graduated, he **had** already **acted** in several movies. *(First he acted; then he graduated.)*
	(Note: The past perfect action is relevant to another point of time in the past. However, the second action—in the simple past— is not always in the same sentence.)	(b) We gave them a surprise party. I **had** never **seen** them so happy.

UNIT 2 *Turning Points*

FORM	Use *had* + **past participle** of the verb.	I **had finished** We **had finished** You **had finished** You **had finished** He/She/It **had finished** They **had finished** (c) He **had seen** that movie once before.
	For questions, use: *had* + subject + **past participle** For negative sentences, use: *had* + negation + **past participle**	(d) **Had** he **finished** the movie when you interviewed him? (e) No, he **hadn't finished** it yet.
TIME WORDS	*just, recently, already, scarcely, barely, ever, never, yet, still*	(f) She was frustrated because after two attempts, she ***still* hadn't won** an Olympic medal. (g) I **had *barely* hung up** the phone when it rang again. (h) He **had *scarcely* warmed up** when the competition began. (i) We **had *never* imagined** such a good performance.
	By the time (that) introduces a time clause with the simple past. The past perfect is in the main clause.	(j) **By the time (that)** I finished, everyone **had already left**.
	The past perfect is optional if *before* or *after* is in the sentence because the sequence of events is already clear.	(k) **Before** he performed in the concert, he **(had) practiced** for three weeks.

3.1 Get in Motion: Past Perfect

Do you know any Elvis Presley songs? Look at the events in Elvis Presley's life. Why were they milestones for him? Make sentences by following the example below.

EXAMPLE
1945   sing at a county fair (sing in public)
In 1945 he sang at a county fair. This was a milestone because he had never sung in public before.

1948   move to Memphis, Tennessee, from a small town in Mississippi (live in a big town)
1954   meet a record producer / ask Elvis to sing on a recording (make a record)
1956   act / first movie "Love Me Tender" (act)
1958   go to Germany with the army (live in another country)
1960   meet Priscilla Beaulieu, 14 years old, in Germany (meet anyone like her)
1967   marry Priscilla (be married)
1968   have daughter, Lisa Marie (have a child)

Elvis Presley

3.2 Recognition: Past Perfect, Simple Past, and Past Continuous

Which sentence is correct in each group? Circle the letter of the correct answer.

1. a. I wasn't hungry by 5:00 because I will eat a big lunch.
   b. I had been hungry by 5:00 because I was eating a big lunch.
   c. I wasn't hungry by 5:00 because I had eaten a big lunch.

2. a. I slept in class because I was staying up late.
   b. I was sleeping in class because I had stayed up late.
   c. I had slept in class because I stayed up late.

3. a. When I met your family, I felt like I had met them before.
   b. When I was meeting your family, I was feeling like I had met them before.
   c. When I met your family, I felt like I was meeting them before.

4. a. I wasn't doing well on the test because I wasn't studying the night before.
   b. I didn't do well on the test because I hadn't studied the night before.
   c. I hadn't done well on the test because I wasn't studying the night before.

5. a. By midnight I was very tired because I was working hard all day.
   b. By midnight I had been very tired because I was working hard all day.
   c. By midnight I was very tired because I had worked hard all day.

3.3 Verb Contrast: Past, Past Continuous, Past Perfect

Underline the best choice to complete each sentence. Circle the time clues.

1. Jacqueline Bouvier (grew / was growing / had grown) up in a wealthy New York City family.

2. She (was / had been) born on July 28, 1929.

3. While she (grew / was growing / had grown) up, her parents (sent / were sending / had sent) her to private schools.

4. By the time she (went / was going / had gone) to high school, her parents (got / were getting / had gotten) divorced.

5. Jacqueline (spent / was spending / had spent) two years at Vassar before she (went / was going / had gone) to the Sorbonne in Paris because she (was always / was always being / had always been) interested in France.

6. When she (returned / was returning / had returned) to the United States, she moved to Washington, D.C., and (graduated / was graduating / had graduated) from George Washington University there.

7. After she (graduated / was graduating) from college, she (got / was getting / had gotten) a job as a photographer and reporter at a newspaper.

8. When she (met / was meeting / had met) John Kennedy in 1951, he (already became / was already becoming / had already become) a member of Congress.

9. Although Kennedy (dated / was dating / had dated) quite a few women, he (didn't meet / wasn't meeting / hadn't met) anyone like Jacqueline.

10. They (got / were getting / had gotten) married in 1953.

*President John Kennedy and Jackie Kennedy
with President and Madame de Gaulle of France*

3.4 Tense Contrast: Past, Past Continuous, or Past Perfect

Complete these sentences with the correct form of the verb in parentheses. Circle the time clues.

1. John Kennedy and Jacqueline Bouvier _____ (never, meet) before 1951.

2. Jacqueline Bouvier _____ (work) for a newspaper when she _____ (meet) John Kennedy.

3. Jackie Kennedy _____ (be) only 31 when her husband _____ (become) President. There _____ (only, be) a couple of First Ladies younger than this before.

4. It is clear now that Jackie _____ (not, like) to campaign. However, she _____ (be) a very popular First Lady.

5. When she _____ (go) to the White House, people in the United States _____ (never, have) such a fashionable First Lady.

6. On November 22, 1963, someone _____ (shoot) President Kennedy while he and Jackie _____ (ride) in a motorcade in Dallas, Texas.

7. People in the United States _____ (never, see) such a tragedy before. It _____ (be) especially shocking because of the live television coverage of the assassination.

(Continued on the next page)

8. Jackie Kennedy _____ (be) only 34 when her husband _____ (die).

9. Five years later, Jackie _____ (marry) Aristotle Onassis, a very wealthy Greek ship owner.

10. People _____ (not, understand) why she _____ (marry) a man who was so much older than she _____ (be).

11. They decided she _____ (marry) him for his money.

12. When Onassis _____ (die) in 1975, he _____ (not, leave) Jackie very much in his will.

13. Although Onassis _____ (not, want) to leave Jackie much, his daughter Cristina later _____ (pay) Jackie $26 million.

14. Unlike many wealthy women, Jackie went to work. She _____ (work) as a book editor for many years.

15. In 1994, Jackie _____ (die) of cancer. At the time of her death, she _____ (live) in New York City.

3.5 Pair Work

Partner A, look at File 5 in Appendix G. Partner B, look at File 12. Ask your partner questions and circle the answer.

EXAMPLE

A: Jacqueline Kennedy was 31 when she became First Lady. _____Had_____ a First Lady _____ever been_____ (ever, be) as young as that before? (yes) no

B: There _____had been_____ (be) two First Ladies younger than Jacqueline Kennedy.

3.6 Optional Writing

Write a composition about one of the following topics.

1. Write about a time in your life when you made a decision that ended up being a major turning point.

2. Go to the library. Look up information about two famous people in the same field. Either (a) write a report on their lives or (b) prepare a poster to illustrate their lives. Emphasize similarities and differences. Share the information with your classmates.

4 PAST PERFECT CONTINUOUS

past 1 2 now future

USE	The **past perfect continuous**: • emphasizes a continued action which happened before another event in the past • emphasizes a repeated event which happened before another event in the past • expresses a temporary action or an action that was interrupted by another action in the past	(a) He **had been practicing** for several hours when he hit his head. (*First he was practicing; then he hit his head.*) (b) He **had been calling** her for days but she never answered. (c) He **had been studying** for a couple of hours when there was a knock on the door.
	The past perfect continuous may not be used with non-continuous verbs. (*See Appendix A for a list of non-continuous verbs.*)	(d) She didn't invite him although they **had known** each other for years.
FORM	Use **had** + **been** + present participle of the verb.	I **had been working** We **had been working** You **had been working** You **had been working** He/She/It **had been working** They **had been working** (e) He **had been competing** for several years when he won his first Olympic medal.
	For questions, use: **had** + subject + **been** + **present participle** For negative sentences, use: **had** + negation + **been** + **present participle**	(f) **Had** they **been looking** long before they found the address? (g) No, they **hadn't been looking** very long.
TIME WORDS	**For** (*a period of time*) and **since** (*a point in time*) often appear in sentences with the **past perfect continuous**.	(h) She **had been practicing** *for* hours when a news reporter arrived to interview her. (i) She **had been practicing** *since* early morning when the reporters came.

UNIT 2 Present and Past Perfect

4.1 Get in Motion: Simple Past or Past Perfect Continuous

Complete the sentences with the correct form of the verb in parentheses. Use the simple past or the past perfect continuous.

1. The king _____ (go) against tradition when he _____ (decide) to marry a commoner. Everyone was surprised because they _____ (not, expect) this.

2. Grace Kelly _____ (act) in movies for several years when she _____ (meet) Prince Rainier of Monaco.

3. Prince Charles _____ (think) about getting married for a long time when he finally _____ (tell) people of his plans to marry Diana.

4. People _____ (expect) Prince Charles to get married for a long time before he _____ (announce) his engagement to Lady Diana Spencer.

5. At the time that Charles and Diana _____ (start) to see each other, Diana _____ (not, live) on her own for very long.

6. When Charles and Diana _____ (announce) their engagement, Diana _____ (stop) working with children, which she _____ (do) for several years.

7. Lisa Halaby _____ (graduate) from Princeton University before she _____ (meet) King Hussein of Jordan.

8. People in England _____ (hope) that King Edward VIII would not marry Wallis Simpson, a divorced woman from the United States, when he _____ (announce) his plans to give up his throne for the woman he _____ (love).

9. How long _____ the king _____ (see) Mrs. Simpson when they _____ (decide) to get married?

10. King George VI, who _____ (take) over when King Edward VIII _____ (give) up the throne, _____ (not, expect) to become the king of England.

46 UNIT 2 *Turning Points*

4.2 Listening: A Modern Princess

A. Before you listen, discuss these questions with a classmate.
Would you want to marry royalty? What are the advantages and disadvantages?

Advantages	Disadvantages
_____	_____
_____	_____
_____	_____
_____	_____
_____	_____

Prince Naruhito and Masako Owada

B. Listen to the story of Prince Naruhito and Masako Owada's engagement. Answer these general questions about the listening.

1. Had Masako Owada always wanted to marry Prince Naruhito? _____

2. Did the Prince have an easy time finding someone to marry? _____

C. Listen again to the tape. Are these statements true or false? Write T or F.

_____ 1. The Prince met Masako Owada in 1992.

_____ 2. The Prince had been looking for a suitable wife.

_____ 3. They fell in love at first sight.

_____ 4. Masako had been working at the Ministry of Foreign Affairs when she went to Oxford University.

_____ 5. Masako and her father worked in the same area.

D. Check your answers with a classmate. Then tell each other the events that happened.

UNIT 2 Present and Past Perfect   47

4.3 Editing Practice

Are the verb tenses in these sentences correct? If not, write the correct verb on the line.

1. When Naruhito began to look for a wife, he was having difficulty finding someone. _____

2. Naruhito's mother was being the first commoner to marry into the royal family in Japan. _____

3. She felt isolated in the strict formality of the royal family. _____

4. In the early 1960s, Empress Michiko, Naruhito's mother, had a nervous breakdown. _____

5. Japan had been passing an equal opportunity law the year that Masako Owada was looking for a job. _____

6. Masako and the Prince had not seen each other for five years when they met again at someone's home. _____

7. Both Masako and Prince Naruhito had been spending several years in universities overseas. _____

8. The Imperial Household did not think Masako had been a suitable match for the Prince. _____

9. Masako's grandfather had taken over a company that was responsible for a terrible pollution problem. _____

10. Masako's longer skirts, slower walk, and lowered eyes were different from the way she had looked and acted before she was becoming engaged. _____

4.4 Past Tense Review

A. Combine these phrases and time expressions into complete sentences that describe a situation in the past.

1. Lisa and John / talk on the phone / last night
2. While Lisa and John / talk on the phone / Lisa's doorbell ring
3. Lisa / go to the door / she hear the bell
4. There / be / a man at the door but Lisa / never / see him / before
5. She / not want to open the door at that time of night
6. When she / ask / the man / what he / want / he / be / very friendly

7. He say / he / try to reach her for two days
8. He tell her / her phone not work all that time
9. Lisa / know / he lie because John / wait for her on the phone at that very moment

B. What happened? Complete the story. The last sentence is "Lisa was very happy that she had met this wonderful person."

5 TROUBLE SPOTS: *MOST, ALMOST, OTHER, ANOTHER*

Most and Almost

most	adjective	(a) **Most** soccer players do not go to the World Cup.
the most	adverb (used in superlatives)	(b) **The most** successful players go to the World Cup.
most of	+ a specific noun or a pronoun	(c) **Most of** the children in my country learn to play soccer in their neighborhoods or at sports clubs.
almost + adjective + of	+ a specific noun or a pronoun	(d) **Almost all of** my friends played soccer. (e) **Almost** twenty **of** them were on teams.

Other and Another

other(s)	there are several more	(f) Some teams practiced the night before; **others** rested.
another	there is one more in addition	(g) One team got to the finals, **another** got to the semi-finals, but the rest were out of the competition.
each other, one another	a reciprocal relationship	(h) They like working with **each other**. (i) They help **one another** prepare for the event.
the others, the other ones	all that remain	(j) Four hundred fans had arena seats; **the others** had standing room only.

5.1 Most, Almost, Other, Another

Underline the best choice to complete each sentence.

1. There are 11 players on our World Cup team. Two are from the Nacional team. The (others / another) (is / are) from Santa Fe.
2. One of the players is an Italian and (the other / another one) is Brazilian but they are playing on the Spanish team.
3. (Most / Almost) kids have memories of playing soccer or some sport as a child.
4. The United States calls the sport "soccer." (The other / Other / Another) countries call it "football."
5. (Almost / The most) all of the radio stations cover the games during the World Cup.
6. (The most / Most) of the players began the sport as children.
7. Three of the players fouled out. One of the players had used bad language and (the others / the other) two had started a fight.
8. After the Olympics, (most / the most) popular sporting event to watch is the soccer World Cup.

UNIT 2 *Present and Past Perfect*

6 PHRASAL VERBS WITH ON

(a) **Try on** this uniform. (*test the fit*)
(b) Improper warming up can **bring on** stress injuries. (*cause*)
(c) My parents always **passed on** my older brother's clothes to me. (*transfer*)
(d) He's **getting on** so well in this event that I think he'll get a gold medal. (*continue*)
(e) Don't forget to **turn on** the alarm before you go to sleep. (*start the power*)
(f) I want to **be in on** the celebration. (*participate in*)
(g) It's hard to **catch on** to the main points when he **keeps on** interrupting the lecture with questions. (*understand*) (*continue*)
(h) My parents expect me to **carry on** the family business. (*continue*)
(i) He can **draw on** his past experiences to face this difficult time. (*use*)
(j) He **fell back on** his family when he was most in need. (*rely on for support*)

For definitions of these and other phrasal verbs, see Appendix D.

6.1 Practice with Phrasal Verbs

Underline the best choice to complete each sentence. Then complete each sentence with the correct form of the verb you choose.

1. My parents didn't believe in wasting money, so they _____ (get / pass) on my brothers' clothing to me. Unfortunately, I was the fifth son. I remember how excited I used to feel when I got to go to a store and _____ (carry / try) on something new. It felt wonderful! Believe it or not, though, I _____ (draw / carry) on the tradition; I make my three daughters wear the same clothes until the clothes are worn out.

2. I was almost out of gas but I _____ (keep / fall back) on driving because I didn't want to be late to the surprise party. I wanted to _____ (be in / turn) on the surprise.

3. I worry a lot about finances. I don't have any money saved so if something happens I don't have any money to _____ (pass / fall back) on.

4. You're studying Chinese, aren't you? How are you _____ (get / catch) on to learning a different language?

5. Musical director is a great job for her. It _____ (bring / draw) on her management background and also her love of music.

6. My English is fairly good but I have a hard time when people tell jokes. It takes me a while to _____ (draw / catch) on to whether people are serious or not.

7. It's dark in here! Where do you _____ (turn / keep) on the light?

8. They always seemed like such a happy couple. I can't understand what _____ (bring / be) on their divorce.

LISTENING TEST

Listen and circle the letter of the statement which best describes the situation.

1. a. They knew each other well.
   b. They went to a friend's wedding.
   c. They did not know each other very long.

2. a. She finished.
   b. She's doing her homework now.
   c. She hasn't started her homework.

3. a. He hadn't started his work yet.
   b. He had started his work.
   c. He had finished his work.

4. a. The speaker used to live at home.
   b. The speaker lives at home.
   c. The speaker is no longer going to school.

5. a. I was early.
   b. I was on time.
   c. I was late.

6. a. The person is doing this interesting activity now.
   b. The person has had a lot of experience with this activity.
   c. The person hasn't tried that before.

7. a. They went to Mexico for the first time last year.
   b. They spent two years in Mexico.
   c. They have been to Mexico many times.

8. a. I knew her.
   b. I did not know her.
   c. I saw her once or twice.

9. a. We didn't hear the news.
   b. We weren't home when we heard the news.
   c. We had been out.

10. a. We were working when you arrived.
    b. We hadn't started working.
    c. We had finished working.

QUIZ YOURSELF

Circle the letter of the underlined verb which is not correct.

1. Nadia Comaneci was a Romanian gymnast in the 1976 Olympic Games in Montreal. She was only 14 years old when she (a) won the gold in balance beam, uneven parallel bars, and the all-around event. No woman (b) was getting a perfect score in the uneven parallel bars before. In 1980 in Moscow she took the gold in balance beam and floor exercise. By 1989 she (c) had defected to the United States.

2. Peggy Fleming and Dorothy Hamill (a) are being well-known names in American figure skating. Both (b) have been skating professionally for some time. They (c) received gold medals in the 1968 and 1976 Olympics, respectively.

3. Three African-American track and field athletes are related. Jacqueline Joyner-Kersee (a) won the gold in 1988 and 1992 in the heptathlon. Her brother, Alfrederick Alphonzo Joyner, (b) was a triple jump gold medalist in 1984. Alfrederick's wife, Florence Griffith Joyner (c) has taken gold medals in the 100 meter, 200 meter, and 4 x 100 meter relay in Seoul in 1988.

4. Although soccer (a) came to the United States in the late part of the 19th century, it (b) hadn't become a college sport until 1959. By the next decade it (c) had become the fastest growing sport in the country.

5. Mary Lou Retton (a) made many breakfast cereal commercials after she (b) was becoming the first American woman to win the all-around event in gymnastics in 1984. In fact, she (c) was the first woman athlete to appear on a box of Wheaties.

6. Pele is probably the most well-known name in soccer. He (a) has led Brazil to World Cup victories in 1958, 1962, and 1970. He (b) retired in 1974, then reentered the game with the New York Cosmos, and (c) re-retired in 1977.

7. Abebe Bikila, an Ethiopian, (a) won the Olympic Marathon in 1960 and again in 1964 at the Tokyo Games although he (b) had had an emergency appendectomy one month before. Five years later he (c) had become paralyzed from a car accident.

8. Russian gymnast Olga Korbut (a) was another Olympics favorite. She (b) won gold medals in team competition, floor, and balance beam before she (c) retiring in 1977.

9. Many soccer games (a) have ended in violence. While Argentina and Peru (b) compete in the Olympics Qualifying match in Lima in 1964, post-game violence killed 309 people and (c) injured 1,000 more.

10. The world (a) had reacted strongly to the deaths and injuries at the European Cup in Brussels in 1985. Such violence (b) did not equal the border war that (c) broke out between Honduras and El Salvador after a qualifying match for the World Cup in 1970.

UNIT 3

Future and Future Perfect

My Future, Our Future

1 FUTURE

```
    past      now     future
 ─────────────|───────●─────
```

USE

In most cases, both **will** and **be going to** express the future.
However, **be going to** is more common in conversation than in formal writing.

	Will	**Be Going to**
promises willingness requests	(a) I'**ll be** on time. (b) Don't worry. I'**ll do** it. (c) **Will** you **pick** it up for me?	
predictions determination	(d) He'**ll be** late. (f) I **will pass** that test!	(e) He'**s going to be** late. (g) I'**m going to pass** it next time!
plans and intentions	(h) I'**ll probably go** away next week. (Note: You may use **will** if you soften it with words like **perhaps, probably,** or **I think.**)	(i) I'**m going to go** home in June. (j) I'**m probably going to go** home in June.
refusals	(k) I **won't do** it!	(l) I'**m not going to do** it!

54

FORM	*will* + **base form** of verb *be going to* + **base form** of verb	(m) She **will finish** tonight. (n) She **is going to finish** tonight.
	For questions, use: *will* + subject + **base form** of verb or *is / are / am* + subject + *going to* + **base form** of verb For negative sentences, use: *will* + negation + **base form** of verb or *is / are / am* + negation + *going to* + **base form** of verb	(o) **Will** you **have** dinner with us? (p) **Is** he **going to come** with you? (q) I **will** not **call** him this late. (r) We **aren't going to be** there on time.
	Shall* + base form** is more formal than *will*. In American English, it is mainly used today in invitations. (*For more information about* ***shall, *see page 103.*)	(s) **Shall** we **go** to a movie after dinner? (t) **Shall** I **get** you a drink?
TIME WORDS	*tomorrow, next week/month/year,* *by . . . , in . . . , at . . .*	(u) They're **going to meet** *next month*. (v) I'll **be finished** *by March*. (w) I'll **have** that for you *by September 6*. (x) I'm **going to see** him *in two weeks*. (y) We'll **talk** about that sometime *in the future*. (z) Is dinner **going to be** *at 8:00*?

1.1 Listening: Pronunciation

In spoken English, the future forms sound different than they look.

EXAMPLES

1. When *will* is contracted (*I'll, he'll*), it is difficult to hear the / ll / sound.
2. When the pronoun is *it*, the / t / changes to a / dt /.
3. In *going to,* the / t / sound also changes to a / dt /. In very fast speech, "What are you going to do?" sometimes sounds like / whaddaya gonna do /.
4. The final / t / sound in *won't* is almost silent.

A. Listen and complete the sentences.

1. _____ go tomorrow.
2. _____ go tomorrow.

(Continued on the next page)

3. Who _____ do it? _____!
4. I _____ worry. I'm sure _____ get here on time.
5. _____ talk about it tomorrow.
6. I think _____ rain.
7. _____ be there and _____ too.
8. What _____ tonight?
9. _____ be great!
10. _____ be fine.
11. _____ make any difference.
12. _____ go.

B. Now practice the pronunciation of the sentences.

1.2 Your Future Plans

Remember that when you talk about future plans, you usually use *going to*. You do not use *will* by itself. However, you can use *will* if you use *I think* or *probably*.

A. Work with a classmate. Complete these sentences about your future plans. Use these expressions:

I'm going to . . .

I think I'll . . .

I'll probably . . .

1. After class today,
2. Tonight
3. Tomorrow
4. On the weekend
5. Next month
6. In a couple of days
7. In a few hours

B. Now ask your classmate questions about long-term plans.

1. When do you think you'll . . . ?
2. What do you think you'll do after . . . ?
3. When are you going to . . . ?
4. What are you going to . . . ?
5. How long are you going to . . . ?

UNIT 3 My Future, Our Future

1.3 Listening: Time Management

A. Todd Jenkins is taking a workshop in Effective Time Management. Listen and write the time management ideas.

1. _Make a list of things to do the next day._

2. _____

3. _____

4. _____

5. _____

6. _____

7. _____

UNIT 3 Future and Future Perfect   57

B. Check your list with a classmate. Look at the description of some of Todd's habits. How will his habits be different if he follows the time management ideas?

Todd wakes up late because he has trouble sleeping. He eats breakfast in his car on the way to work because he's usually late.

At work, he goes through all the papers in his "in box" and puts the most urgent ones in a pile to take care of that day. About once a month he goes through this "urgent" pile and throws away letters that are old.

At home, Todd looks through his mail. If he has time, he pays any bills that he receives. Sometimes he remembers that he has to pay a bill. He has to go through his pile of letters to find the bill. Todd usually plans to exercise, but he can't find the time. Todd hardly ever starts big projects because he knows that he doesn't have the time to finish them.

C. How about your time management? Make some plans to get better organized. Tell a classmate what you will do differently.

1.4 Will versus Be Going to

Cross out any inappropriate future forms. In some cases, both forms may be appropriate.

1. A: We need someone to head our recycling committee.
   B: (I'll do it. / I'm going to do it.)
   A: Thanks. I can always count on you to volunteer.

2. A: I'm tired of not getting my work done. This year (I'm going to change / I'll change) the way I use my time!
   B: What (are you going to / will you) do differently?
   A: (I'm going to / I'll) look at what I have to do and break it into smaller tasks. Then I (won't / am not going to) feel so overwhelmed with work.

3. A: (Are you going to / Will you) go to the library today? (Are you going to / Will you) get some information on food production for me?
   B: Sure. Just give me the topics you want me to look up.

4. A: (I will / I'm going to) go to Mexico during spring vacation.
   B: Sounds great. (Is anyone going to / Will anyone) go with you?

5. A: This project (will / is going to) work if you make a major effort. Can we count on you?
   B: I promise (I'm going to / I'll) work hard this time.

6. A: I (am going to / will) try to remember to look at each piece of mail once and then deal with it.
   B: (Will that / Is that going to) make a difference in how much you get done?
   A: I think (it will / it's going to). Usually I make piles of things and then I never want to sort through them and work doesn't get done.

7. A: Food shortages are a world problem.
   B: I feel confident that we ('ll / 're going to) find a solution if we keep trying.

8. A: (Will you / Are you going to) leave on Friday?
   B: That's my plan, but I'm not sure we (will / are going to) be ready.

9. A: I need volunteers to help on this project. Who wants to do it?
   B: (I'm going to / I'll) do it!

10. A: They say that changes in the rain forest (will / are going to) affect the world's climate.
    B: I don't think it (will / is going to) happen in our life time.

2 PRESENT TENSES FOR THE FUTURE

Use **present tenses** (simple present, present perfect) in time and conditional clauses to express the future. Use the future in the main clause. *(For more practice with the conditional, see Unit 14.)*	(a) After I **graduate**, I'll **look** for a job. (b) While I **am looking** for a job, I'll **live** with my family. (c) When I **have finished**, I'll **call** you. (d) If I **study**, I'll **do** well on the test.
Use the **simple present** or **present continuous** to express the future with: • verbs related to scheduled or planned activities • transition verbs, such as *arrive, come, depart, go, head, leave, sail, start, fly* These sentences usually have a future time expression.	(e) I **graduate** in June. *(statement of fact about the future)* (f) I **am graduating** in June. (g) We **leave** at 7:00 a.m. tomorrow. (h) We're **leaving** at 7:00 a.m. tomorrow. (i) The term **starts** in September. (j) The flight **leaves** in 30 minutes.

2.1 Get in Motion: Expressing Results

With a partner, complete these sentences to show cause-effect relationships. Use the word cues. Make sure you give the correct form of the verb.

1. If we don't recycle garbage, we / HAVE / problems disposing of it.
2. If we / POLLUTE / the water, the fish / DIE.
3. If we / CUT / down too many trees, the earth / GET / hotter.
4. If we don't buy plastic, there / BE / less garbage.
5. Fewer trees / BE / cut down if we / USE / two sides of every paper.
6. If we eat more vegetables than beef, we / not NEED / to use so much land for cattle.
7. If we / DEVELOP / plant life in the oceans, we / HAVE / more food to eat.
8. If there / BE / more oil spills, we / DESTROY / more sea life.
9. People / HAVE / problems with their lungs if we / POLLUTE / the air.
10. If all countries meet to discuss the problem, they / FIND / solutions.

2.2 Causes and Effects

Look at the illustrations about the causes and effects of deforestation. Complete the sentences to explain these causes and effects.

EXAMPLE

country with trees → timber at dock → $$$$

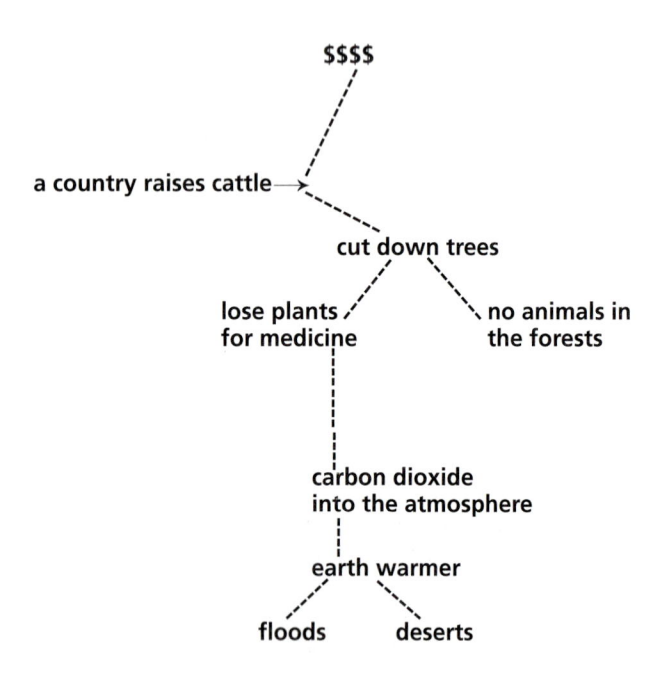

```
            $$$$
             /
            /
a country raises cattle →
              cut down trees
         lose plants /     \ no animals in
         for medicine        the forests
              |
         carbon dioxide
         into the atmosphere
              |
           earth warmer
           /        \
        floods      deserts
```

If a country has timber, people __will sell__ (sell) it. If they sell timber, they __will make__ (make) money.

(1) If a country _____ (raise) cattle, it _____ (make) money, but it _____ (also, cut down) trees. (2) If they _____ (cut down) trees, they _____ (lose) plants for medicine. (3) The animals that live in the forests _____ (also, not, survive).

(4) Trees also absorb carbon dioxide, so if there _____ (be) no trees, carbon dioxide _____ (go) into the atmosphere. (5) If carbon dioxide _____ (go) into the atmosphere, the earth _____ (get) warmer. This is called the "greenhouse effect." (6) If the earth _____ (get) warmer, we _____ (have) more floods. (7) And if the earth's temperature _____ (get) even hotter, there _____ (be) more deserts. If . . .

Can you continue with more causes and effects?

2.3 Future Plans

Your class has received a memo from the head of your program about waste reduction. Read the memo and work in a small group to complete the tasks.

> TO: All Students and Teachers
> FROM: Program Director
> SUBJECT: Waste Reduction
>
> Some students have suggested that we are not very aware of environmental concerns. I agree that we need to be more aware of how we use resources. I have listed some ideas for waste reduction below.
>
> Decide which actions will be most effective in reducing waste and energy. Decide what action your group will take. Please report to your teacher and the rest of your class.
>
> Possibilities for energy and waste reduction.
>
> Recycle white paper
> Recycle colored paper
> Use two sides of every paper
> Appoint a recycling supervisor in each class
> Recycle aluminum cans
> Use washable dishes for food instead of plastic, paper, or Styrofoam
> Buy and sell used textbooks instead of new ones
> Do homework in the textbook instead of on other paper
> Keep the lights off
> Reduce the amount of heat or cooling

Can you think of any additional ideas?

A. In your group, identify which ideas will have the most significant result in your program.

EXAMPLES
Recycling white paper **will** *make a big difference.*
If we recycle white paper, it **will** *cut down on garbage.*

B. Decide which solutions you will take.

EXAMPLES
We **will** *recycle white paper.*
We **won't** *keep the lights off.*

C. Then report on your plans to the rest of the class.

We have decided to _____.
We are going to _____. We are not going to _____.

EXAMPLES
We have decided to recycle white paper.
We are not going to keep the lights off.

UNIT 3 *Future and Future Perfect*

3 FUTURE CONTINUOUS

	past　　now　　future
USE	Use the **future continuous** for: • an action which will last for some time in the future • a repeated future action • a temporary condition (Note: The future continuous of *finish* is not necessary in (d) because *while they are finishing* is a time clause. See Box 2 on page 59.)	(a) Students **will be using** computers a lot more in the classrooms of the future. (b) I **will be working** on that project from time to time. (c) She **will be working** at the front desk next week rather than at her usual job. (d) We **will be teaching** while they **are finishing** their exams.
	The future continuous is **not** used with non-continuous verbs. (See Appendix A for a list of non-continuous verbs.)	(e) After three days of camping, we **will appreciate** our comfortable beds. (f) I suppose our grandchildren **will like** different music than we do.
FORM	***will be*** + present participle of the verb ***be going to be*** + present participle is less common because of its length	(g) I'**ll be studying** until midnight. (h) He **is going to be taking** calculus.
	For questions, use: ***will*** + subject + ***be*** + present participle of the verb For negative sentences use: ***will*** + negation + ***be*** + present participle of the verb	(i) **Will** he **be studying** at the university next year? (j) I **won't be working** with them on that project next month.

3.1 Get in Motion: Future Continuous

Work with a partner. You are each going to a conference in Paris on Feeding the World. Partner A's schedule is in File 24 in Appendix G. Partner B's schedule is in File 14 in Appendix G. Find a time when you can meet.

A: Where will you be staying?

B: At the _____. How about you?

A: I'll be staying at the _____. Are you free on Wednesday?

62　UNIT 3 My Future, Our Future

B: What time?

A: 12:30?

B: No, sorry, I'll be _____ ing _____ then. How about 3:30?

A: No, I'll be _____ ing _____ then. How about...?

3.2 Predictions

Write predictions of what we will be doing in 50 years to deal with food shortages. Make the sentences negative if you do not agree with them.

EXAMPLE:
we   eat insects for protein
We will be eating insects for protein.

1. we   produce more bread than rice
   _____

2. the United Nations   manage all aspects of food production
   _____

3. countries with food   provide food aid to those without
   _____

4. scientists   research new disease-resistant plants and stronger pesticides
   _____

5. people   consume more meat than fish
   _____

6. sea farmers   grow new edible plant life in the oceans
   _____

7. schools   educate farmers on new agricultural techniques
   _____

8. consultants   train small farmers regarding high-yield crops
   _____

9. we   prepare more meat than vegetable dishes
   _____

10. governments   promote smaller families so that everyone will have food
    _____

11. unfortunately, people   probably still fight wars against each other
    _____

UNIT 3 *Future and Future Perfect*

3.3 Talk It Over and Optional Writing

Do you agree or disagree with the statements below? Discuss them with your classmates. Then write a composition about one of the topics.

1. Students' success will determine a country's success.
2. When you educate women, you are educating the nation.
3. World hunger will not exist in the 21st century.
4. Solving the world garbage problem begins at home.

4 FUTURE PERFECT AND FUTURE PERFECT CONTINUOUS

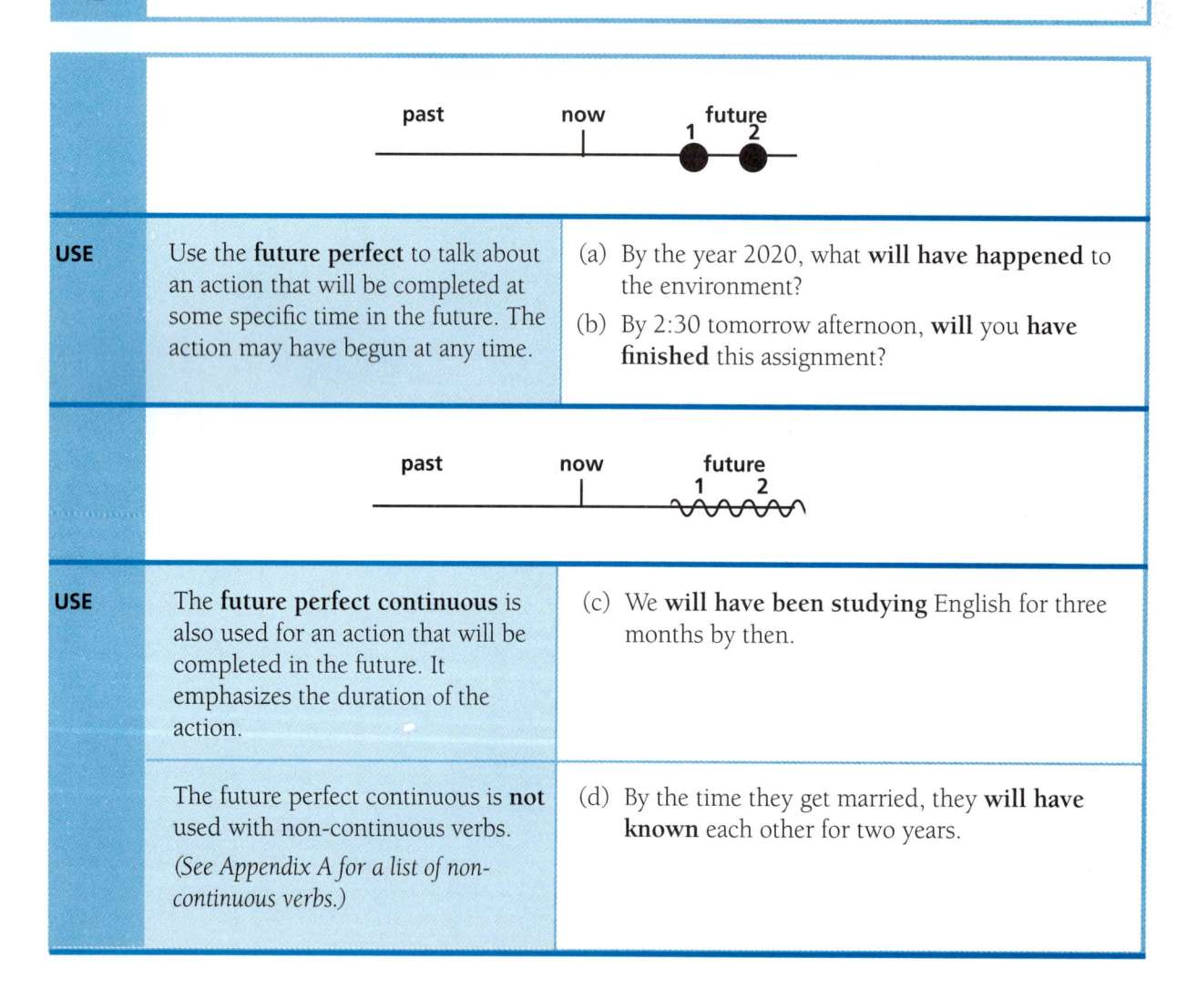

past — now — future 1 2

USE	Use the **future perfect** to talk about an action that will be completed at some specific time in the future. The action may have begun at any time.	(a) By the year 2020, what **will have happened** to the environment? (b) By 2:30 tomorrow afternoon, **will** you **have finished** this assignment?

past — now — future 1 2

USE	The **future perfect continuous** is also used for an action that will be completed in the future. It emphasizes the duration of the action.	(c) We **will have been studying** English for three months by then.
	The future perfect continuous is **not** used with non-continuous verbs. *(See Appendix A for a list of non-continuous verbs.)*	(d) By the time they get married, they **will have known** each other for two years.

UNIT 3 *My Future, Our Future*

FORM	Future perfect: ***will have*** + **past participle** of the verb	(e) I **will have finished** my course by then.
	Future perfect continuous: ***will have been*** + the **present participle** of the verb	(f) We **will have been studying** for three months by then. (g) By the time both our children graduate, we **will have been paying** tuition for 10 years.
	For questions, use: ***will*** + subject + ***have (been)*** + **past participle** of the verb For negative sentences, use: ***will*** + negation + ***have (been)*** + **past participle** of the verb (Note: The past perfect continuous is not common in questions or negatives.)	(h) **Will** you **have finished** by then? (i) I **won't have finished** my degree by then.
TIME WORDS	***By the time (that)*** (Note: Use the simple present in the time clause to indicate the future.) ***By*** (*a time*)	(j) **By the time** the year ends, her students **will have participated** in several conservation projects. (k) We'll **have finished by** 6:00.
	For (*a period of time*) and ***since*** (*a point of time*) often appear in sentences with the future perfect continuous.	(l) By the time that he retires, he **will have been teaching** in that school *for* ten years. (m) By the time he retires, he **will have been teaching** *since* 1975.

4.1 Get in Motion: Future Perfect Continuous

A. Write down three things that you are doing right now.

sitting in class _____   _____

_____   _____

B. Now answer this question: By the time you finish these activities, how long will you have been doing these things?

I will have been sitting in class for (time).

C. Ask a classmate: What are some things you will have done in your life by the year 2015?

I will have completed my education.

UNIT 3 Future and Future Perfect

4.2 Tense Contrast

Complete the sentences with the correct form of the verb in parentheses. Use simple present, present continuous, future, future continuous, future perfect, or future perfect continuous. Circle the time expressions.

1. A: How _____ (you, be able) to do all the reading when you're in the university next year?
   B: I _____ (not, worry) about it. By then I _____ (study) English in the United States for three years.

2. A: _____ (you, plan) on getting a job using your English?
   B: Yes. By the time I _____ (go) back to my country, I _____ (study) English for two years. I think I _____ (be able) to communicate just fine in English.

3. I _____ (want) to buy a car next year. By then I _____ (save) enough money to get one.

4. If we _____ (continue) to use our natural resources this way, we _____ (use) them up and we _____ (not, have) alternative sources.

5. My husband and I _____ (plan) to retire in six years. By then our children _____ (finish) college and _____ (find) jobs.

6. This is our plan. We _____ (sell) our house and _____ (buy) a smaller one.

7. Don't be late tonight! If you _____ (come) later than 5:30, we _____ (already, leave) for the airport.

8. I _____ (probably, work) until I _____ (be) 65. After I _____ (retire), I would like to travel.

9. By age 65 I _____ (work) for more than 40 years. I _____ (be) ready to stop working! I hope that I _____ (have) enough money saved to live well.

10. By the time they _____ (get) married next year, they _____ (know) each other for three years.

UNIT 3 My Future, Our Future

4.3 Predictions

Are you an optimist or a pessimist? Make predictions about the future with the affirmative or negative form of the verb. Use the future perfect or future perfect continuous. You may have to add *not*, prepositions, and articles. Begin with "By the year . . . ,".

EXAMPLE
CO_2 deplete   the ozone layer
By the year 2020, CO_2 will not have depleted the ozone layer.

1. global warming   change   the climates

2. air   become   too polluted   to breathe

3. tropical rain forest   become   totally deforested

4. oil spills   destroy   waters and animal life

5. there   be   too much disposal of hazardous waste

6. acid rain   pollute   forests, rivers, and lakes

7. cities   become   too crowded to live in

8. scientists   discover   new uses for recycled waste

9. scientists   invent   a non-polluting, fast car

10. robotics   totally   replace factory workers

4.4 Talk It Over and Optional Writing

Discuss these questions with a group of classmates. Then write a composition based on your discussion.

1. Is there an environmental problem near you or near your hometown? Describe the problem.

2. What plans do people / the government have to take care of it?
   Use the future perfect to describe when these plans will have been carried out and what will have changed in the situation. If there are no plans to take care of the problem, describe what will happen.

5 FUTURE IN THE PAST

USE	There are different ways to state that an action was intended in the past. It may or may not have eventually happened.

FORM	*was / were going to* + **base form** of verb *(very common)*	(a) They **were going to meet** with their study group.
	was / were to + **base form** of verb if the action is under human control	(b) The president of the class **was to address** the students.
		(c) The project **was to start** in September of 1991.
	was / were about to + **base form** of verb for a future plan that is immediate	(d) We **were about to take** a test when the fire alarm went off.
	would + **base form** of the verb to describe a second, future action in the past	(e) They **would realize** too late the importance of studying throughout the quarter. *(First, they didn't realize the importance; then at a future time, they did.)*
		(f) They were to start an experiment that **would last** for two years. *(First, the experiment started and then it lasted for a period of time.)*

5.1 Get in Motion: Future in the Past

Complete these plans about events that were supposed to take place. Give a reason why they were interrupted or never happened.

EXAMPLE
They were going to go to a meeting when *their car broke down.*

1. They were about to leave for dinner when . . .
2. We were to be at the meeting at 8:00 a.m. but . . .
3. I was going to finish the project by summer but . . .
4. He was going to become a vegetarian but . . .
5. Our class was about to begin an experiment when . . .
6. They were going to collect food for the hungry but . . .
7. They were to meet with the director of the project the next day but . . .
8. The plane was to arrive at 6:00 but . . .
9. We were going to stay at a great hotel but . . .
10. I was going to sleep late but . . .

5.2 Listening: Biosphere 2

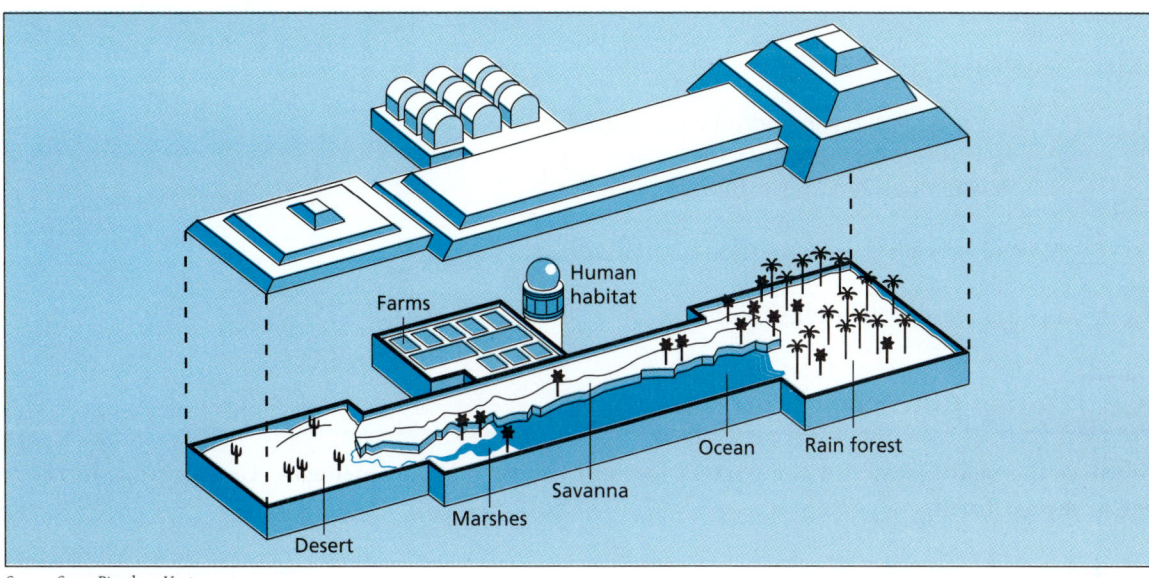

Source: Space Biosphere Ventures
Gannett Newspapers/Seattle Times

A. Before you listen, look at the illustration. Complete the sentences with words from the list.

environment	experiment	inhabitants
living	out of balance	pesticides
sealed off	self-sufficient	

1. Scientists planned to study Biosphere 2, an environmental _____.

2. The word "biosphere" has two parts. "Bio-" means _____. "Sphere" means ball. Biosphere 2 is named after Earth, "Biosphere 1."

3. Scientists _____ Biosphere 2 from the outside atmosphere. No air from the outside was supposed to enter Biosphere 2.

4. Biosphere 2 had its own atmosphere and the people inside planned to live off the crops they grew inside on their farms. Biosphere 2 was supposed to be _____.

5. With its rain forest, ocean, and desert, Biosphere 2 tried to establish an _____ just like that in the real world.

6. On the farms, the Biosphere _____ hoped to produce all their own food.

7. The Biosphere did not use any _____, so insects were a problem on the farms.

8. The amount of oxygen in the air declined and the amount of carbon dioxide increased. The atmosphere got _____.

B. Listen and take notes about the Biosphere project.

UNIT 3 Future and Future Perfect   69

C. Listen again. Put an X next to the plans that did not succeed in the Biosphere experiment.

_____ 1. lasted two years

_____ 2. eight people lived in a sealed-off space

_____ 3. had enough oxygen and little carbon dioxide

_____ 4. grew enough food for eight inhabitants

_____ 5. had enough communication with friends

Check your answers with a classmate.

5.3 Tense Contrast

Complete the sentences with the correct form of the verb in parentheses. Use a future in the past or a past form.

1. In September of 1991, Jane Poynter _____ (leave) the larger world for two years and live in a small "mini-world" with seven other people.

2. In that world, called Biosphere 2, they _____ (find out) if scientists could make a sealed-off space self-sufficient.

3. The plan was that the Biosphere _____ (be) self-sufficient.

4. It _____ (provide) everything necessary to sustain eight people for two years.

5. The idea was that it _____ (keep) a balanced atmosphere.

6. They felt sure it _____ (work).

7. Biosphere 2 _____ (not, work) perfectly.

8. The Biosphere's farms _____ (feed) its inhabitants but problems with insects and bad weather resulted in less successful crops.

9. This two-year experiment _____ (be) the first stage of a longer experiment.

10. The entire Biosphere 2 project _____ (last) 100 years.

11. Originally, Biosphere 2 _____ (remain) totally sealed.

12. One resident _____ (have to leave) Biosphere 2 for a medical visit.

UNIT 3 My Future, Our Future

6 TROUBLE SPOTS: NON-COUNT NOUNS

Non-count nouns are nouns that cannot easily be counted because they have smaller parts (like "rice") or they cannot be touched (like "advice"). Many of them are abstract nouns that express ideas, feelings, and actions that we cannot touch. These nouns are always singular.	*homework* *research* *technology* *advice* *waste* *information* *history* *management* *damage* *anger* *luck* *love* *safety*
Add **expressions of quantity** to make non-count nouns countable. We rarely use **a (an)** with non-count nouns, but the article **the** is possible.	(a) We have **a lot of** homework to do tonight. (b) Please give us **some advice** on this matter. (c) Their culture has **thousands of years of** history. (d) **The** information they gave me was correct. (e) I'd like to talk to **the** management.

Little / Few

Use **a little** + a **non-count noun** and **a few** + a **plural count noun** to express a positive sense even though it is a small number.	(f) **A little research** has been done on the problem. *(It's not much but we are happy with what we have.)* (g) **A few teachers** have experience working with non-native speakers. *(There are not many but at least some have this kind of experience.)*
Use **little** + a **non-count noun** or **few** + a **plural count noun** to express a negative sense with a small number.	(h) **Little research** has been done into that problem. *(This is not enough research. We need more.)* (i) **Few teachers** have the training to work with non-native speakers. *(We need more experienced teachers. This is not enough.)*
Use **quite a lot / a few / a little** to make the number higher.	(j) The schools need **quite a few** new **teachers**. (k) **Quite a lot of research** has been done on how to learn a foreign language.

UNIT 3 Future and Future Perfect

6.1 Count or Non-Count?

Write NC next to the nouns that are usually non-count. Circle the appropriate quantifier.

_____	1. knowledge	a great deal of	several
_____	2. idea	thousands of	much
_____	3. work	many	a lot of
_____	4. oil	100 barrels of	a few
_____	5. suitcase	several	too much
_____	6. milk	few	a glass of
_____	7. transportation	many	two kinds of
_____	8. advice	lots of	one
_____	9. story	some	much
_____	10. truth	some	three

6.2 Little / Few

Underline the best choice to complete each sentence.

1. (Little / A few) progress has been made on the problem. We need quite (a few / few) more people working on the project.
2. There is (a little / little) possibility that he will be here on time. We might as well begin without him.
3. (A few / Few) committee members have been meeting to study the problem. There are not many but they are getting a lot of work done.
4. With (little / a little) more effort, you will succeed. It won't take much.
5. (A few / Few) people from my committee are coming to the meeting. I am disappointed.
6. Quite (a little / a few) new students showed up for the recycling meeting. We didn't expect to get so many new members.
7. Quite (a lot of / a little) money is necessary to finance the project. The original budget is not enough.
8. (A few / Few) times I have called him for advice and he has been very helpful.
9. Do you need any help with your project? Yes, we'd appreciate (a little / a few) help.
10. The planning committee listed quite (a little / a few) ideas.
11. Wait (a little / a few) more minutes. I need (a little / a few) more time.
12. It's too bad that they worked so hard but were only able to finish (quite a few / a few) things on their list.

UNIT 3 My Future, Our Future

7 TROUBLE SPOTS: ARTICLES

Do not use *the* for the names of countries, continents, states, and cities; streets and avenues; or colleges and universities.	(a) **Thailand** is in **Asia**. (b) We live on **45th Avenue**. (c) He attends **Boston University** but his sister goes to **Carleton College**.
Use *the* for *the Sudan*, countries which are plural, and countries which begin with *Union, United, Republic,* or *Kingdom*.	**the** Philippines, **the** Netherlands, **the** United States, **the** People's Republic of China, **the** Kingdom of Saudi Arabia
Use *the* with colleges and universities which have *of* in their names.	**the** University **of** New Mexico **the** College **of** the Pacific

7.1 Articles

Write the names of 12 countries and 12 colleges and universities. Be careful to include *the* when necessary.

UNIT 3 *Future and Future Perfect*

8 PREPOSITIONS AND PHRASAL VERBS

Prepositions of Time

In winter   *On* Monday   *At* noon / midnight

in	a period of time	**in** winter, **in** May, **in** 1999; **in** the morning, evening; **in** five minutes, **in** the future; **in** time for (*within a period of time*)
on	a day or date	**on** Monday, **on** March 5; **on** weekends; **on** time (*punctual*)
at	a point in time	**at** midnight, **at** noon, **at** night, **at** 12:30, **at** the opening of the ceremony; **at** a time, **at** any time, **at** the end of the year

Phrasal Verbs

(a) **Jump at** that chance! It's worth it. (*be eager for*)
(b) **Keep at** it! (*continue*)
(c) He's **coming at** it from a very strange direction. (*advance*)
(d) We have to **go at** the problem from a different direction. (*attack*)
(e) I can't **get at** it. Can you help me out? (*reach*)

For definitions of these and other phrasal verbs, see Appendix D.

8.1 Practice with Prepositions

Look at the following times. Decide which preposition would be used: *in*, *on*, or *at*.

1. _____ January 4
2. _____ early November
3. _____ twenty minutes to 11:00
4. _____ Friday afternoons
5. _____ my birthday
6. _____ the Fourth of July
7. _____ the time
8. _____ good weather
9. _____ the daytime
10. _____ this holiday

74   UNIT 3 *My Future, Our Future*

8.2 Practice with Phrasal Verbs

Match the best meaning for each item. If necessary, refer to Appendix D.

A.

_____ 1. I will look into that.
_____ 2. I will look at that.
_____ 3. I will look in on her.
_____ 4. Count on me.
_____ 5. Count me in.

a. examine
b. depend on
c. include my participation
d. research / find out more about
e. go by to see / visit

B.

_____ 1. He said to go on in.
_____ 2. He said to go on.
_____ 3. I put in my two cents.
_____ 4. I put on my coat before I left.
_____ 5. I forgot to turn in my work.
_____ 6. I forgot to turn on the lights.

a. hand in / give the teacher
b. enter / go inside
c. switch on / put on / supply electricity or power
d. contributed
e. continue
f. covered my clothes with my coat

C.

_____ 1. She always jumps at the opportunity.
_____ 2. She always jumps on me for that mistake.
_____ 3. She always jumps in when needed.
_____ 4. If he can get in on the action, he will.
_____ 5. If he can get on with her, he will marry her.
_____ 6. If he can get at the problem easily, he will solve it.

a. reach
b. gets irritated with / criticizes
c. volunteers
d. participate in / have a part of
e. get along with / be content with
f. is eager for

D.

_____ 1. She never let on that she was so ill.
_____ 2. She never let her cats into the house again.
_____ 3. We kept at it for days.
_____ 4. He keeps on doing it. It bothers me.
_____ 5. Let's go at it from another way.
_____ 6. He's coming at it from the wrong perspective.

a. approaching
b. continued
c. told anyone
d. continues
e. attack
f. admitted (permitted inside)

LISTENING TEST

Listen and circle the letter of the best restatement or answer.

1. a. We are flying now.
   b. We are planning to go.
   c. We have already left.

2. a. I'm going to be there.
   b. I want to be there.
   c. I'm not going to be there.

3. a. I have finished.
   b. I'm going to work on it while you're here.
   c. I'm going to finish it before you come.

4. a. Tom has plans to help us.
   b. I think Tom is willing to help us.
   c. I'm not sure that Tom will help us.

5. a. I haven't called her yet.
   b. I have already called her.
   c. A letter will arrive first.

6. a. We're living in a new house.
   b. We're leaving our new house.
   c. We're going to move.

7. a. I have studied English for about thirteen years.
   b. I have studied English for about twelve years.
   c. I have studied English for about eleven years.

8. a. I'm going to help.
   b. Sure. I'd be glad to help.
   c. Are we going to help?

9. a. I always go to the university.
   b. I am attending the university.
   c. I am going to go to the university.

10. a. We are going to eat.
    b. We heard the news as we were eating.
    c. We heard the news right before we planned to eat.

QUIZ YOURSELF

Circle the letter of the expression which has the same meaning as the underlined words.

1. To solve the global waste problem, we <u>will begin</u> on a local level in our own homes this month.
   a. are beginning
   b. were to begin
   c. begin

2. Buying refillable bottles <u>has cut down</u> on the amount of packaging which people throw away.
   a. will have cut down
   b. had cut down
   c. has been cutting down

3. From now on we <u>will be reusing</u> our butter containers to store leftovers and other food.
   a. would reuse
   b. will reuse
   c. will have been reused

4. If you buy fresh vegetables, rather than prepackaged ones, you <u>will be decreasing</u> the amount of packaging waste.
   a. were going to decrease
   b. will have decreased
   c. are going to decrease

5. Buying repairable items <u>will cut down</u> on the amount of non-recyclable garbage.
   a. will have cut down
   b. has been cutting down
   c. is going to cut down

6. Composting leaf, plant, and grass waste as well as food waste <u>will provide</u> you with fertilizer for your garden and decrease the amount of garbage in your city.
   a. provides
   b. is providing
   c. is going to provide

7. My plan <u>was to stop</u> asking for a bag in stores, but I always forgot.
   a. was going to be to stop
   b. stopped
   c. was stopping

8. We <u>were going to donate</u> items we didn't use to a charity.
   a. will be donating
   b. would donate
   c. will have donated

9. By the year 2010 families in our city <u>will have been using</u> recycle bins for 20 years.
   a. will use
   b. have used
   c. will have used

10. By the time they are grown, our children <u>will have</u> always <u>lived</u> in a home where we recycle paper, metal, glass, and newspaper. They won't know family life without recycling.
    a. are living
    b. will have been living
    c. have lived

UNIT 3 Future and Future Perfect

UNIT 4

Modals and Related Structures: Advice, Obligation, Expectation

Parents and Children

1 ADVICE AND OPINION

should, ought to	*Should* and *ought to* indicate the speaker / writer thinks something is a good idea, but the listener / reader has a choice to follow the suggestion or not. You can make advice more indirect by using **maybe**, **perhaps**, or **do you think . . .**	Advice: (a) You **shouldn't do** that. (b) You **ought to talk** to her about it. (c) **Perhaps** you **should talk** to his mother first. Opinion: (d) Parents **should provide** their children with a loving home. (e) Parents **shouldn't hit** their children. (f) A child **ought to have** a secure home environment.
had better	*Had better* implies that something bad will happen if you don't act. It is not appropriate to say **had better** to someone who has more status or power than you do (for example, someone older than you). It is used more in spoken English than written English.	(g) You**'d better ask** your parents before you do that. (h) **Hadn't** you **better** telephone your parents? They'll be worried about you. (i) You**'d better not** do that! You'll get in a lot of trouble.

FORM	Use the **base form** of the verb after these modals. For questions, use: **should** + subject + **base form** of the verb The question form with **had better** is always negative. For negative sentences, use: **should / had better** + negation + **base form** of the verb (Note: **Ought to** is not commonly used in negatives or questions.)	(j) You **should / ought to talk** to her. (k) You'**d better do** it soon. (l) **Should** you **be** doing that right now? (m) **Hadn't** you **better talk** to her first? (n) You **shouldn't do** that. (o) You'**d better not do** that.

1.1 Get in Motion

What are these parents saying to their children? Use the words below each picture.

1. ought to / backpack

2. should / straight

3. had better / next test

4. should / loud

(Continued on the next page)

UNIT 4 Modals: *Advice, Obligation, Expectation*

5. had better / milk / strong bones

6. ought to / bed

7. had better / to school today

8. should / junk food

1.2 Speaking Practice: Advice in the Present and Future

Give advice to these parents.

1. Our 3-year-old child is throwing a temper tantrum at a restaurant.
2. We love going to movies, but our baby sometimes wakes up and starts to cry. The other people in the theater get irritated with us.
3. When our teenage son came home last night, we smelled alcohol on his breath.
4. Our 12-year-old daughter wants to go to a party at a friend's house, but we don't know that friend and we don't know if her parents are going to be home.
5. Our 17-year-old daughter wants to travel in Europe for the summer with a friend. We want her to get a job to save money for college.
6. Our teenage son has saved quite a lot of money and wants to buy a used car when he gets his driver's license next month.
7. Our 16-year-old daughter wants to go out with a 22-year-old man.
8. Our daughter is going to the university in our city, but she wants to get her own apartment with friends. (Is your advice the same if it's a son?)
9. Our youngest son is 26 years old. He has a good job, but every day after work, he comes home (he lives with us) and watches TV. Even on weekends he spends most of his time with us. We are worried about him because he doesn't seem to have a life of his own.
10. Our daughter is 18. She is starting to spend time with a young man whom we don't like. We are worried that she is going to want to marry him.

UNIT 4 *Parents and Children*

3. Marty is too young to have a driver's license, but he took his parents' car out last weekend and he ran into the garage when he came back. His parents are out of town for two weeks.
   a. Marty shouldn't have _____.
   b. He'd better _____.
   c. His parents shouldn't have _____.

4. When his parents were out last weekend, Bailey had a party. His parents didn't know until they came home. They were furious!
   a. Bailey shouldn't have _____.
   b. He'd better _____.
   c. His parents had better _____.

5. Joo forgot to tell his parents that he had a baseball game after school on Friday. When he didn't arrive home, they were very worried.
   a. Joo shouldn't have _____.
   b. He ought to _____.

2.3 Talk It Over

Discuss this question with your classmates.

What did your parents usually tell you?
You'd better (not) . . . . You should always (never) . . . .

UNIT 4 Modals: Advice, Obligation, Expectation

3 OBLIGATION AND NECESSITY

has / have to	*Has / have to* shows that something is necessary or required now or in the future.	(a) Parents **have to feed** and clothe their children. (b) She **has to take care** of him.
must	*Must* is used to explain rules or laws. It is used more in writing than in speaking and it is not as common as *have to*. The past tense of *must* is *had to*.	(c) All students **must wear** the same uniform. (d) When Jean was a child, girls **had to wear** skirts to school.
have got to	*Have got to* is used in speaking only and is somewhat informal. It has the same meaning as *have to*.	(e) I **have got to go** now. (f) He**'s got to be** home by 10:00.
Imperatives	Imperatives are strong commands that are used to give orders, directions, or warnings. They imply that the listener has little choice because of the power the speaker has.	(g) **Go** to your room right now! (h) **Don't talk** to me that way! (i) **Be** more careful around your baby sister! (j) **Get** me a paper towel, quickly! (k) **Don't let** me see you do that again!
FORM	These modal expressions are followed by the **base form** of the verb. For questions, use: *do / does / did* + subject + **have to** + **base form** of the verb *must* + subject + **base form** of the verb For negative sentences, use: *do / did* + negation + **have to** + **base form** of the verb *do* + negation + **base form** of the verb *Have got to* is rarely used in the negative or in questions. *(See Box 4 for negatives of have to and must.)*	(l) I **must talk** to you right away! (m) **Do** I **have to do** it? Yes, you do. (n) **Must** you **make** so much noise? (o) We **don't have to be** home early tonight. (p) **Don't do** that!

3.1 Get in Motion: Obligation

Who is responsible for these child-rearing activities? The father, the mother, both parents, teachers? Circle F, M, or T. You may circle more than one.

1. F M T keep children safe
2. F M T teach children the difference between right and wrong
3. F M T discipline children
4. F M T give children a good education
5. F M T teach children to read
6. F M T teach children how to interact socially
7. F M T show children not to use drugs and alcohol

3.2 Listening: Discipline

A. Listen and complete the sentences.

MOTHER: Michael, _____ do that!

FATHER: What's he doing?

MOTHER: He's pulling on the cord. Michael, _____!

FATHER: I'll make him stop.

MOTHER: _____ him!

FATHER: He _____ learn discipline.

MOTHER: Yes, but you _____ hit him!

B. In the United States, most parents agree with the mother in this dialogue: Parents should not hit their children. What is your opinion? Discuss this with your classmates.

3.3 Talk It Over

Interview a classmate. Make questions to ask his / her opinion.

EXAMPLE
parents / yell at their children (should)
Do you think parents should yell at their children?
I think that sometimes a parent has to . . . What do you think?
I don't think parents should . . .

1. parents / hit their children (should)
2. when children misbehave, parents / lock them in their rooms (ought to)
3. When teenagers misbehave, parents / ground them (should) ("ground" means keep someone at home, keep them from going out with their friends)
4. children / be seen, not heard, when they are eating dinner with their parents (should)
5. If young children don't want to eat dinner, parents / force them to eat (had better)
6. teenagers / stay out later than 11 p.m. (should)

UNIT 4 Modals: Advice, Obligation, Expectation

4 ABSENCE OF NECESSITY

must not	**Must not** shows that something is important not to do. It is also used to show that something is prohibited by society's rules or by law.	(a) Children **must not yell** at their parents. (b) Students **must not bring** alcohol into the dormitory.
doesn't / don't have to	**Doesn't / Don't have to** shows the absence of necessity	(c) Teenagers **don't have to have** a baby-sitter when their parents go out. (d) An adult **doesn't have to drink** as much milk as a child does.
FORM	These modal expressions are followed by the **base form** of the verb.	(e) Stop that! You **must not do** that! (f) You **don't have to do** it right now.

4.1 Get in Motion: Absence of Necessity

Complete the sentences with *has / have to*, *doesn't / don't have to*, or *must not*.

1. Young people _____ have a job before they can support children of their own.

2. If they want to get good jobs, teenagers _____ quit school.

3. Parents _____ support their children financially once they graduate from college, but most help them until they find jobs.

4. Children _____ play with fire.

5. A family _____ be rich in order to raise happy and healthy children.

6. In my opinion, parents _____ hit children when they misbehave.

7. In my country, children in elementary schools _____ wear uniforms to school.

8. In my country, if a child has a learning disability, the public school _____ provide for that child to have special help.

9. In my country, if a child has a physical disability, the public school _____ provide access and help for that child.

86   UNIT 4 *Parents and Children*

4.2 *Must Not* versus *Don't Have to*

Complete the sentences with your ideas.

1. Parents must _____.

2. Parents don't have to _____.

3. Parents must not _____.

4. Young children must _____.

5. Young children must not _____.

6. Young children don't have to _____.

7. Teenagers must _____.

8. Teenagers must not _____.

9. Teenagers don't have to _____.

4.3 Optional Writing

A. Write a composition discussing one of these statements:

> Spanking is physical abuse.
> Parents should be very strict with children.
> Some public places and events are not appropriate places for children.

B. Write a story about an experience from your childhood when you were fairly or unfairly punished for misbehaving. Write it from the third-person perspective. Include the lesson your character learned from the experience.

4.4 Listening: Child Divorces Parents

Gregory Kingsley

(Continued on the next page)

A. Match the word and the definition.

_____ 1. abused   a. an institution for children with no parents
_____ 2. adopt   b. split up
_____ 3. adoption   c. harmed or injured
_____ 4. allowed   d. become a child's legal parent
_____ 5. custody   e. a person who helps people in trouble
_____ 6. divorce   f. permitted
_____ 7. foster parents g. the legal end to a relationship
_____ 8. orphanage   h. temporary legal guardians
_____ 9. protection   i. safety from some danger
_____ 10. separated   j. the process of becoming a child's legal parent
_____ 11. social worker k. guardianship of a child

B. Listen and complete the sentences with one of the words above. Then check your answers with a classmate.

(1) When Gregory Kingsley was three years old, his parents _____.
(2) His father had _____ of Gregory. (3) When he was living with his father, his father _____ him. (4) A _____ _____ found out about Gregory's problems and took him away from his father. (5) His mother decided to put him up for _____. (6) The government agency that took care of the child was a child _____ agency.

(7) Gregory lived in a(n) _____ _____ for a short time. (8) Then he went to live with _____ parents, George and Lizabeth Russ. (9) When he told his mother that the Russes wanted to _____ him, his mother changed her mind and decided to keep Gregory. (10) Gregory filed for _____ from his parents. (11) The judge has to decide if a child should be _____ to divorce his or her parents.

UNIT 4 Parents and Children

C. Sue and Carlos are sitting with their daughter Michelle watching the news on TV. They are discussing the judge's decision in the Gregory Kingsley case. Listen to the next part of the listening exercise and identify who has what opinion.

_____ 1. Judge   a. Gregory should not have sued his parents.
_____ 2. Sue (mother)   b. Gregory's parents should never have had children.
_____ 3. Carlos (father)   c. Gregory ought to be able to divorce his parents.
_____ 4. Michelle (daughter) d. Children must always obey their parents.

D. What is your opinion? Discuss your ideas with your classmates.

4.5 Modal Review

Which of the choices best describes the meaning of the underlined part of the sentence?

1. Gregory's parents should never have had children.
   a. a law
   b. an action that has a bad consequence
   c. an opinion about a past action

2. Gregory's mother should give her son up for adoption.
   a. an action that has a bad consequence
   b. an opinion of a present action
   c. a strong command

3. The judge had better decide against Gregory. Otherwise, a lot of children will try to divorce their parents.
   a. a law
   b. a strong opinion because of a possible bad consequence
   c. an opinion of a past action

4. Gregory's father should not have abused Gregory.
   a. advice
   b. an opinion of a past action
   c. an obligation

5. The judge had to make a decision.
   a. a strong command
   b. an obligation
   c. an opinion of a past action

6. Gregory's mother didn't have to give him to his father.
   a. an opinion
   b. the absence of necessity
   c. an action that has a bad consequence

7. Gregory's parents should have provided a stable home life.
   a. an opinion about a past action
   b. an action that has a bad consequence
   c. a strong command

8. The legal system must protect parents' rights as well as children's rights.
   a. an action that has a bad consequence
   b. some advice
   c. an obligation

9. I've got to tell you about this case of a child divorcing his parents.
   a. a necessity
   b. an opinion
   c. an action that has a bad consequence

10. Gregory's father ought to have treated him better.
    a. an opinion of a past action
    b. a necessity
    c. a law

UNIT 4 Modals: Advice, Obligation, Expectation

5 EXPECTATION

be supposed to	This expression shows that someone else (a person, society, or organization) expects a certain action or behavior.	(a) Children **are supposed to obey** their parents' decisions. (b) Children **aren't supposed to miss** school.
be to	*Be to* shows a more definite expectation than *be supposed to*. It is more formal and less common than *be supposed to*.	(c) Children **are to bring** a medical report when they start school. *(expected procedure)* (d) The judge **is to make** the decision soon. *(expected schedule)*
FORM	These modal expressions are followed by the **base form** of the verb. For questions, use: *am / is / are* + subject + *(supposed to)* + **base form** of the verb For negative sentences, use: *am / is / are* + negation + *(supposed to)* + **base form** of the verb	(e) You **are supposed to be** there by 7:30. (f) **Are** we **supposed to wear** our uniforms? (g) **Are** we **to be** there by 8:00? (h) We **aren't supposed to sit** in this area. (i) You **aren't to say** a word to anyone!

5.1 Get in Motion: Expressing Expectation

Answer the questions. Use the words in parentheses.

1. Do you have any plans with friends or family for tonight / this weekend / in the future? (be supposed to)
2. How long do your parents or family expect you to study? (be to)
3. What are your plans for tonight? Do you have any homework to do? (be supposed to)
4. In the note on the right, what are the parents' plans? (be to) (be supposed to)
5. In the note, what do Andy's parents expect him to do? (be supposed to)

> Andy,
> We've got an appointment to meet with your teacher at 5:30. We'll be home by 7:00. Please put the meatloaf in the oven by 6:00 and start working on your HOMEWORK!!
>
> Love,
>
> Mom

UNIT 4 Parents and Children

5.2 Expectations

Look at the picture below and read Jim's parents' expectations. Make sentences explaining what is wrong.

EXAMPLE
Jim is supposed to do his homework.

Jim's parents work. When they come home . . . at 5:30

. . . they expect that Jim has:
- done his homework
- not had friends over
- set the table for dinner

. . . they don't expect that Jim has:
- had friends over
- made a mess in the house
- ruined his appetite from snacks

UNIT 4 Modals: Advice, Obligation, Expectation

6 EXPECTATION IN THE PAST

was / were supposed to	*Was / were supposed to* expresses an obligation in the past that was not fulfilled.	(a) They **were supposed to call** home. *(but they didn't)*
was / were supposed to have	The perfect form (*have* + past participle) shows an obligation or expectation in the past that was not met. It often has the same meaning as *was / were supposed to*.	(b) I **was supposed to have called** my parents before 10:00. *(but I didn't)* (c) They **weren't supposed to have taken** their parents' car. (d) They **weren't supposed to take** their parents' car.
	However, if the sentence refers to two events which happened at different times in the past, use *was / were supposed to have* + the **past participle** to make the time clear.	(e) The plane **was supposed to leave** at 8:30. (f) The plane **was supposed to have left** by then, but it was late.
had better have	*Had better have* implies that if an action did not happen, a bad consequence may be the result, such as anger.	(g) You**'d better have finished** your homework by the time I come back home! (h) They**'d better have fixed** my car by now! (i) You**'d better not have ruined** the sweater you borrowed from me!
FORM	These expressions are followed by a **past participle** of the verb. For questions, use: *was / were supposed to* + subject + *have* + past participle For negative sentences, use: *was / were* + negation + *supposed to* + *have* + past participle *had better* + negation + *have* + past participle (Note: *Had better have* is not used in questions.)	(j) You **were supposed to have finished** by now. (k) What **was I supposed to have done**? (l) You **weren't supposed to have told** him. (m) You**'d better not have told** Dad!

UNIT 4 *Parents and Children*

6.1 Get in Motion: *Be Supposed to*

Discuss these questions.

1. When you were a child, did your parents expect you to do chores around the house?
2. As a teenager, did you have a curfew, a time your parents wanted you to be home at night? Was it different on week nights or weekends? What happened if you were late?

6.2 *Had Better*

Complete these threatening responses. Use the expressions given.

EXAMPLE
Your son is not a good student. Last night he went to a concert. You just found out he had a test today.

| had better have | had better not have | had better | had better not |

a. You '*d better have* passed that test!
b. You '*d better not have* failed that test!
c. You '*d better not* his kind of chance in the future.

1. Your sister borrowed your mother's new blouse without asking permission.
   a. She _____ spilled anything on it.
   b. She _____ put it back before Mom gets home.

2. Your daughter used your car. Now she can't find the car keys.
   a. She _____ lost them!
   b. She _____ be more careful in the future or she won't get to use the car.

3. You took $500 out of the bank yesterday. Now you can't find it.
   a. I _____ be careful with money I withdraw from the bank.
   b. I _____ lost it.

4. Your daughter is supposed to be studying tonight. When you come home, she is not in the house.
   a. She _____ finished her homework.
   b. She _____ gone out to a party.
   c. She _____ do this again!

5. I had some important papers on my desk. Yesterday I cleaned my desk and now I can't find the papers.
   a. You _____ thrown them out.
   b. You _____ be more careful with your important papers in the future.

UNIT 4 Modals: Advice, Obligation, Expectation

6.3 Expectations

Complete these sentences with the affirmative or negative form of *be supposed to*, *be supposed to have*, or *had better have*. More than one answer may be possible.

1. My sister left yesterday for a visit to New York, Los Angeles, and San Francisco. She _____ (call) when she arrived in New York, but we haven't heard from her yet. She _____ (arrive) by now. My parents are worried.

2. I am on my way to the hospital where my wife is having a baby. She _____ (not, have) the baby until next week. She _____ (not, have) the baby before I get there!

3. My car won't start, so we're going to be late. What time _____ we _____ (be) at the party?

4. My son borrowed my car three hours ago. He _____ (be) home two hours ago! I don't know whether to be angry or worried. He _____ (not, forget) or I'm never going to lend him the car again!

5. I told my mother a secret. She _____ (not, tell) my father, but I think she did. She _____ (not, tell) him or I'll never tell her another secret in my whole life!

6.4 Modal Review

Restate the sentences using modals and related structures to comment on disciplining children.

EXAMPLE
It's not a good idea to criticize children for bad behavior because that reinforces the bad behavior.
Parents *shouldn't criticize* their children for bad behavior because that reinforces the bad behavior.

1. Society expects parents to discipline their children so that they learn what behaviors are appropriate and also feel loved.
   Parents _____ their children so that they learn appropriate behaviors and have the feeling of being loved.

2. It's not a good idea for parents to get into fights with their children about who is in charge.
   Parents _____ power struggles with their children.

3. You should not threaten a punishment unless you are ready to carry out the consequence.
   You _____ not threaten a punishment if you are not ready to carry the consequence out. Otherwise, the threat has no meaning to a child.

94 UNIT 4 *Parents and Children*

4. It is wise to praise children for good behaviors rather than always reminding them of the things they do wrong.

   You _____ children when they behave well instead of reminding them when they behave badly.

5. You are expected to model behaviors you want your children to have.

   You _____ the way you want your children to behave.

6. I've said this before: We, as parents, are obligated to use nonviolent methods of disciplining children.

   As I've said before, we parents _____ our children in peaceful ways.

6.5 Talk It Over and Optional Writing

A. In a small group, discuss the questions below.

1. How did your parents punish you when you misbehaved?
2. What responsibilities / obligations did you have when you were a teenager?
3. In your family, did you have a reputation as a well-behaved teenager or a wild teenager?
4. Did your family have very strict rules that you had to follow? What were they? How did your parents punish you or enforce these rules?
5. Did your parents like your friends?
6. Was your relationship with your grandparents close? Could you go to talk to them when you had problems or did you have a more formal relationship with them?
7. Did your parents influence which children you could play with?
8. What was the strongest message about behavior that your mother and/or father gave you?

B. Write a composition about one of these questions.

1. What do you think it was like for your parents to raise you?
2. If you have children, how will you raise them? What will you do differently from the way your parents raised you?
3. If you are a parent, what has been the most difficult part of being a parent?

7 TROUBLE SPOTS: WORD CHOICE; ARTICLES

suppose, be supposed to	*Suppose* means to believe or consider whereas *be supposed to* expresses expectation.	(a) They **supposed** she was coming to the party. *(belief)* (b) She **was supposed to come** to the party. *(expectation)*
that / this kind / sort / type (of)	Use with a singular noun to refer to a type or sort.	(c) **That sort** is hard to deal with. (d) **This type of** problem is difficult to handle. (e) **That kind of** party is always fun. (f) We don't want **that sort of** disruptive person at our party.
those / these kinds / sorts / types (of)	Use with a plural noun to refer to a type or sort.	(g) **Those kinds of** behavior problems drive me crazy. (h) **Those sorts of** children are difficult to deal with. (i) **These types of** problems are difficult for parents. (j) We are having a lot of problems with the caterer for the party. **These kinds of** problems really frustrate me. (NOT: **these kind of**)
Articles	Do not use *the* in front of names of people or places, such as mountains, islands, or lakes except when you are referring to groups of them.	(k) Mary Brightman BUT **the** Nickersons (l) Mt. Shasta BUT **the** Rocky Mountains (m) Catalina Island BUT **the** Hawaiian Islands (n) Crystal Lake BUT **the** Great Lakes

7.1 Editing Practice

Correct the error in each sentence. There is only one error in each sentence.

1. Those kind of children are always a pleasure to have on trips.
2. They supposed to provide a school bus for the trip, but parents had to drive instead.
3. Andes are a mountain chain in South America.
4. Lake Louise is set in a beautiful part of Canadian Rockies.
5. Orkneys are a group of islands which belong to the United Kingdom.

6. Kains are coming to dinner tonight.
7. The Robert Kain is our new manager.
8. Kain family lives in the city of Tacoma, Washington.
9. Los Angeles is a very smoggy city and so is the Mexico City.
10. These kinds of editing question are not very hard.

8 PREPOSITIONS AND PHRASAL VERBS

Prepositions of Time, Space, Degree		
about, around	all around; on all sides approximate	**about** 5:00; **around** 70 *(degrees)*
above, over	higher than	**above** 90 *(degrees)*, **over** $300, **over** 30 minutes
under, underneath; below, beneath	lower than	**under** an hour, **under** $20, **below** freezing, **below** average, **underneath** the desk, **beneath** the covers
Common Adjectives Followed by About		angry, careful, certain, disappointed, doubtful, glad, honest, positive, right, sensitive, serious, uncertain, wrong

Phrasal Verbs

(a) It is not easy to **bring about** change in his behavior. *(cause)*

(b) How did that **come about?** How did the military **take over** so quickly? *(happen)* *(take control of)*

(c) Let's **play around** with the idea. We can **talk it over** some more, and if we don't like it, then we can **turn** it **over** to a committee. *(try in different ways)* *(discuss)* *(give possession of)*

(d) I am trying to **get over** it, but I keep **going over and over** the series of events. *(recover emotionally)* *(review)*

See Appendix D for more phrasal verbs.

UNIT 4 Modals: Advice, Obligation, Expectation

8.1 Practice with Prepositions

Complete the sentences with the correct prepositions of time, space, and degree.

1. Fifty-nine minutes is _____ an hour.
2. His temperature is 101°. That's _____ normal.
3. Changing a baby's diaper is _____ his dignity. He won't do it because he feels it's not dignified.
4. It's going to cost you _____ $3,000. I don't know the exact number. Will you have enough money?
5. I feel that when interest gets _____ 8%, we should buy a house.
6. When the temperature gets _____ 90°, she's miserable, especially if the humidity is _____ 60%. For instance, there was 80% humidity last week.
7. When it gets _____ freezing, tomato plants will die.
8. I think there are going to be _____ 50 people, but I'm not exactly sure.
9. I'd say it's _____ time they got some professional advice. Their daughter is out of control.
10. We like to drive _____ town and see all of the different styles of homes.

8.2 Prepositions and Phrasal Verbs

Ask your partner these questions to practice prepositions and phrasal verbs.

1. What are you serious about these days?
2. What has been the hardest thing to get over in your life?
3. What kinds of changes would you like to bring about in your life?
4. What was the last thing you were really wrong about?
5. What are you usually right about?
6. What was the last thing you got really angry about?
7. What are you careful about in relationships?
8. How did taking this class come about?
9. What grammar points would you like to go over before the test?
10. What are you most positive about in life?

LISTENING TEST

Listen and circle the letter of the statement that has the most similar meaning.

1. a. She is going to go to the party.
   b. She cannot go to the party.
   c. She doesn't think it's a good idea for her to go.

2. a. They are meeting.
   b. They are planning to meet.
   c. They met already.

3. a. They left today.
   b. They had to leave today.
   c. They planned to leave today.

4. a. It's not necessary to wait.
   b. You must not wait.
   c. You'd better not wait.

5. a. It's a good idea to call them now.
   b. I called them.
   c. I didn't call them.

6. a. I'm giving you advice.
   b. I'm warning you.
   c. I'm afraid you are going to lose it.

7. a. I talked to her.
   b. It's a good idea to talk to her.
   c. It's necessary to talk to her.

8. a. It's a bad idea to do that.
   b. It's important to do that.
   c. It's not necessary to do that.

9. a. I didn't meet them.
   b. I am going to meet them.
   c. It's a good idea to meet them.

10. a. It's a good idea to meet with the teacher.
    b. It's necessary to meet with the teacher.
    c. Parents have a choice.

QUIZ YOURSELF

Circle the letter of the best answer to complete each sentence.

1. In the past, parents _____ punish bad behavior rather than reward good behavior. Today, parents are expected to reward good behavior.

    a. had to
    b. were supposed to
    c. must

2. In my grandmother's day, children _____ be good out of fear of punishment.

    a. expect to
    b. had better
    c. were to

3. When children behave well, they need social rewards such as kind words or praise. According to psychologists, they also may receive gifts or money but parents _____ give these less often than social rewards. That is, it's not a good idea to always give something for good behavior.

    a. ought not
    b. should
    c. must

4. The timing of praise is important. Late praise might be less effective than immediate praise. This means you _____ give praise in the first five minutes after the good behavior.

    a. ought
    b. should
    c. must have

5. Another way to reinforce good behavior is to keep a chart of what the child _____ (for example, brush teeth, make bed) and reward him or her with stickers. The child can later "cash in" the stickers for a special treat.

    a. is supposed to do
    b. must have done
    c. had better have done

6. Small children _____ be kept waiting for a reward. If they have to wait, they will lose interest.

    a. must not
    b. did not have to
    c. prefer to

7. When setting goals, remember it's hard for a child to be perfect all day. Children _____ be able to fulfill the goals that you set and sometimes make mistakes.

    a. suppose to
    b. ought to
    c. had better have

100   UNIT 4 *Parents and Children*

8. Parents _____ make sure that their expectations of children are realistic. Otherwise, the reward system won't work because children will not be able to fulfill their expectations.

   a. had better
   b. have
   c. ought to have

9. _____ make your reward system so complicated that a child becomes confused.

   a. Don't
   b. Let's
   c. Why should you

10. You _____ involve your children in the design of the rewards so that they will want to work for them.

    a. should
    b. had better have
    c. ought

UNIT 5

Modals and Related Structures: Suggestion, Invitation, Possibility

Socializing

1 SUGGESTION

let's, let's not, why don't I / we + base form of verb	These suggestions include the speaker.	(a) **Let's go** tomorrow. (b) **Let's talk** about this later, OK? (c) **Let's not watch** TV. (d) **Why don't I meet** you there?
why don't, why doesn't + base form of verb	These suggestions are for other people.	(e) **Why don't you call** me first? (f) **Why doesn't he take** his car?
how about, how about not + gerund	These suggestions are not specific about who is involved.	(g) **How about going** tomorrow? (h) **How about not inviting** so many people this time?
could, might + base form of verb	These present a possibility and an indirect suggestion.	(i) I **could call** to see if there are any tickets left. (j) We **could go** to a play. (k) We **might think** about going to a movie.
maybe we should, maybe you could, maybe you should + base form of verb	These give polite advice as a suggestion.	(l) **Maybe we should meet** earlier. (m) **Maybe you could pick** me up in your car. (n) **Maybe you shouldn't tell** your parents.

1.3 Role Play

Take the role of these family members. Make suggestions for a week's vacation.

Mother:	likes to go to museums and baseball games
Father:	likes to golf and go to baseball games
Teenage Son:	likes to skateboard and listen to music; likes to be with his friends
Teenage Daughter:	likes to listen to music; likes to golf and go to museums
Younger Son:	likes to swing and play in parks; likes movies, games, and swimming

2 INVITATION

let's, **why don't you / we,** **maybe we could** + base form of verb **how about** + gerund	These are used to make suggestions that are invitations.	(a) **Let's go** to a movie this weekend, OK? (b) **Why don't you come** over for dinner tonight? (c) **Why don't we go** to a movie? (d) **Maybe we could go** to a concert next week. (e) **How about going** to a movie?
would you like to, **do you want to** + base form of verb	These request someone's preference while making an invitation. *Do you want to* is a little less formal.	(f) **Would you like to go** out for dinner tonight? (g) **Do you want to go** out for Thai food?
have you + past participle **are you interested in** + noun phrase / gerund	Some phrases indirectly set the stage for an invitation.	(h) **Have you seen** that new movie at the Metro? (i) **Are you interested in** baseball? playing baseball?

2.1 Get in Motion: Invitation

Underline the expressions in the dialogue that are invitations or suggestions.

Victor and Pam met each other in a class. They are walking out of the building together and have this conversation.

PAM: Say, Victor, are you interested in going to a movie tonight?
VICTOR: Oh, hmm . . . Uh . . . Well, sure! What movie?
PAM: Well, there are a couple I haven't seen yet. Why don't we meet at the coffee shop at the Metro Theaters and decide which one we want to see?

(Continued on the next page)

VICTOR: OK. I guess they probably all start around 9:00, so how about meeting at about a quarter of?
PAM: Well, maybe we should meet earlier in case any are sold out. We could have some coffee while we decide.
VICTOR: All right, that's a good idea. So let's meet at 8:00.
PAM: OK, That sounds good. I'll see you then!
VICTOR: OK. 'Bye!

2.2 Speaking Practice

A. Invitations between friends are often suggestions that follow simple comments. Work with a partner. Make some plans for the weekend. Partner A, look at File 19 in Appendix G. Partner B, look at File 15.

EXAMPLE
A: It's going to be a nice weekend.
B: Yes, I think it is.
A: Maybe we should go out for a hike or something.
B: Well, sure, that sounds like a good idea. When do you want to go?
A: How about . . . ?

B. Invitations between people who do not know each other very well or who know each other through business are more direct. You and your partner are business people. You are meeting in New York for two days with several other people. Partner A, look at File 16 in Appendix G. Partner B, look at File 18.

2.3 Talk It Over and Optional Writing

A. Discuss these questions with a classmate.

1. Do people "date" in your group of friends or do they just go out in groups?
2. Are people chaperoned if they go out alone as a couple?
3. Who pays for the activities on a date?
4. In the dialogue in 2.1, Pam asked Victor to go out. Do women ever invite men out in your group of friends?

B. Choose one of these topics and write a composition about it.

1. At what age do young people date in your country? Are group activities more popular than dates?
2. Describe an ideal evening on a date or with friends in your country.
3. Do you think it is OK for women to invite men out on dates or should they wait for men to make the invitation? Why?
4. Does it matter who pays for the date? Why?

3 POSSIBILITY AND PROBABILITY IN THE PRESENT OR FUTURE

may, **might,** **could** + base form of verb OR **modal** + **be** + present participle	These show possibility and negative possibility in the present or future.	(a) She **may say** no. (b) They **may not like** it. (c) It **might not be** a good idea to go there. (d) We **could see** if she wants to go to the party. (e) We **could be seeing** more of them in the future.
must + base form of verb OR **modal** + **be** + present participle	***Must*** presents logical conclusions about present situations you are fairly sure of. It is also used to show empathy.	(f) He **must be** Mike's son. He looks just like him. (g) They look unhappy. They **must not like** each other. (h) They are getting dressed up. They **must be going** to the party. (i) You **must be** exhausted! You've worked so hard today.
Adverbs: ***maybe,*** ***probably***	These adverbs also express probability or possibility. ***Maybe*** is used at the beginning of a sentence. ***Probably*** is used in the middle.	(j) **Maybe** we'll stop for ice cream. (k) We'll **probably** pick up some fast food before the play.

3.1 Get in Motion: Possibility and Probability

At 8:15 at night, Tom sees a friend named Victor outside the coffee shop at the Metro Theaters.

(Continued on the next page)

UNIT 5 Modals: Suggestion, Invitation, Possibility 107

Underline the expressions in this dialogue that present a possibility or make a suggestion.

TOM: Victor! Hi! What are you doing here?
VICTOR: Well, I'm supposed to meet Pam Barnett here. You haven't seen her anywhere, have you?
TOM: No, I sure haven't. Maybe you're in the wrong place.
VICTOR: I might be. Or maybe I have the time wrong.
TOM: You could try telephoning her apartment.
VICTOR: Well, I'll wait a few more minutes.
TOM: Boy! Look at that line! Oh, isn't that Pam in the line there?
VICTOR: Oh yeah, you're right. Maybe she decided to get in line so we'd get tickets. I'll see you later! Hi, Pam!

3.2 Possibilities

Consider these ways to meet people. What are the possible risks or "payoffs" in each case?

EXAMPLE
Someone in one of your classes asks you out.
You might have a terrible time and then you will feel embarrassed in class.

1. Your best friend's brother / sister asks you out.
2. A friend arranges a blind date for you.
3. A dating service arranges a lunch date for you.
4. Your mother arranges for you to go out with her friend's son / daughter.
5. You answer an advertisement in the "personals" section of the newspaper.

3.3 Modal Contrast

Lillian and Peter are on a blind date. Look at the illustration and discuss the questions with a classmate. Use the words in parentheses in your answer.

1. How's the weather? (must)
2. How do Lillian and Peter feel about each other? (must)
3. They look like they don't know what to say to each other. Suggest some topics of conversation for them. (could)
4. What do you think they are thinking about? (might)
5. What do you think the waiter assumes? (probably)

108   UNIT 5 *Socializing*

3.4 Modal Contrast

Read the situations and answer the questions. Use the words in parentheses in your answer.

A. Richard and Angela went out together several times: to a movie, to a party with some friends, and then to dinner. They seemed to have a lot in common and Angela commented that she couldn't remember having such a good time. Then Richard told Angela some things about his life before he met her. He said that he had been married once for a year when he was a teenager. He had a son whom he never sees because his ex-wife moved to another country. The next time Richard called Angela to ask her out, she said that she couldn't go. He called again and again she refused.

1. How do you think Richard feels? (must)
2. Why do you think Angela is refusing to go out with Richard? (might)
3. Is there anything for Richard to do in this situation? (could)

B. Marie and Frank work at the same office. On Tuesday Frank asked Marie to go to the movies on Saturday night. She accepted and Frank said he would pick her up at 8:00. It is now 9:30 on Saturday night and Marie is still waiting.

1. How do you think Marie feels? (must)
2. What do you think happened to Frank? (maybe)
3. What should Marie do when Frank arrives? (ought to)
4. If Frank doesn't show up or telephone, what do you think Marie should do when she sees Frank in the office on Monday? (should)

C. Ken and Jean have been seeing each other for a couple of months. They have a lot of fun together and Jean is getting fairly serious about Ken. However, Ken talks a lot about his former relationships.

1. Why do you think Ken talks about former relationships? (may)
2. Jean never mentions previous involvements to Ken. How do you think Ken's behavior makes Jean feel? (could)

3.5 Talk It Over and Optional Writing

Discuss these questions with your classmates. Then choose one of the topics to write a composition on.

1. Have you ever been on a blind date? Was it a success or not?
2. Do you think it's appropriate to talk about old boyfriends or girlfriends with someone you are dating? Why or why not?
3. Are personal ads in a newspaper a good way to meet people to date? Why might they be a good or bad idea?
4. When should you introduce a boyfriend or girlfriend to your parents? When is it important for parents to meet their son or daughter's romantic interest?
5. What kind of rule did your parents have regarding dating or socializing with friends? For example, what time did you have to come home? Were some activities and locations prohibited?

4 POSSIBILITY AND PROBABILITY IN THE PAST

may have, might have, could have + past participle	These present a possibility in the past.	(a) They're late. They **may not have left** on time. (b) They **might have run** into a lot of traffic. (c) We **could have gotten** here earlier, but I forgot the directions.
can't have, must have + past participle	These present probability or logical conclusions about past situations. *Must have* is a very common way to show empathy for a past experience.	(d) He **can't have gotten** lost. It's easy to get here. (e) It **must have been** a great party. Everyone stayed very late. (f) That **must have been** a terrible experience.
Adverbs: *maybe,* *probably*	You can also use these adverbs to express probability or possibility in the past. *Maybe* is used at the beginning of a sentence. *Probably* is used in the middle.	(g) **Maybe** they forgot the party. (h) They **probably** got delayed in bad traffic.

4.1 Get in Motion: Possibility and Probability in the Past

Match these situations with the comments at right.

EXAMPLE
Sandy seemed quieter than normal yesterday.
He might have been upset.

1. Everyone is wearing dressy clothes.
2. The highway looks like a parking lot.
3. Everyone is here except the Johnsons.
4. Grant was in a bad accident.
5. The plane left three hours late.
6. Amy looks tired.
7. I never heard from Carl.
8. The classroom is empty.

He might have been upset.
She might not have gotten much sleep.
They must have been at a party.
The teacher could have taken the class to the library.
There must have been an accident.
That must have been a terrible experience for him.
He may not have gotten your message.
Maybe they forgot.
It might have had mechanical problems.

UNIT 5 *Socializing*

4.2 Recognition of Meaning

Decide if these sentences (a) make suggestions, (b) give advice, (c) describe an obligation, or (d) express probability. Write the letter or letters on the line. One item has more than one answer.

_____ 1. We could take some flowers when we go to their house for dinner.

_____ 2. Since it's a dinner party, we'd better arrive on time.

_____ 3. Why don't we take the pictures of our vacation? They'll want to see them.

_____ 4. Shall we leave?

_____ 5. You must be very tired from all that cooking.

_____ 6. Try a little of everything so the hostess will not be offended.

_____ 7. It is not necessary to take a gift, but you might bring something to drink.

_____ 8. You shouldn't feel bad if you don't take a gift. It's not expected.

_____ 9. Maybe you should talk to the hostess to find out how we should dress for this dinner party.

_____ 10. We must have stayed too late because the hostess kept yawning.

4.3 Sentence Completions

Complete the sentences with one of the expressions below.

be feeling nervous	be unhappy	have gone this afternoon	will get married
be shy	go out to dinner	have hurt	
be tired	have forgotten about it	have had a fight	

1. Arlene is crying. She must _____.

2. Jeff is yawning. He must _____.

3. Mary is going to sing a solo in a concert tonight. She must _____.

4. Mike and Ann used to see each other every night. Now they don't even talk to each other. They must _____.

5. Edward never talks to girls. He must _____.

6. Mac and Celine have been seeing each other for over a year now. Maybe they _____.

7. Scott hit his finger with a hammer. That must _____.

8. I don't know what we're going to do. We might _____.

9. I wonder why Andy didn't come to the party. He might _____.

10. We didn't have to go tonight. We could _____.

4.4 Modal Contrast

Complete these dialogues with modals or related expressions and the verb in parentheses.

1. A: Did you know Sally is pregnant?
   B: Really? She and Mike _____ (be) excited!
   A: Mike's away on business. He _____ (know) yet.
   B: I bet he does. She _____ (telephone) him!

2. A: Where's Alice? She was supposed to be here at 6:30.
   B: I don't know. Maybe she _____ (be) lost.
   A: Or she _____ (have) car trouble.
   B: I hear a car. It _____ (be) her.

3. A: Whitney is going to tell her parents tonight she's getting married.
   B: She _____ (be) excited.
   A: Well, her parents don't like her boyfriend, so she _____ (be) nervous.

4. A: Jefferson's not seeing his girlfriend any more.
   B: Really? What happened?
   A: I'm not sure. I think she _____ (meet) someone else.
   B: I saw her last week with someone. He _____ (be) her new boyfriend.
   A: It's possible. What did he look like?

5. A: Lyn's parents won't let her go out with Alex anymore.
   B: I wonder why.
   A: I'm not sure. Maybe they _____ (like) Alex.
   B: That's possible. Or Alex and Lyn _____ (do) something her parents didn't like.
   A: It _____ (be) pretty serious.

4.5 Listening: Weekend Plans

A. Marty and Anna are discussing possibilities for the weekend. Listen and put a check next to the options they discuss. Then write Anna's final plans on her calendar.

Possibilities

_____ Drive to the mountains   _____ Take a picnic to the park   _____ Drive to Lake Shasta

_____ Go to a movie   _____ Stay home

_____ Go to the street fair   _____ Eat in a restaurant

112   UNIT 5 Socializing

SATURDAY 22 APRIL		Lunch	Dinner
SUNDAY 23 APRIL		Lunch	Dinner

B. Listen again and complete the sentences.

MARTY: Are you doing anything exciting this weekend?

ANNA: Well, I thought I _____ to the street fair in the university district on Saturday.

MARTY: Oh yeah?

ANNA: Mm hmm. _____ go?

MARTY: Well, actually I was thinking about driving out to the mountains on Saturday.

ANNA: Oh. That sounds nice. It _____ to be a beautiful weekend.

MARTY: Uh huh. _____ like to go?

ANNA: Well, I have to be back home by 2:30, so I _____ enough time to do that.

MARTY: Oh. We _____ just go as far as the lake. Lake Shasta is only a 30-minute drive.

ANNA: OK. That'd be great. I _____ to the street fair on Sunday.

MARTY: I went to the lake a couple of weeks ago, but it was a disaster.

ANNA: Really? How come?

MARTY: Well, we had a nice day, but that night every single one of us got sick!

ANNA: Really? That's terrible.

MARTY: Mm hmm. We took a picnic lunch with us and . . . I don't know . . . maybe the sandwiches were bad . . . or we _____ too much . . . but we all felt terrible afterwards.

ANNA: That _____ awful.

MARTY: It was! Anyway, _____ I pick you up around 10:00?

ANNA: That sounds fine. I guess you don't want to take a picnic lunch?

MARTY: No! _____ go to a restaurant on the way back.

ANNA: OK. I'll see you Saturday.

UNIT 5 Modals: Suggestion, Invitation, Possibility

5 TROUBLE SPOTS: ARTICLES

When you are talking about a specific count noun, use **a / an** for the first mention. Then when you mention it again, use **the**.	(a) There's **a** party tonight. Do you want to go? What time does it start? (b) **The** party's at 7:00 so we'd have to get some dinner first.			
Use **the** for aspects of our lives that everyone knows. We are specific with these because there is no confusion about what we are talking about.	**the** air **the** moon **the** sky **the** sun	**the** earth **the** universe **the** wind **the** present	**the** world **the** solar system **the** weather **the** past	**the** Koran **the** Bible **the** future

5.1 Articles

A. Complete the sentences with the missing articles: *a*, *an*, *the*, or X (no article).

(1) Ways of greeting _____ people vary around _____ world. (2) In _____ Greece, for example, _____ person may shake hands, embrace, or kiss when they greet _____ friends. (3) In _____ Iceland it is impolite to call _____ person by his or her last name. (4) That is, you would use _____ person's first name to greet him or her. (5) While _____ handshake is common in most Asian countries, _____ Thais use the *wai* (6) _____ person places _____ both hands in _____ praying position at _____ chest. (7) The higher _____ hands, the more respect _____ person is showing. (8) In _____ Middle East, _____ handshake is customary outside of _____ home, but, inside, a host may give _____ male guest _____ kiss on both cheeks. (9) _____ embrace or _____ two-handed handshake is not uncommon among _____ acquaintances in _____ Latin American countries. (10) In _____ Australia, after _____ handshake or _____ beer, you will probably be on _____ first name basis with _____ person.[1]

---

[1]Adapted from Roger E. Axtell, ed., *Do's and Taboos Around the World* (New York: John Wiley & Sons, 1985).

B. Discuss these questions with a classmate. Be careful to use *a* for the first mention, *the* for the second mention.

1. How do people greet each other for the first time in your culture? Consider possibilities such as types of handshakes, embracing, types of kisses, and bowing. Is it different when greeting someone of the opposite sex?
2. How do they greet each other when they know each other better?
3. How close do you stand to a person you are meeting for the first time? Does this distance change when you meet the person again?
4. Do you consider your culture to be one where people have a lot of physical contact when socializing or not?
5. How about you? Are you a high contact or low contact person?
6. Is the way you greet someone or the distance you stand from someone determined by your age or your relationship? For example, do you stand as close to a close relative such as your mother or father as you do to an older relative such as a grandparent?

C. Write a summary of your greeting customs and your partner's.

5.2 Article or No Article?

Write the definite article *the* if it is necessary.

_____ 1. Andes

_____ 2. Mediterranean Sea

_____ 3. Gulf of Mexico

_____ 4. world

_____ 5. Union of South Africa

_____ 6. Koran

_____ 7. Rio de Janiero

_____ 8. poor

_____ 9. Oxford University

_____ 10. Mars

_____ 11. United Kingdom

_____ 12. Canary Islands

6 PREPOSITIONS AND PHRASAL VERBS

Prepositions of Direction		to → ■ → from
to	direction in time or place	**to** church; **to** jail, **to** prison; **to** bed; **to** class, **to** school, **to** work; a quarter **to** 12:00 BUT **not** "to downtown": I am **going downtown** towards noon.
towards	in the direction of	**towards** noon; **towards** town
from ... to	until	**from** noon **to** 4:00; **from** the library **to** the dorm
from	indicating a source or cause	**from** the bank; **from** the news
Adjectives with to and from		different **from** across **from** absent **from** close **to** able **to** contrary **to** equal **to** essential **to** good **to** (someone) harmful **to** interesting **to** evident **to** subject **to** obvious **to** sensitive **to** similar **to**
Note: Sometimes **to** is followed by a **gerund** rather than the base form of the verb. (See Unit 10 Trouble Spots, page 000, for more information.)		(a) Small class sizes are **essential to providing** a good education. (b) The experience was **similar to discovering** a new world. (c) I didn't **get around to inviting** him.
Phrasal Verbs		(d) I haven't **gotten around to** inviting him yet, but I'll **see to** it soon. *(finally do) (take care of)* (e) I can always **turn to** him for help. *(ask)* (f) If it **comes to** over $100, we can't afford it. *(total)*

UNIT 5 *Socializing*

6.1 Practice with Phrasals

Discuss these questions with a partner.

1. What haven't you gotten around to doing lately?
2. How are you different now from five years ago?
3. How many times have you been absent from class this term?
4. What kind of stress have you been subject to lately?
5. What habits are most harmful to your health?
6. What would be interesting to do this weekend?
7. Are you more sensitive to temperature or lights?
8. Who are you closest to in your family?
9. What kind of music do you like to listen to?

6.2 Phrasal Review

Underline the best choice to complete each sentence.

1. I can't (get around / come to) the fact that most people don't want this to happen.
2. He must have (gotten around / gotten over) her because he's got a new girlfriend and he seems very happy.
3. It's late. Why don't we (come to / get on with) this so we can all go home.
4. Let's (talk this over / speak over this).
5. They must have (said / spoken) to the teacher because he mentioned it in class.
6. We've asked him to (look on / look into) ways to improve education.
7. He must have (listened / listened in on) our conversation because he knew exactly what we were talking about.
8. I didn't (catch on to / carry on) the point of his story until later. Then I understood.
9. If it should (turn to / come to) that, I won't continue to fight it.
10. We need to (bring on / draw on) our past experience to solve this problem.
11. If you take care of the telephoning, I'll (see to / turn to) the room arrangement.
12. I've been so busy that I haven't (come to / gotten around to) that yet.
13. What's the total going to (come to / get around to)? I hope I have enough money with me.
14. Their parents didn't (catch on to / turn to) what the children were doing until the damage had already been done.

UNIT 5 Modals: Suggestion, Invitation, Possibility

LISTENING TEST

Listen and circle the letter of the best response or restatement.

1. a. That's a good idea.
   b. How about going to a movie?
   c. What do you want to do tomorrow?

2. a. You must be tired.
   b. You didn't go to sleep early.
   c. You might not have slept very well.

3. a. That sounds like a good idea.
   b. No, you're wrong.
   c. Where do you want to go?

4. a. Yes, they must.
   b. No, they decided not to go.
   c. That's probably right.

5. a. Someone might break it.
   b. Someone must have broken it.
   c. The window must be broken.

6. a. They might be here.
   b. He might not have been able to come.
   c. Sara must have been late.

7. a. I had a choice.
   b. I was obligated to take it.
   c. I won't take it.

8. a. Should you?
   b. You might have talked to your parents.
   c. Why don't you ask your father for advice?

9. a. Sure. That would be nice.
   b. I want to have dinner with you tonight.
   c. Let's have dinner together.

10. a. I had to do that.
    b. Did I?
    c. Yes, I did.

UNIT 5 *Socializing*

QUIZ YOURSELF

In each dialogue, circle the underlined phrase that is incorrect.

1. A: They're having a lot of trouble with their son. He wants to watch TV six hours a day. He shouldn't watch that much.
   B: Why don't they limit the amount of time he might have watched?

2. A: I'm worried about the programs my daughter could be watching on TV when I'm not around.
   B: Maybe the government should rate TV programs. Then parents should have known what programs are truly for children.

3. A: I read that children who watched two to three hours of TV daily performed higher on standardized tests than those who watched no TV.
   B: How could that be?
   A: It may have been because children with no hours have no TV. Maybe they may not have books or magazines in their homes either.

4. B: How about children watching more than three hours?
   A: It said children watching four to six hours did the worst on the tests.
   B: They must have not have time to do homework.
   A: Maybe you're right.

5. A: Lynn and David's children have always been very successful in school. They are also very creative children.
   B: That could be because they have a lot of books and magazines. They spend a lot of time reading.
   A: Let's try a month without TV, shall we? We might even have had a regular family reading time each night.

6. A: It drives me crazy that our daughter watches so much TV.
   B: What could you do about it, though?
   A: I could limit her TV time but the problem is my husband watches so much.
   B: He must have set a better example.

7. A: Do you think there's a relationship between TV violence and Sam's behavior?
   B: There might have be.
   A: Maybe we shouldn't let him watch cartoons. They're so violent.
   B: Why don't we monitor what he watches and see if it makes a difference?

8. A: My wife and I argue a lot about having the TV on during mealtimes. I want the news on at dinner and she thinks dinner should be a relaxing time.
   B: How about not have it on at dinner but only at breakfast?
   A: We could try that.

9. A: When I was a child, I must do my homework before I could watch any TV.
   B: It must have been a good motivation to get your homework done.

10. A: You may be a child in the 1950s. Did you watch a lot of TV then?
    B: No, we couldn't because like most people, we didn't even have a TV until I was older.
    A: When you did get one, you must have watched a lot.
    B: Some kids might have but I didn't. There weren't as many programs as there are today.

UNIT 5 Modals: Suggestion, Invitation, Possibility

UNIT 6

Modals and Related Structures: Requests, Preference, Ability

Living Together

1 IMPERATIVES AND REQUESTS

Imperatives	Use to give directions, orders, or warnings	(a) **Go** outside. (b) **Don't smoke** in here. (c) **Please have** a seat. (d) **Watch** out!
	Using an imperative with **will / would you** as a tag softens the command in the imperative form. It makes it more of a request. It may also show that the speaker assumes the other person will help.	(e) **Give** me a hand here, **will you?** (f) **Get** the door, **would you?**
Requests	Situation and tone of voice determine how polite or forceful requests are. Using **please** and such distancers as **will you, would / could you, would you mind** make requests increasingly more polite. (Note: **Would you mind** is followed by a present participle of the verb.)	(g) **Will you stop** that! (h) **Will you help** me? (i) **Will you give me** a hand here? (j) **Would you please shut** the window? (k) **Could you turn** down the radio? (l) **Would you mind turning** down the radio?

Do you think you could is very tentative and therefore a good form to use for a sensitive request.	(m) **Do you think you could** do a little cleaning?
Will is not a future tense marker here but rather an indication of willingness.	(n) **Will** you talk to him about it? I'm too embarrassed.

1.1 Get in Motion: Levels of Politeness

Rank these expressions according to levels of politeness: 1 = the least polite, 2 = average, 3 = the most polite.

EXAMPLE

   1   a. Lend me a quarter, would you?

   3   b. Would you mind lending me a quarter?

   2   c. Could you lend me a quarter?

1. _____ a. Please take the garbage out.
   _____ b. Do you think you could take the garbage out?
   _____ c. Would you mind taking the garbage out?
2. _____ a. Could you open this for me, please?
   _____ b. Open this for me, would you?
   _____ c. Would you open this for me?
3. _____ a. Could you give me a call when you get a chance?
   _____ b. Give me a call when you get a chance.
   _____ c. Would you mind calling me when you get a chance?
4. _____ a. Wash the dishes!
   _____ b. Could you wash the dishes?
   _____ c. Would you please wash the dishes?
5. _____ a. Could I borrow $20?
   _____ b. Do you think I could borrow $20?
   _____ c. Lend me $20, OK?

1.2 Requests

Write a request for each of the following situations.

1. Your little brother is bothering you.

   _____

2. A visitor arrives in your office and you want him or her to sit down.

   _____

(Continued on the next page)

3. You are at the dinner table. The salt and pepper are on the other side of your little sister.

4. You are at the dinner table. The salt and pepper are on the other side of your grandfather.

5. You are walking in the door with a huge box that is about to fall. Your roommate is sitting in the room.

6. Your spouse has the TV on very loud.

1.3 Request Role Play

Work in pairs. You are roommates in an apartment in the United States. Act out these situations.

Role Play 1:

Person 1: You are a strict vegetarian and never eat meat.
Person 2: You love to cook and eat everything.
Situation: Person 1 sees Person 2 cutting up chicken with the knife and cutting board you usually use to cut vegetables.

Role Play 2:

Person 1: You love to have parties and have friends over to the apartment to listen to music and to play guitars.
Person 2: You are a student in medical school. You spend all your time working, studying, or sleeping and it is *very* important for you to have a quiet place to live.
Situation: Person 1 has some friends over. They are in the living room listening to music. A couple of people are playing guitars and singing along with the music. Person 2 comes home after working at the hospital for 30 hours straight.

UNIT 6 Living Together

2 PERMISSION

Permission	When asking for permission, your tone of voice and the situation influence the degree of politeness. *Distancers*, such as *could, would, do you think, possibly,* remove the speaker from the request for permission and make it more polite.	(a) **May I go** now? (b) **Could I borrow** your car tonight? (c) **Do you mind if I ask** you a question? (d) **Would he mind if I borrow** his car? (e) **Would it be all right if some friends come** over for dinner tonight? (f) **Is it all right if I smoke?**
	Please adds a level of politeness.	(g) **Can I please stay** out until 2:00?
	Using three distancers is a very polite way to ask for a request that you are not sure will be granted.	(h) **Do you think I could possibly borrow** your car?
Responses to Requests for Permission	*That's fine.* *No problem.* *Sure.* *Go ahead.*	*Well . . . I'd rather you didn't.* *I don't think that would be a good idea.* *No, you can't.* *No, you may not!*

2.1 Get in Motion: Permission

You are a guest in your roommate's family's house. Use one of the expressions above to request permission in the following situations.

EXAMPLE

You want to smoke, but you don't see ashtrays. Ask your roommate's father.
Is it all right if I smoke?

1. You want to use the washer and dryer to wash your clothes. Ask your roommate's mother.

2. The TV is on, but the volume is very low and you want to turn it up. Ask your roommate's sister.

3. You want to use the washer and dryer to wash your clothes. Ask your roommate's brother.

4. It is 4:30 p.m. You want to take a bath, but you're not sure it is appropriate to take one now. Ask your roommate's mother.

5. It's 10:30 p.m. and you want to go to bed, but everyone is still talking. Ask the family.

6. At breakfast, you want some more coffee. Ask your roommate's mother.

7. When it's time to leave, you would like to borrow a book that you started to read. Ask your roommate.

8. Your roommate's father is driving you home. You want to stop at a drugstore. Ask him.

2.2 Listening: Conversations

A. Listen and circle the situation that matches the conversation.

Conversation 1:	permission	request	hesitant / polite request
Conversation 2:	demand	hesitant / polite request	permission
Conversation 3:	hesitant / polite request	permission	request
Conversation 4:	hesitant / polite request	demand	permission
Conversation 5:	permission	request	hesitant / polite request

B. Listen and complete the conversation.

A: Carol, do you remember the $50 I lent you last week?

B: Oh, yeah. _____ I haven't paid it back yet.

A: That's all right, but _____ pay me tomorrow?

B: Oh, sure. No problem.

(the next day)

A: Carol, _____ get my $50?

B: Oh, I forgot to go to the bank! I'm sorry! _____ it to you tomorrow?

A: Oh. Well, all right, but don't forget, OK?

(the next day)

A: Hi, Carol. _____ my $50?

B: Oh, no! I forgot again.

A: Look, Carol, just _____ the $50, OK? I need it!

B: Yeah, sorry.

C. How does the language change in these requests from day to day? Why?

3 PREFERENCE

prefer	Use **prefer** to state a preference which is a general fact for that person. It does not need **would** before it.	(a) Everyone **prefers** relaxing to working.
		(b) I **prefer** to go dancing.
	Use **to** to make the comparison. However, it is more common to use "I **like** . . . **better than** . . ."	(c) I **prefer** jazz **to** rock.
		(d) I **like** jazz **better than** rock.
	Prefer may be followed by a **gerund, noun,** or **infinitive form**. Be careful to use the same kind of structure after **to** as you use before it.	(e) I prefer **walking** to **running**. (NOT: I prefer walking to **run**.)

124 UNIT 6 *Living Together*

would prefer, would rather	Use these to show a preferred behavior or action at a specific moment.	(f) I **would prefer not to sit** in the smoking area. (g) I **would prefer to eat** on the deck. (h) What **would you rather do**—go to the library or have lunch? (i) We**'d rather not talk** about that right now.
	When you state both options, **would rather** is followed by **than**.	(j) I**'d rather** go swimming **than** go for a walk.
prefer that	In formal English, **prefer that** is followed by a **subject** and the **base form** of the verb.	(k) I**'d prefer that** you **be** on time. (l) We**'d prefer that** he **smoke** outside. (m) I**'d prefer that** you **not smoke** in here. (n) I**'d prefer that** he **not do** that.
prefer it if . . .	Use **prefer it if** to state a condition with the preference. In formal English, the verb following **if** changes from present to **past tense**, from past to **past perfect**.	(o) I**'d prefer it if** you **did** your own work. (p) I**'d prefer it if** you **didn't have** your friends over so often. *(referring to a present / general situation)* (q) I**'d have preferred it if** you **had been** on time. *(referring to a past situation)*

3.1 Get in Motion: Preference

Answer each of these requests negatively by expressing a preference.

EXAMPLE
Would you mind if I open the window?
I'd prefer it if you didn't.
I'd prefer that you left it closed.
I'd rather you didn't.
I'd prefer it to be closed.

1. Is it all right with you if I have some people over for dinner tomorrow night?

   _____

2. Do you mind if I turn on some music?

   _____

3. How about going out to dinner tonight?

   _____

(Continued on the next page)

4. Do you think I could possibly borrow your car tomorrow?

   _____

5. Would it be all right if you cooked dinner tonight?

   _____

6. Would you mind if I put some things in your bookcase? I notice you aren't using all the shelves.

   _____

7. Could I borrow that jacket sometime? It would look great with this sweater I bought.

   _____

8. Let's go to dinner late tonight. I ate a huge lunch!

   _____

3.2 Listening: A Smoking Question

A. Alex and Maria are discussing plans to entertain John, a friend of theirs. Listen and answer the questions.

1. Who suggests having John over for dinner? _____

2. What habit of John's are Maria and Alex discussing? _____

3. Do they feel that they can talk with John about this problem? _____

4. What plans do they make to entertain John? _____

UNIT 6 Living Together

B. Listen again and complete the dialogue.

ALEX: (1) Maria, _____ I invited John over for dinner this weekend?

MARIA: (2) You know _____ we took him out to dinner instead of having him here. You know he smokes like a chimney and the house just smells terrible when he's been here.

ALEX: (3) I _____ eat here than at a restaurant.
(4) _____ we ask him not to smoke in the house?

MARIA: (5) What _____ to say. . . . "Here's an ashtray. . . . Go outside?"

ALEX: Well, no. . . . (6) We _____ say, "_____ smoking so much. . . ." (7) No, I guess we _____ say that either.

MARIA: (8) No. Even if he asked, "_____ I smoke?" I wouldn't say, "Yes, I mind!"

ALEX: No, you're right. Let's go out to dinner then. (9) _____ the reservations?

MARIA: No, that's fine. Is the Lido Café all right?

ALEX: (10) I _____ Anthony's _____ .

MARIA: All right. (11) Call and _____ he can come, _____ ?

ALEX: OK. I'll ask him tomorrow.

C. Identify expressions in the conversation that express request, permission, possibility, expectation, or preference. Write one on each line below.

Request: _____

Permission: _____

Possibility: _____

Expectation: _____

Preference: _____

D. Discuss the questions below with your classmates.

1. Do you know many people who smoke?
2. Is smoking acceptable or do people consider it a bad habit?
3. Maria and Alex don't want John to smoke in their home. This is not uncommon in the United States. What about in your group of friends?
4. Do you think that Maria and Alex could invite John to their home and ask him not to smoke?

UNIT 6 Modals: Requests, Preference, Ability

4 ABILITY

can	**Can** expresses ability or a real possibility in the present. **Can't** or **cannot** expresses inability or impossibility in the present.	(a) He **can speak** English better than Cambodian. (b) We **can walk** or **take** a taxi. (c) You **can't buy** candy for five cents now.
be able to	**Be able to** expresses ability or real possibility. You may use **be able to** after these modals: **will, won't, would, should, may, might, must**. Change the form of **be** to fit the appropriate tense.	(d) He's **not able to come** to the phone right now. (e) We **will be able to go** to outer space. (f) We **won't be able to use** cars. (g) We **should be able to travel** very fast in the future. (h) **Were** you **able to walk** to school when you lived in the country? (i) We **weren't able to fly** there in one day. (j) We **haven't been able to contact** them for some time.
could	**Could** is the past tense form of **can**. However, its use to show ability is limited. You can use **could** to show a general condition or ability to do something in the past. However, you cannot use the affirmative of **could** to talk about the ability to do something at **one specific time in the past**. In that case, it is necessary to use the past of **be able to**. In the negative, you can use **could** for a specific situation. **Could** also shows an opportunity. This opportunity is a possibility for the present or future, so the past <u>form</u> of **can** does not always indicate past <u>tense</u>.	(k) I **couldn't do** the math homework. It was too difficult. (l) I **could stand** on my head when I was a child. (m) In the old days, people **could leave** their houses unlocked. (n) We **were able to eat** together last night because my dad came home early from work. (NOT: We **could eat** together last night.) (o) Last night **I was able to finish** my homework before I fell asleep. (NOT: Last night I **could finish** my homework before I fell asleep.) (p) Last night I **couldn't finish** my homework. I was too tired. (q) They **couldn't fly** there. They had to drive. (r) I **could go** tomorrow if you can't make it today. (s) We **could study** French.

UNIT 6 *Living Together*

4.1 Get in Motion: Ability

Complete the sentences with the affirmative or negative form of *can, could,* or *be able to*.

1. A: I'm sorry you _____ come to dinner with us last night.
   B: I am, too. I hope I'll _____ go next time you go out.

2. A: Hey, Antonio, would you turn down that music? I _____ study!
   B: What? I _____ hear you.

3. A: I feel great today, for a change. I finally _____ sleep well last night.
   B: Oh really? Why have you been having trouble sleeping?
   A: My roommate has been staying up late to study and the light bothers me.
   B: _____ you ask her to study at the library or something?
   A: I guess I _____, but I don't want to cause bad feelings.
   B: But it's your room, too! You should _____ sleep there!

4. A: Why are you moving so slowly?
   B: I _____ exercise yesterday. If I _____ exercise every day, I get very sluggish.
   A: That's too bad.

5. A: Helen, would you like some bread?
   B: No, thank you. I _____ eat bread. I'm allergic to wheat.
   A: That's terrible!
   B: Well, I don't miss bread because I've had this allergy all my life. I _____ never _____ eat wheat products.
   A: I _____ imagine life without bread.

6. A: I almost missed the test this morning. I _____ start my car this morning.
   B: How did you get here then?
   A: I was really lucky. I _____ get a ride with a friend.

UNIT 6 Modals: Requests, Preference, Ability

4.2 In Other Words

Circle the letter of the expression which has the same meaning as the underlined words.

1. My parents grew up in the country so they <u>could not have</u> the city experiences I had as a child.
   a. weren't able to
   b. cannot have
   c. did not prefer to have

2. <u>Could you</u> turn down that rap music? It's making me crazy. In my day, we listened to more relaxing music.
   a. I'm inviting you
   b. Are you able to
   c. Would you

3. If there's a problem at home, <u>you could talk</u> to your parents and try to resolve your differences.
   a. you may talk
   b. would you mind talking
   c. why don't you talk

4. You <u>can go</u> to your friend's house after school, but you need to be home by dinner time.
   a. How about going
   b. You may go
   c. Would you mind going

5. Her mother <u>could take</u> free English classes but she is too shy to go out alone in a foreign country.
   a. should take
   b. wasn't able to take
   c. has an opportunity to take

5 UNFULFILLED POTENTIAL OR POSSIBILITY

Could have + past participle of the verb	*Could have* shows an opportunity in the past that you did **not** take. It can also show a possibility that did **not** happen.	(a) I **could have studied** in Australia. (b) You **could have hurt** yourself with that knife.

130　UNIT 6　*Living Together*

5.1 Get in Motion: Unfulfilled Potential or Possibility

Older people often see dangers that younger people don't worry about. Yesterday, almost everything Martina did worried her grandmother. What did her grandmother say to her?

EXAMPLE

Martina climbed up on the roof.
You could have fallen.

1. Martina crossed the street without looking.
2. She drove over the speed limit on her way to school.
3. She gave a friend a ride home and drove through a dangerous part of the city.
4. She went to visit a friend who is very sick with the flu.
5. She went on a picnic in the woods with some friends and had a campfire.
6. She ate wild mushrooms that a friend picked in the woods.
7. She walked through the woods at night.

5.2 Problem Solving

Work in a small group. Read the following situation and answer the questions.

Julie and Yasuhiro met and got married in San Francisco six years ago. Two years later Yasuhiro's father died. His mother announced that she was moving in with Julie and Yasuhiro. Julie was pregnant at the time and thought that it would be great to have someone living with them to take care of the baby while she went back to work, so she didn't say anything against the idea.

However, life with Yasuhiro's mother was different than Julie had expected. Yasuhiro's mother was not very nice to Julie. (She had never wanted Yasuhiro to marry someone who wasn't Japanese.) She did not help Julie in the house and, in fact, wanted Julie to serve and take care of her. She criticized Julie and spoiled the baby.

Julie is very unhappy about this situation.

1. What could Julie have done differently when Yasuhiro's father died?
2. What could she have done differently when Yasuhiro's mother moved in with them?
3. What could Yasuhiro have done differently?
4. What can Julie and/or Yasuhiro do now to change the situation?

5.3 Talk It Over and Optional Writing

Discuss these questions with a group of classmates. Then write a paragraph about a decision you made.

Think of a time in your life when you had a big decision to make about your future. How would your life have been different if you had decided differently than you did? What could you have done differently?

6 PAST HABIT

used to + base form of the verb	**Used to** expresses a past habit or action, a past situation, or a repeated action.	(a) My grandmother **used to read** to me every night after dinner. *(past habit, repeated action)* (b) My grandmother **used to live** with us. *(situation, not repeated action)*
would + base form of the verb	**Would** is only used with repeated actions.	(c) My grandmother **would read** to me every night after dinner. *(repeated action)* NOT: My grandmother **would live** with us.

6.1 Contrast: *Could, Had to, Used to, Can, Would*

Circle the best choice to complete each sentence.

(1) Before the 1970s, life in university residence halls was very different from the way it is now. Women and men (didn't use to / didn't have to) live in the same residences. (2) In fact, men (couldn't / wouldn't) even *enter* the women's dormitories! It was against school rules. (3) They (could / would) usually meet their dates at the front desk. (4) Women (had to / could) leave campus if they got permission from the person in charge. (5) When they left at night, they (used to / had to) be back in the dorms at a certain time. (6) A woman (could / can) be grounded — restricted to the dorm — for a weekend if she got a lot of "late minutes." (7) Of course, a lot of people (could / used to) try to get around the rules. (8) Men and women (would / had to) sneak in and out windows and back doors and friends (had to / used to) sneak out and sign in for friends. (9) However, it (used to / could) be difficult to arrange all this.

(10) The university (used to / can) relax this rule one day a year, on "Open House Day." (11) This was the only day that men (would / used to) visit women's rooms, but the door (could / had to) be left open or the women (would / had to) get in trouble. (12) Chaperones (could / used to) patrol the halls to make sure that everyone was behaving. (13) Life in residence halls in those days (used to / had to) be very strict! (14) Students today (can't / used to) believe how different it was.

6.2 Talk It Over and Optional Writing

Discuss this question with a group of classmates. Then write a paragraph about a decision you made.

How is life for younger people different now than it was in your parents' generation?
Try to use *can, could, be able to, used to,* or *would* in your discussion.

7 TROUBLE SPOTS: *USED TO* VERSUS *BE* OR *GET USED TO*; ARTICLES; MORE NON-COUNT NOUNS

used to + base form of the verb	expresses a past habit or past situation		(a) I **used to ride** my bicycle to work. (b) I **used to live** in the center of the city.
be / get used to + present participle of the verb	means "to be or get accustomed to something"		(c) I'm **not used to having** a lot of freedom. (d) I **wasn't used to living** by myself. (e) It took time **to get used to living** alone. (f) I couldn't **get used to waking** up at 4:30 a.m.
Articles for Generalizations	with a count noun	Use *a* or *an* with a singular noun or no article with a plural noun.	(g) **A non-smoker** would not be happy in that restaurant. (h) **Non-smokers** would not be happy in that restaurant.
	with a non-count noun	Do not use an article.	(i) **Smoke** can harm people even if it's second-hand **smoke**.
More Non-Count Nouns	natural conditions		weather dirt fog rain mud earth
	liquids and gases		wine milk gas oil
	things in small pieces		sand rice grain

UNIT 6 Modals: Requests, Preference, Ability

7.1 In Other Words

Circle (G) if the sentence is a generalization. Circle (S) if the sentence refers to something specific. If the sentence is a generalization, rewrite it, if possible, changing the underlined words from singular to plural or from plural to singular.

EXAMPLE

(G) S   A <u>cat</u> makes <u>a wonderful house pet</u>.
          Cats make wonderful house pets.

G S 1. It is possible to get <u>cancer</u> from <u>second-hand smoke</u>.
G S 2. If you are a <u>medical student</u>, it is impossible to get much <u>sleep</u>.
G S 3. Would you mind taking out the <u>garbage</u>?
G S 4. I don't see an <u>ashtray</u>.
G S 5. A <u>friend</u> in need is a <u>friend</u> indeed.
G S 6. It's hard to find good <u>baby-sitters</u>.
G S 7. She gives us a lot of <u>homework</u>.
G S 8. The <u>homework</u> for tonight is too difficult.
G S 9. She drove over the <u>speed limit</u>.
G S 10. <u>A university dormitory</u> can be very noisy.

7.2 Generalizations

Rewrite these generalizations in another way, if possible.

EXAMPLE
A roommate can be challenging.
Roommates can be challenging.

1. Having a roommate is sometimes difficult.
   _____

2. I hate looking for an apartment.
   _____

3. However, if you move in with someone, the person thinks the apartment is his or hers.
   _____

4. A difficult situation sometimes arises.
   _____

5. Sometimes no other person can help you with your problem.
   _____

6. You just have to change your apartment.
   _____

134   UNIT 6 Living Together

7. Problems with roommates sometimes seem worse when you are living in other countries.

   _____

8. Sometimes language problems can cause interpersonal problems.

   _____

7.3 Used to versus Be or Get Used to

Underline the best choice to complete each sentence.

1. Before I moved to the suburbs, I (used to / was used to / got used to) live in the center of the city.
2. When I lived in the city, I (used to / was used to / got used to) being close to everything: stores, my job, entertainment.
3. When I moved to the suburbs, it was difficult for me (used to / to be used to / to get used to) living there.
4. I (used to / was used to / got used to) have a lot more time when I lived downtown.
5. I don't know if I'll ever (used to / be used to / get used to) spending two hours a day commuting. It's terrible!
6. However, now that I (used to / am used to / get used to) seeing more trees and open space here in the suburbs, I would probably have a hard time (used to / being used to / getting used to) living in the city again.
7. I miss all the music and art shows I (used to / was used to / got used to) attend.
8. I don't miss the noise of the city. When I lived downtown, I (used to / was used to) the noise, but now the city seems incredibly loud. I wonder how I (used to / was used to) be able to sleep with all the noise!

7.4 Non-Count Nouns

Write NC next to the nouns which are usually non-count. Circle the appropriate expression of quantity for each word.

1. _____ word	one	three of	
2. _____ salt	two	a teaspoon of	
3. _____ green paint	three	a can of	
4. _____ vocabulary	ten	a list of	
5. _____ rice	a cup of	two cups	
6. _____ snow	two feet	a foot of	
7. _____ cheese	a pound of	three	
8. _____ cookie	a small amount of	one	
9. _____ meat	a ½ lb. of	two kilos	
10. _____ silk	a yard	a yard of	
11. _____ weather	a lot of bad	three days bad	
12. _____ smoke	a cloud of	one cloud	

UNIT 6 Modals: Requests, Preference, Ability

7.5 Talk It Over and Optional Writing

Discuss these questions with a classmate. Then choose one to write about.

1. Have you ever visited or lived with anyone from another culture?
2. What do you think are the most difficult things about living with people from another culture?
3. What do you think would be difficult if someone from the United States came to live with your family? What advice would you give your guest about things to do or not do?

8 PREPOSITIONS AND PHRASAL VERBS

Prepositions of Direction and Location	*up*	*upon*
up	shows movement in a direction	**up** north
	often appears with other prepositions to show location	**up** on the roof; **up** in the attic; **up** on the shelf
upon	indicates location	**upon** the roof; **upon** the shelf
Phrasal Verbs	(a) It isn't hard to **give up** cleanup duty. I hate doing dishes. *(stop)*	
	(b) Could you **wipe up** that spilled juice? *(remove with a cloth)*	
	(c) The costs have **gone up** but will they **stay up**? *(increase) (remain at a high level)*	
	(d) How long will that old car **hold up**? *(last)*	
	(e) The rain hasn't **let up** this morning. *(decrease)*	
	(f) What time do you **get up** in the morning? *(arise)*	
	(g) He'll never **grow up**. He's so immature. *(become mature)*	
	(h) Let's **clear up** this mess. *(put in order)*	
	(i) If the weather **clears up**, we can go to a picnic. *(become less bad)*	

See Appendix D for more phrasal expressions.

8.1 Practice with Prepositions

Up, over, and *above* often appear in set or idiomatic phrases. Match these phrases with the definitions. Then write sentences on a separate piece of paper using each.

_____ 1. 21 and over
_____ 2. over 200
_____ 3. up and down
_____ 4. up against
_____ 5. up to me
_____ 6. all over the place
_____ 7. came up for air
_____ 8. above all
_____ 9. over and done with
_____ 10. mentioned above

a. most importantly
b. facing
c. finished
d. everywhere
e. more than (a number)
f. older than (an age)
g. written about earlier in the text
h. higher and lower
i. got his breath
j. my responsibility

8.2 Practice with Phrasal Verbs

Circle the appropriate verb. Consult Appendix D, if necessary.

1. Don't (hold / give) up! If you can just (hold / give) on for another year, you'll graduate.
2. I didn't (get / bring) around to discussing the problem with my roommate. I'll (get / bring) it up tomorrow night.
3. If the rain (falls / lets) up, we can go biking. If not, we can (fall / let) back on plan B, to watch a video.
4. He's had a terrible time (getting / taking) over his homesickness and he has let it (get / take) over his life. He's miserable.
5. Sometimes you just need to (go / put) on a happy face and (go / put) along with your life as if nothing were the matter.
6. The cost of most things usually (gives / goes) up every year, but sometimes new technology gets less expensive.
7. The weather (cleared / got) up, so we were able to go for a hike.
8. I'm trying to (give / go) up smoking.
9. When the rain (clears / lets) up, let's go outside.
10. That blind is broken. It won't (get / stay) up.

LISTENING TEST

Identify what the speaker is expressing in each statement. Circle the correct letter.

1. a. making a request
   b. asking permission
   c. explaining a past habit

2. a. expressing a possibility in the past
   b. expressing a present ability
   c. expressing a preference

3. a. making a request
   b. asking about a past opportunity
   c. asking permission

4. a. making a request
   b. explaining a past habit
   c. expressing a preference

5. a. making a request
   b. giving a warning
   c. giving directions

6. a. expressing ability
   b. making an offer
   c. asking permission

7. a. asking about ability
   b. asking permission
   c. making a request

8. a. expressing inability
   b. stating a preference
   c. asking permission

9. a. expressing a preference
   b. making a request
   c. expressing a past habit

10. a. expressing a preference
    b. expressing ability
    c. asking permission

QUIZ YOURSELF

Circle the letter of the expression which has the same meaning as the underlined words.

1. My dad <u>would</u> always <u>establish</u> good relationships with people because he had good communication skills.
   a. would rather
   b. would prefer to establish
   c. used to establish

2. Active listening is one of the best ways that <u>you can tell</u> a person that her problem is being heard.
   a. you are able to tell
   b. you should tell
   c. you prefer to tell

3. <u>Would you mind not talking</u> until I'm finished?
   a. Do you think you could not talk
   b. You may not talk
   c. You aren't able to talk

4. <u>Look</u> the person in the eye while he is talking.
   a. May you look
   b. You ought to look
   c. Should you look

5. It is a real skill <u>to be able to</u> hear the feelings behind the words the person is expressing.
   a. if you can
   b. if you are supposed to
   c. if you might

6. <u>You could show</u> your concern for their problem by asking questions and paraphrasing what they say.
   a. You have got to show
   b. You might show
   c. Would you mind showing

7. If I don't understand, <u>do you think I could</u> ask some questions afterwards?
   a. would I
   b. is it all right if I
   c. possibly I could

8. Second, <u>you can paraphrase</u> what you hear them say.
   a. you used to be able to paraphrase
   b. you could paraphrase
   c. would you mind paraphrasing

9. <u>We are used to giving</u> advice, rather than simply listening to what a person is saying.
   a. We would give
   b. We are accustomed to giving
   c. We could give

10. Most people <u>would prefer to be heard</u> rather than be lectured to.
    a. would mind being heard
    b. would prefer it if they listened
    c. would rather be heard

UNIT 7

Passives

Technology

1 ACTIVE VOICE VERSUS PASSIVE VOICE

USE	The sentences you have studied so far have all been in the **active voice.** They usually have the structure **subject + verb + object.** The most important part of the sentence is first: the subject or the doer of the action.	(a) Many **people have bought VCRs** in recent years.
	Another way to look at an action is to see how the object or receiver of the action is affected. This is the **passive voice.**	(b) **VCRs have been bought** by many people in recent years.
	The **passive voice** is used when the object is more important than the subject, we don't know the subject, or we don't want to identify who the doer of the action is. It is used in everyday English but is especially common in academic writing.	(c) Thousands of **videos are rented** each day in the United States.
FORM	*be* + the **past participle** of the verb	(d) VCRs **were developed** for consumer use in the 1970s.
	The "doer" of the action is often given in the *by* phrase.	(e) The first commercially successful VCR was developed **by the Sony Corporation** in Japan.

1.1 Get in Motion: Active or Passive?

Write A if the sentence is in the active voice and P if it is in the passive voice.

_____ 1. In the future, TV viewers will be able to interact with the TV.

_____ 2. In interactive TV, the technology of TV, computer, and telephone is combined.

_____ 3. Interactive TV will be common in the future.

_____ 4. Viewers will participate in game shows while they are sitting at home.

_____ 5. Political and social issues will be decided by voters touching their TV sets.

_____ 6. Banking will be done at home using computer screens to make choices.

_____ 7. Videos will be selected for home viewing without leaving one's home.

_____ 8. Your dream home can be toured via TV without leaving your home or beginning construction.

_____ 9. Viewers will have more control over the content of programs on TV.

_____ 10. Many options will be available on interactive TV.

1.2 Listening: Passive or Active?

Listen and decide if the sentences you hear are active or passive. Write A if the sentence is in the active voice and P if it is in the passive voice.

1. _____   4. _____   7. _____   10. _____

2. _____   5. _____   8. _____

3. _____   6. _____   9. _____

UNIT 7 Passives

2 FORMS OF THE PASSIVE

be + past participle of the verb	The passive is used in all verb tenses and with modals. Here are the most common uses:
Simple Present	(a) Households are transformed by electronic technology.
Present Continuous	(b) are being transformed
Simple Past	(c) were transformed
Past Continuous	(d) were being transformed
Present Perfect	(e) have been transformed
Past Perfect	(f) had been transformed
Future	(g) will be transformed
Future Perfect	(h) will have been transformed
Modal	(i) can be transformed

2.1 Get in Motion: Passive

Look at the sequence of pictures in each part. Make passive sentences. Use the words under each picture. Be sure to use the correct tense.

A. 1.

In earlier times messages / send / smoke signals.

2.

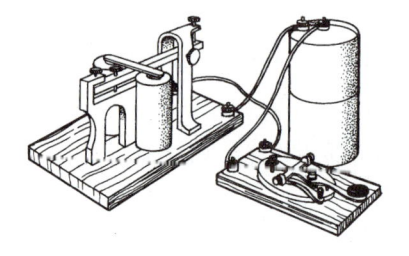

In the 19th century the telegraph / use / for long-distance communication.

3.

By the mid-20th century the telegraph / replace / the telephone.

4.

Today the cellular phone / use / more and more people.

B.

1. In the past portraits / paint.

2. By the mid-20th century cameras / commonly use / to preserve memories.

3. Today people's faces and actions record / camcorders.

4. In the years to come, memories / ???

C.

1. In ancient times bread / bake / in stone ovens.

2. By the mid-20th century brick ovens / replace / electric ovens.

3. Today cooking time / cut considerably / microwave technology.

4. In the next century food / ???

UNIT 7 Passives 143

D.

1. In olden times messages / hand-deliver.

2. In this century delivery time / dramatically reduce / air mail.

3. At present sending messages / greatly simplify / electronic mail.

4. By the year 2020 messages / ???

E.

1. In the past music / perform / live.

2. At the turn of the century, previously live performances / can hear / phonograph records.

3. By the 1970s cassette tapes / play / around the world.

4. Today compact discs / sell.

2.2 Passive Forms

Complete the sentence with the appropriate tense of the verb *be*.

1. Some people have trouble understanding how to work their VCRs. Their VCRs _____ (never) used.

2. In order to tape a TV show, someone has to program the VCR. It _____ (have to) programmed so that the right TV show _____ (can) taped.

3. My mother has never figured out how to open the control panel of the VCR. It _____ (never) opened.

4. She telephoned me and said that the instruction manual showed a different VCR. She thought the wrong VCR _____ packed in the box.

5. My uncle will probably never use the VCR his children gave him. The VCR _____ (only) set up if someone else does it for him.

6. People who don't understand new technology need special classes. Classes in using new technology _____ (should) offered.

7. People are trying to make new technology easier to use. New ideas to simplify technology _____ developed all the time.

8. A company invented VCR Plus, a gadget that did the VCR programming for people. VCR Plus _____ invented to program the VCR for people.

9. I gave a VCR Plus to my mother. The directions for programming it are complicated and so it _____ (not) used yet either.

10. My mother says, "You can't teach an old dog new tricks," but it is not just older people who have trouble. Even young people _____ (can) confused by new technology.

11. My father says that he is going to read the instructions and try to use the VCR. He says that the VCR _____ used someday.

12. I'll believe it when I see it. I think their VCR _____ (may, never) used.

13. Oh well. It was a nice gift. The VCR _____ given to my parents as a gift.

14. Thousands of people probably buy VCRs as gifts. Thousands of VCRs _____ (probably) given as gifts.

2.3 Talk It Over and Optional Writing

A. Discuss these questions with your classmates.

1. Do you know people who have trouble programming their VCRs? How about you? Are you a "techno-phobe" (someone who fears technology)?
2. What new technologies have you had to adjust to in the last 5 years?
3. What technologies have been introduced in your country since you were a child?
4. What kinds of consumer technology are you interested in? What do you own or what have you considered buying?

B. Write a composition about your experience or feelings about new technology. Include at least five passive verbs.

2.4 Passive Forms

Complete these sentences with the correct form of the verb in parentheses, active or passive voice, depending on the situation. Pay attention to the verb tense.

(1) VCRs _____ (be) as popular today as color TVs _____ (be) in the 1960s. (2) It is hard to believe that this technology _____ (have) its start in the late 1800s when audio-magnetic recording _____ (first, investigate) by the science community. (3) During World War II, important advances in magnetic recordings _____ (make) in Germany and these techniques _____ (improve) on in the United States in the 1920s and 1930s. (4) The first commercial VCR _____ (introduce) in 1956. (5) In the late 1970s, the VCR equipment market _____ (control) by Sony, a Japanese company.

(6) Some years later, using a VCR at home _____ (make) easier when the VHS (Video Home System) _____ (introduce) by the Victor Company, also of Japan. (7) VHS tapes soon _____ (outsell) Sony's one-hour Betamax tapes because they offered two hours of video time.

(8) Today VCRs _____ (be) popular because they _____ (record), _____ (play) back, and _____ (freeze) or _____ (slow) down the motions on the screen. (9) Home movies _____ (can, play) on them. (10) However, most consumers say they _____ (buy) a VCR because TV programs _____ (can, tape) when they _____ (be) away from home or watching a different channel. (11) In addition, the rapid growth in video outlets _____ (mean)

146 UNIT 7 *Technology*

thousands of movies _____ (can, view) at home. (12) "Commercial zapping" machines _____ (can, buy) so the viewer _____ (can, delete) commercials from recorded programs.

(13) In the future the sound and picture quality of VCRs _____ (improve). (14) Entertainment rooms with large video screens and high-tech stereo equipment _____ (install) in more and more homes. (15) _____ the movie theater business _____ (destroy) by the VCR? (16) So far, this _____ (not, be) the case. (17) in fact, studies show that people who _____ (have) VCRs _____ (be) still frequent movie-goers. (18) The social aspect of movie-going _____ (not, disappear). (19) It _____ (be) still enjoyable to be with someone in a theater and to see a newly released film.

2.5 Listening: The History of TV

A. Listen and take notes on your own paper about the development of television.

B. Now ask each other questions about the development of TV. Use these cues in your questions. Change the verb in parentheses to active or passive.

1. when / television / (invent)
2. 1939 / how many hours of programming / (offer)
3. who / (write) / the first programs
4. by 1945 / how many TVs / (sell) / in the United States
5. how much / television / (cost) / 1945
6. when / color television / (develop)
7. in what year / color television / (outsell) / black and white TVs

2.6 Passive Voice Questions

Ask your partner questions to complete this chart about inventions. Your partner will look at File 22 in Appendix G.

Invention			fax machine
When	1854		
Who		George de Mestral	Alexander Bain
Where	the United States		Scotland

UNIT 7 Passives

2.7 Optional Writing

Choose one of these topics and research about it in the library. Then write a composition about it.

1. Write a report about a famous invention and its impact on the world.
2. Write a report about a famous inventor and his or her process of discovery.
3. Research and write about how new technology has developed from wars. Some examples are radar and antibiotics.
4. How has new technology been destructive to the environment in a country you are familiar with?
5. How important is electronic technology to the rock music industry? Support your argument with examples.

3 MORE ABOUT PASSIVES

The **passive** is only used with **transitive verbs**, that is, verbs which take objects.	(transitive) (a) This invention **will change** our lives. (b) Our lives **will be changed** by this invention. (intransitive; no passive possible) (c) This new technology **seems** confusing.
However, not all transitive verbs work in the passive.	(d) I **had** computer training last quarter. (NOT: Computer training **was had** last quarter.) (e) She **helped** me understand the new technology. (NOT: I **was helped** by her to understand the new technology.)
You can change the **direct object** or **indirect object** to the subject in a passive sentence.	(active) (f) The director is showing **us the new technology**. S V I.O. D.O. (passive) (g) **The new technology** is being shown now. (h) **We** are being shown the new technology.
Causatives **have** and **get** are often used in spoken English with a passive meaning.	(i) She **had** her VCR repaired last week. (j) She **got** her VCR repaired last week.

3.1 Get in Motion: Transitive or Intransitive?

Can the sentences below about virtual reality be changed into passive sentences? Write *Yes* or *No*.

_____ 1. In 1965 Ivan Sutherland first used the term "virtual reality."

_____ 2. Virtual reality means a computer-created reality.

_____ 3. It puts the user into computer graphic scenes.

_____ 4. The user puts on special equipment, an "eyephone" and "datagloves."

_____ 5. The user then enters a three-dimensional world.

_____ 6. The user feels like a part of the computer scene.

_____ 7. The distance between the user and the computer seems to disappear.

_____ 8. The user can touch and move the things in the computer screen.

_____ 9. Virtual reality will change computer use in the future.

_____ 10. Teachers are interested in its possibilities to provide experiential learning.

_____ 11. Scientists have created a virtual forest for children.

_____ 12. In it, children experienced being a tree, a bird, or an earthworm.

_____ 13. Will virtual reality have a greater impact on society than TV?

_____ 14. Just as the microscope and telescope opened new worlds, virtual reality opens our creativity.

_____ 15. Physical and political boundaries will not matter.

_____ 16. Virtual reality means that we can all work together on the same projects.

3.2 Active to Passive Transformations

Change the sentences below from active to passive. Use the *by* expression only if it is necessary.

1. Scientists, doctors, and businesses use virtual reality.
   Virtual reality _____

2. Space scientists are already using it to simulate space work and exploration.
   _____ to simulate space work and exploration.

3. Doctors may diagnose a patient's body via virtual reality.
   _____ via virtual reality.

(Continued on the next page)

4. Kitchen designers in Japan use it to show buyers their new kitchen.

   _____ to show buyers their new kitchen.

5. It saves countless hours in the design and manufacturing process.

   _____ in the design and manufacturing process.

6. Car designers can check rear window visibility in new model designs.

   _____ in new model designs.

7. Companies are training assembly workers using this new technology.

   _____ using this new technology.

8. We have used flight simulators, an early form of virtual reality, for years.

   Flight simulators, an early form of virtual reality, _____

   _____.

3.3 Talk It Over and Optional Writing

Discuss these questions with your classmates. Then write a composition with your ideas. Use at least five passive verbs.

1. What do you believe are the advantages and disadvantages of creating an artificial world such as virtual reality does?

2. Use your imagination to design an ideal virtual reality. What would the user be able to experience?

4 ACTIVE AND PASSIVE PARTICIPIAL ADJECTIVES

Adjectives which have an **active -ing** form and a **passive -ed** form are often confusing. It is important to remember who the doer of the action is and who the receiver is.

Active Adjective	(a) The movie was very **boring**.	The movie bored me. **The movie** was the doer of the action.
Passive Adjective	(b) I was **bored** by the movie.	The movie bored me. **I** was the receiver of the action.

4.1 Get in Motion: Active and Passive Adjectives

Complete the sentences with the correct adjective.

1. confused / confusing

   I didn't like the movie because it had a _____ plot. I was

   _____ about the story line.

150   UNIT 7 Technology

2. frightened / frightening

   We don't let our young son go to _____ movies. When he is too _____, he can't sleep at night.

3. interested / interesting

   I am _____ in buying a VCR. This new brand has _____ features.

4. bored / boring

   We were _____ with the movie so we left early. A movie with too much dialogue and not enough action is _____ to me.

5. amazed / amazing

   Steven Spielberg used some _____ techniques in his new film. I am _____ at his impact on the movie industry.

6. heartened / heartening

   We were _____ by their commitment to the project. It was _____ to see so many people work hard to make the film a big success.

7. shocked / shocking

   It is _____ to see how much violence there is in movies today. The children were not _____ by the violence because they see it every day.

8. excited / exciting

   The ending was so _____ that the audience was holding its breath.
   The children were so _____ that they couldn't sit still.

4.2 Passive or Active?

Complete the sentences with the active or passive form of the word in parentheses. Use verb and adjective forms.

1. Christopher _____ (cannot, walk). He is _____ (disable).

2. Christopher was born with cerebral palsy. He _____ (never, be able to, walk).

3. In the past, wheelchairs were not _____ (motorize). Someone always _____ (have to, push) the wheelchair.

4. _____ (motorize) wheelchairs _____ (give) disabled people more independence.

(Continued on the next page)

UNIT 7 Passives

5. However, learning how to use a wheelchair can be a _____ (frustrate) experience.

6. Young children _____ (usually, push) in the wheelchair by someone else.

7. Some children _____ (teach) to be helpless.

8. In recent years virtual reality _____ (help) children learn to use a wheelchair.

9. Able-bodied people _____ (cannot, imagine) what it is like to use a wheelchair. Virtual reality _____ (may, also, use) to show other people the experience of using wheelchairs.

10. A friend of mine would like to have a special wheelchair _____ (design) to go on hikes outside where the surface is bumpy. Then he would be able to enjoy a hike in the woods.

11. Virtual reality _____ (seem) real, but it is not.

12. Adults who are _____ (injure) in accidents have less trouble than children when they _____ (learn) to use wheelchairs.

13. In some countries public buses _____ (have) automatic ramps for wheelchairs. Wheelchairs _____ (lift) into the bus or train on a moveable ramp.

14. Ramps _____ (have to, build) in sidewalks in the United States so that wheelchairs _____ (can, get) on and off sidewalks easily.

15. All public buildings also _____ (have to, have) wheelchair entrances.

4.3 Describing Experiences

Describe orally or in writing experiences you have had. Use as many adjectives as you can.

EXAMPLE
It was *depressing* to see so many poor people living on the streets when I was . . .
Traveling in . . . was *frightening* because . . .
I was very *excited* when I first . . .

depressing	embarrassing	excited
frightening	frustrating	interested
surprising	tired	worried

UNIT 7 Technology

5 TROUBLE SPOTS: NUMERICAL RELATIONSHIPS; MORE NON-COUNT NOUNS; ARTICLES

Expressing Numbers and Numerical Relationships	hundreds	125	one hundred twenty-five
	thousands dates (up until the year 2000 are always given using hundreds)	1230 1895	twelve hundred thirty eighteen hundred ninety-five (NOT one thousand eight hundred ninety-five)
	millions	100,000,000 1.2 million	one hundred million one "point" two million
	percentages	15% 1.5% 20% **of** households	fifteen percent one "point" five percent or one and five tenths percent
	numerical changes or contracts	(a) The number of programs **changed / increased / decreased / rose / fell / dropped from** X **to** Y. (b) The number **increased / grew / decreased / rose / fell / dropped (by)** 5 **percent** or 16 **units.**	
Non-Count Nouns	Some **non-count nouns** have times when their meaning makes them countable.	(c) There has been a lot of computer **crime** recently. *(illegal activity in general)* (d) He will be punished for his computer **crimes.** *(individual illegal acts)* (e) VCR **technology** has advanced rapidly. *(the knowledge of VCRs)* (f) It is hard to imagine what computer **technologies** will exist in 50 years. *(processes)* (g) There was a lot of **damage** done to his eyes from too much computer work. *(harm)* (h) The court made the manufacturer pay one million dollars in **damages.** *(money paid for damage done)*	

(Continued on the next page)

Articles	Use the article **the** for names of	deserts, oceans, seas gulfs, bays (except if there is no "of" in the name of the bay)	**the** Gobi Desert **the** Mediterranean Sea **the** Bay of Fundy BUT: San Francisco Bay	**the** Pacific Ocean **the** Gulf of Thailand
		gardens, zoos	**the** Tivoli Gardens	**the** San Diego Zoo
		tunnels, buildings	**the** Chunnel	**the** Parliament building
		companies if "company" is in the title	**the** Boeing Company BUT: Benetton	
		ships	**the** Queen Elizabeth II	
		newspapers	**the** Wall Street Journal BUT: Vogue magazine	
		periods of history	**the** Middle Ages	
		directions if they are the name of a region	**the** Southwest BUT: southwest of here	

154   UNIT 7 *Technology*

5.1 Listening: Practice with Numbers

Listen and fill in the information on the chart about sales of cellular telephones.

YEAR	NUMBER
1984	
1986	
1989	
1991	
1992	

5.2 Practice with Numbers

Work with a partner to find out the missing statistics. Partner A, look at this page. Partner B, look at File 23 in Appendix G.

Year	Number of Home Computers Sold
	2,000,000
1984	
	5,000,000
1991	
Year	**Percent of Households with Computers**
	23%
1992	

UNIT 7 Passives

5.3 Countable or Not?

Circle the correct form of the word in parentheses.

1. A number of children commit computer (crimes / crime) each year.
2. Their parents have to pay (damages / damage) if they are found guilty of those (crimes / crime).
3. We need more (information / informations) about the new systems.
4. I'm hungry. Let's run out and get some (food / foods).
5. He wants to get into some field of (technology / technologies).
6. The (technology / technologies) involved in processing salt water into drinkable water and irrigating deserts (is / are) vital to countries like Kuwait and the Sudan.
7. Look outside! There are about 10 inches of (snow / snows).
   This was one of our heaviest (snow / snows) in years.
8. I need to get some new ski (equipment / equipments) this year.
9. They are having a big sale on (software / softwares) this weekend.

5.4 Articles

In a small group, complete the sentences. Use the choices below. Add the definite article, when necessary.

| Madagascar | Wall Street Journal | National | Gobi | Alps | Titanic |
| Hudson | World Trade Center | Chunnel | Tivoli| Borneo | Mexico |

1. The largest desert in Mongolia is _____ Desert.
2. _____ is the largest island of Indonesia.
3. The largest bay in Canada is called _____ Bay.
4. _____ Building is the tallest building in New York.
5. The British ship which hit an iceberg in 1912 was called _____.
6. _____ Gulf of _____ is the body of water on the west coast of Florida.
7. A large mountain range in South-Central Europe is called _____.
8. _____ is the largest island in the Indian Ocean. It is located off the southeast coast of Africa.
9. _____ is a tunnel under the English channel. England and France are connected by this tunnel.
10. _____ is a daily financial newspaper. It is published in New York.
11. A world-famous garden in Copenhagen is called _____ Gardens.
12. _____ Zoo is the name of the zoo in Washington, D.C.

156   UNIT 7 Technology

6 PHRASAL VERBS WITH *UP*

(a) Be sure to **back up** any work you do on the computer. (*make a copy*)
(b) One movie was called "Honey, I **Blew Up,** the Kids!" (*explode*)
(c) We should get our tank **filled up.** We have a long trip. (*make full*)
(d) He's working hard so he will be able to **catch up** with the others. (*get to the same level*)
(e) Don't **make up** excuses! Tell me the truth. (*fabricate*)
(f) If you **keep up** the good work, you will succeed. (*maintain*)
(g) Should I **bring up** the problem in the meeting? (*introduce*)
(h) **Look** that **up** in the user's manual. (*research*)
(i) Could you **pick** me **up** on your way? (*collect*)
(j) Make sure no problems **come up.** (*happen*)

6.1 Differences in Meaning?

Discuss these sentences with a partner. Consult Appendix D if you don't know the meanings of these phrasal verbs.

EXAMPLE
a. This problem keeps coming up.
b. This problem keeps coming back.
Coming up means happening. *Coming back* means returning.

1. a. He still has time to catch up.
   b. He is having trouble catching on.

2. a. Hold on to her. She's a great person.
   b. Don't hold up the line.
   c. That bank has been held up again. They got a million dollars.

3. a. Look at the ideas he comes up with.
   b. He'll come around to our point of view.
   c. We finally came to a decision.

4. a. I should look in on her and see how she's doing.
   b. Let's look around for a better deal on a computer.
   c. We need to look over the results to see if they are accurate.
   d. Could you look that up in your dictionary?

5. a. They are going to bring in a new consultant.
   b. They brought up the subject of damages.
   c. When they brought on the dancing bears, everyone applauded.

LISTENING TEST

Listen and circle the letter of the statement which best describes the situation.

1. a. CD developed it.
   b. Philips developed it.
   c. CD played it.

2. a. She cut it.
   b. It hadn't been cut in six weeks.
   c. Someone else cut it.

3. a. I know who stole it.
   b. It's possible that someone stole it.
   c. It was stolen by a thief.

4. a. They were made in two different countries.
   b. They are the same model.
   c. They belong to my friend.

5. a. You can buy the car here.
   b. Ten years ago you could buy the car here.
   c. The car isn't produced anywhere at this time.

6. a. I was frustrating.
   b. I was frustrated.
   c. It wasn't as bad as other experiences I've had.

7. a. I painted it.
   b. I haven't painted it yet.
   c. Someone else painted it.

8. a. I am not interested in what he says.
   b. Something bores him a lot.
   c. It puts everyone to sleep.

9. a. I should finish it.
   b. I think it's done.
   c. It's a good idea to finish it.

10. a. Someone delivered the flowers after I got to the office.
    b. The flowers were placed on my desk.
    c. It is clear who brought the flowers.

QUIZ YOURSELF

Circle the letter of the best answer to complete each sentence.

1. More technologically advanced computer crimes _____ along with new developments in technology.
   a. have been coming
   b. were came
   c. have come

2. Computer programs _____ by computer "viruses" — programs designed to cause damage to your software.
   a. can secretly enter and destroy
   b. can be secretly entered and destroyed
   c. can be secretly entering and destroying

3. It is alarming that highly important government computer systems _____ by student-made viruses.
   a. have been invaded
   b. have invaded
   c. invaded

4. Also, in 1990, German computer users _____ enter computer data in the United States military computer system.
   a. are able to
   b. had been able to
   c. were able to

5. This kind of user _____ a "hacker."
   a. called
   b. call
   c. is called

6. Computer crimes are difficult to investigate because they _____ in a second and may be committed thousands of miles away.
   a. are happened
   b. happened
   c. happen

7. Viruses _____ from someone's home computer onto national computer networks.
   a. can be designed and sent
   b. are designing and sending
   c. design and send

8. By the time the hacker was caught, a great deal of damage _____ to the computer system.
   a. was done
   b. had been done
   c. was doing

9. Some computer crimes _____ to court since the "criminals" were children. They did not realize the harm they were doing.
   a. have not be brought
   b. have not brought
   c. have not been brought

10. However, no matter what age, children _____ to respect other users and their computer systems.
    a. have to teach
    b. have to be taught
    c. have been taught

UNIT 7 Passives

UNIT 8

Review

Work

1 REVIEW OF VERB TENSES

The verb tenses in English are divided into three **time periods**: past, present, and future.

Aspect: Our attitudes as speakers, how we look at the experience, are also reflected in the verb tense system: How long was the experience? Does it relate in time to other experiences?

Simple	in that time period	simple **past** simple **present** simple **future**	(a) I **worked** there two years. (b) I **work** from 9 to 5 daily. (c) I **will work** there after I graduate.
Continuous	during a time period	**past** continuous **present** continuous **future** continuous	(d) She **was working** when she met him. (e) I **am working** in the cafeteria this year. (f) He **will be working** on this project for the next two months.
Perfect	before another time period	**past** perfect **present** perfect **future** perfect	(g) I **had** already **worked** in my field when I started my master's degree. (h) She **has worked** here for the past ten months. (i) In January, you **will have worked** here long enough to get medical benefits.

Perfect Continuous	continuous before another time period	**past perfect continuous** **present perfect continuous** **future perfect continuous**	(j) He **had** already **been working** here for several years when I started. (k) She **has been putting in** many hours of overtime on that project. (l) By next month, we **will have been working** on this project for two months.

Note: **Non-continuous verbs** are not usually used in the continuous aspect.
See Appendix A for a list of common non-continuous verbs and their exceptions.

1.1 Get in Motion: Review of Verb Tenses

A. Complete the sentences with the correct form of the verb in parentheses.

1. Peter Hougen _____ (look) for a job. He _____ (be) unemployed since his company _____ (go) out of business.

2. Lisa Mathews _____ (also, try) to find a job right now.

   She _____ (just, graduate) from the university last month.

   She _____ (want) to work in the architecture field although

   she _____ (not, have) any experience in this area. Someday Lisa

   _____ (probably, go) back to school and _____

   (get) a graduate degree in architecture. She _____ (hope) that by the time

   she _____ (go) back to school, she _____ (save)

   enough money to pay for her education. Lisa's parents _____ (pay) for her

   undergraduate education, but they _____ (want) Lisa to pay for her own

   graduate education.

3. For the past five years the airline industry _____ (experience) financial

   problems and they _____ (not, buy) new airplanes. Last year Boeing

   _____ (lay) off 20,000 workers. Cary Tanaka _____

   (use) to work at Boeing. Now he _____ (be) unemployed.

   Before his layoff, Cary _____ (work) as a Boeing engineer.

   (Continued on the next page)

He _____ (work) there for ten years. While Cary _____ (work) at Boeing, he _____ (save) 25 percent of his income each month. He _____ (recently, use) that money to open a coffee shop and bakery now that he _____ (be) unemployed.

4. Last week Pedro _____ (apply) for a job, but he _____ (be) too late. They _____ (fill) the position.

5. I _____ (get) a business degree in 1982. For three years I _____ (manage) the finance department at a small bank. However, I _____ (want) to make more money, so I _____ (go) to another company. They _____ (give) me a higher salary. I _____ (now, consider) changing jobs again. A "headhunter" _____ (call) me last week. He _____ (tell) me about a job at a larger company that _____ (pay) very well. I _____ (think) I _____ (apply) for that job. This is the first time a headhunter _____ (ever, call) me.

1.2 Listening: Choosing a New Police Chief

A. You are members of a committee that is in charge of hiring a new police chief in your city. Listen to the information and take notes about these three candidates.

Craig Hobson

162   UNIT 8   *Work*

Norman Lewis

Mary Gantz

B. **Now work in small groups. Decide which candidate is the best person for the job. Here is some more information about your city and its police force.**

City	650,000 people 15% minority	This is a fairly quiet city. Violent crime is not a major problem, but crimes such as theft and robbery are increasing. Residents are worried about crime, particularly drug-related crime. They were very angry about a scandal that involved the police.
Police Force	400 members 20% minority 15% women average age 31	The current police chief resigned because of that scandal—illegal businesses in the city paid the police money and the police did not close down the businesses. Twenty police officers were involved.

1.3 Verb Contrast

Complete the sentences with the correct form of the verb in parentheses.

BOB: (1) Hello, Mei, how _____ you _____ (do)?

MEI: (2) I _____ (be) fine! I _____ (not, see) you for a long time.

BOB: (3) I know. I _____ (think) the last time I _____ (see) you, we _____ (just, finish) high school!

MEI: (4) That's right. It's amazing how time _____ (fly)!

(Continued on the next page)

BOB: (5) So, what _____ you _____ (do) now? _____ you _____ (work)?

MEI: (6) Yes, I _____ (work) for my father in his car dealership.

BOB: (7) Oh, that's great. _____ you _____ (like) it?

MEI: (8) Yes, it's fine. How about you? Where _____ you _____ (work)?

BOB: (9) Well, I _____ (not, work) right now. I _____ (look) for a job. (10) I _____ (work) at Aldus Computers, but they _____ (sell) the company and _____ (lay) off a lot of people.

MEI: (11) Oh, that's too bad. I _____ (hope) you find something soon.

BOB: (12) Thanks. Tomorrow I _____ (have) a job interview at Microsoft. (13) And then next week I _____ (spend) some time in Vancouver. (14) I actually _____ (not, mind) being unemployed for a while, but I _____ (run) out of money if I _____ (not, find) a job pretty soon!

MEI: (15) Listen, give me a call when you _____ (get) back from Vancouver, OK? (16) I _____ (look) through my address book and _____ (see) if I _____ (know) anyone at any computer companies.

BOB: (17) Thanks. I _____ (definitely, give) you a call when I _____ (be) back in town.

1.4 Talk It Over

Ask a classmate some of these questions about jobs and work.

When you were young, what kind of job did you want?
Do you have / Have you ever had a job?
What is your ideal job?
"Work keeps a person young. I will always work, no matter how rich I am." Do you agree or disagree?

2 REVIEW OF THE PASSIVE

All of the common verb tenses can be expressed in the passive voice to show that the doer of the action is unknown or not important. However, only verbs which take objects—transitive verbs—can be used in the passive voice.

Simple Tenses	(a) She **was employed** by Microsoft. (b) She **is employed** by Microsoft. (c) She **will be employed** by Microsoft.
Continuous Tenses	(d) They **were being interviewed** by Sony. (e) They **are being interviewed** by Sony.
Perfect Tenses	(f) He **had been employed** by Boeing. (g) He **has been employed** by Boeing. (h) He **will have been employed** by Boeing for 30 years when he retires.
Modals	(i) They **should be fired** for that behavior! (j) They **might be fired**. (k) They **should have been fired**.

Note: The **passive** is not common in many continuous tenses: future continuous, future perfect continuous, past perfect continuous, or past continuous.

2.1 Get in Motion: The Passive

Work in pairs or teams. Make questions in the passive or active voice with the phrases below. The answers are in File 21 in Appendix G. How many questions can you answer?

EXAMPLE
who / call / "the best driver who ever lived"
Who was called "the best driver who ever lived"?
Ayrton Senna of Brazil

1. who / imprison / 27 years / and later / elect / president of his country

2. who / kill / San Marino Grand Prix / 1994

3. who / give / the Academy Award for Best Director in 1991 for a movie he acted in

4. who / name / Mr. Europe in 1966 and Mr. Universe in 1968, 1969, and 1970

5. what princess / design / swimsuits

6. what woman / with a famous smile / paint / Leonardo da Vinci

7. what people / employ / as guides on mountain expeditions in the Himalayas

8. what computer company / start / by two college dropouts

Cesar Chavez demonstrating with farm workers

2.2 Form of the Passive

Complete the sentences with the correct form of the verb in parentheses.

(1) Cesar Chavez was a man whose life _____ (devote) to making a better life for migrant farm workers who moved from one area of the country to another to harvest whatever was in season. (2) The farmers often _____ (live) in tents; (3) the children _____ (rarely, educate) because their families _____ (move) so frequently and because the children _____ (also, employ) as farm workers. (4) Chavez himself _____ (never, complete) high school and said that as a child he _____ (go) to more than 30 grade schools.

(5) Chavez _____ (feel) that farm workers _____ (exploit) by growers. (6) In 1962, he _____ (start) the National Farm Workers Association. (7) When California grape growers _____ (not, affect) by a strike in 1965, Chavez _____ (organize) a national boycott. (8) He also _____ (go) on a 25-day hunger strike that _____ (cover) by all the newspapers and TV reporters. (9) By 1969, 12 percent of the people in the United States _____ (join) the boycott and _____ (refuse) to buy grapes. (10) In 1970, growers _____ (give) in to union demands and the first farm workers' labor contract _____ (sign).

(11) Chavez _____ (die) in 1993. (12) He _____ (still, fight) with growers, this time over the use of pesticides on farms.

UNIT 8 Work

2.3 Editing Practice

Find the errors in the sentences. Write the correction on the line.

1. Today we are deal with a world economy.

2. Boundaries have been disappeared because of the number of multinational companies, the international aspects of many companies, and each country's dependence on imports, exports, and even foreign workers.

3. A U.S. product may have been making in Mexico with parts from Taiwan.

4. The work force became more educated as well since then.

5. People without skills are finding it harder to get a job which support their families.

6. Workers today want work to be rewarding. They are expecting their employers to be sensitive to their responsibilities for child and elder care.

7. The work ethic is changed recently. More and more people feel that work is not as important as leisure.

8. In the future, human resource departments will have played an even more important role in helping workers with family and work conflicts.

9. Service-oriented jobs have increased greatly in the past few years. At the same time manufacturing jobs had decreased in tremendous numbers.

10. In fact, manufacturing jobs will probably decrease in the future in the same way that farming jobs have been in the past.

11. The U.S. work force has become more diverse. More women and minorities represent in the workplace.

12. Women workers constitutes 50 percent of the work force.

UNIT 8 Review

3 MODALS AND RELATED STRUCTURES

Modal auxiliaries add extra meaning to verbs. They may express the speaker's perception, intention, or attitude. Modal auxiliaries do not change endings in the third person singular or past forms of the verbs. They often have several meanings and they may express present, future, or past time.

Advice / Opinion	(a) You **should** prepare a good resume. (b) You **ought to** apply for that job. (c) You**'d better** talk to your boss. He's angry! (d) You **shouldn't have** sent that out without his approval. (e) You **ought to have** talked to him first.
Obligation / Necessity	(f) I **have to** get this letter out. (g) I **must** get it mailed before 4:00. (h) I **have got to** get some stamps.
Lack of Obligation	(i) I **don't have to** be at work until 9:00.
Expectation	(j) She**'s supposed to** fax that today. (k) She **was supposed to have** sent that fax. (l) She **had better have** sent it or we'll lose that contract!
Invitations / Suggestions	(m) **Let's** go out for a drink after work. (n) **Why don't** we invite our new officemate? (o) Maybe we **could / should** get some dinner, too? (p) We **could / might** see a movie, too. (q) **How about** having a drink after work? (r) **Shall we** meet after work tonight? (s) **Would you like to** go out for lunch?
Possibility	(t) He **could / may / might** get a promotion. (u) We **could / may / might have** moved if he had gotten the promotion.
Probability	(v) That company **must** be doing well. Its stock is up. (w) That company **must have** had a good year. Its stock is up.

168 UNIT 8 Work

Requests	(x) **Will** you talk to the boss about it?
	(y) **Would you mind** talking to him?
	(z) **Could** you discuss this with him?
	(aa) **Do you think you could** talk to the Director of Human Resources about this?
Permission	(bb) **Can / may / could** I take tomorrow off?
	(cc) **Will** your boss **mind if** you do?
	(dd) **Would it be all right if** I don't come in?
	(ee) **Do you think I could** have the day off?
Preference	(ff) **I'd prefer** to work a four-day week.
	(gg) **I'd rather** not work on weekends.
Ability	(hh) She **can / could** do that job well.
	(ii) He **isn't able to** handle the responsibilities of that job.
Unfulfilled Potential or Possibility	(jj) I **could have** gotten that job if I had had more computer experience.
Past Habitual Action	(kk) I **used to** work there but now I'm retired.
	(ll) I **would** get up every morning and commute for one hour to work.

3.1 Get in Motion: Listening

A. Do you know the meanings of these words and expressions?

| cash register | ring up a sale | pocket the money |

B. "Let's Talk" is a radio talk show. Today's topic is "Trouble at Work." Listen and write down the problems for one listener.

_____
_____
_____
_____
_____

C. Complete these sentences about the situation and discuss your answers with a classmate.

1. Lucas and John work _____.

2. They are supposed to _____.

3. John thinks that Lucas might _____.

4. Even if John is innocent, he _____ lose his job because his boss _____.

5. In my opinion John _____ talk to Lucas. John should _____.

170   UNIT 8 Work

3.2 Problem Solving

You are human resource managers at a large bank. You are in charge of hiring and training new employees. You also deal with employee complaints. Choose <u>one</u> of the following situations to discuss in your group.

1. Marie is physically handicapped. She has the use of her upper body (from her waist up) and sits in a wheelchair. She is 23 years old, has graduated from a university, and has excellent qualifications.

   a. What kinds of jobs can Marie do? What can't she do?
   b. Should you hire her?
   c. Will anything have to be changed at the bank to accommodate Marie?
   d. Should changes like this be made just to accommodate one employee?

2. You have enough money in your training budget to send one person for advanced training. Two people have applied to do the training. Jack is 50 years old and has been with the company for 25 years. Anna is 25 years old. She has been in the company for three years.

   a. Who should you choose to go to the training? Why?
   b. What can you say to the person you don't choose?

3. Three years ago you hired someone who spoke English as a second language. He worked in the check processing department for two years and did very well. When a job opened in the customer service area, he applied for the job. Since your policy is to promote people who work in the bank, you gave him the job. However, within a month, his supervisor started complaining about him. She said she couldn't understand him and he couldn't understand her instructions. Last week he misunderstood a customer and gave the customer some wrong information. His supervisor overheard this and fired him.

   a. How must the employee have felt when he got fired?
   b. Was there anything you could have done differently in this situation?
   c. What should you have done? What should the supervisor have done? What should the employee have done?

3.3 Modal Contrast

Complete the following sentences with one of the modals given. Use each one only once.

1. Monica, Howard, and Lee are often late for work.

can't	had better not	has to	should be able to

   a. Monica _____ arrive late for her job if she still gets her work done.

   b. Howard _____ be late without losing money because he _____ turn in a time sheet in order to be paid.

   c. Lee _____ be late again or he will lose his job.

(Continued on the next page)

2. That company mainly hires part-time employees.

| must   might have   should |

   a. I think they _____ hire full-time employees if they want to get real worker commitment.

   b. Experience has taught them that they _____ have a number of part-time employees who they can lay off—let go from work—during hard economic times.

   c. I _____ taken a part-time job with them if they had offered me benefits, but I'm not sure.

3. Worldwide, women often work longer hours at the same job as men but for less money.

| could not   ought   should |

   a. Some people think women _____ not be paid the same as men because men have to support families.

   b. Some people think women _____ to be paid less than men because women's work is often temporary.

   c. Even though Maria was unhappy about her salary, she _____ do anything about it. She was afraid of losing her job.

4. In many countries it is common for women to stop working when they get married and begin a family.

| doesn't have to   are not able to   can |

   a. People are often surprised if a wealthy woman works when she _____.

   b. Women in my country _____ continue to work when they get married if they want to. It's up to them.

5. In some countries there is a very high mortality rate on the job.

| must not   ought to have   should |

   a. I think companies _____ pay more attention to job safety.

   b. The government _____ passed laws to force companies to be safer. Then so many workers would not have died last year.

   c. That factory _____ care about safety because its mortality rate is the highest.

172   UNIT 8   Work

6. England has a 15 percent absenteeism rate in factories.

| could | had better | might not |

   a. One way to reduce this rate is that companies _____ provide buses to pick up workers.

   b. This problem _____ be carefully studied.

   c. If factory workers were bored by their work, they _____ want to go to work every day.

3.4 Verb Review

The following passages discuss ideas about business in different cultures. Complete the sentences with the correct form of the word in parentheses. Which perspective matches the general description? Which perspective is most like your culture?

A. (1) Many business people _____ (feel) that time _____ (be) something that _____ (modal of ability) _____ (save) or _____ (spend).

(2) You _____ (modal of advice) _____ (arrive) on time to a meeting. (3) Business people _____ (plan) in advance and _____ (keep) a tight schedule to meet with clients.

Perspective 1: (4) I _____ (live) in country X for six months when I finally _____ (get) an important account. (5) I _____ (have) a lunch appointment with the client and I _____ (wait) for him for one hour in the restaurant. (6) While I _____ (sit) there, I _____ (become) angrier and angrier because I _____ (know) I _____ (waste) my time.

(7) When he finally _____ (show) up, I _____ (try) to hurry through the business because I _____ (modal of obligation) _____ (get) back to work by 4:00. (8) Unfortunately, the meeting _____ (go) badly and I _____ (lose) the account!

(Continued on the next page)

Perspective 2: (9) Americans _____ always _____ (hurry)! (10) In my country, we _____ (need) more time to develop a good relationship before we _____ (agree) on a business deal. (11) I _____ (have) a lunch meeting with an American last week that _____ (be) a disaster. (12) The American _____ (try) to force me to make a commitment before we _____ (have) a chance to get to know each other. (13) I _____ (not, feel) trust in that hurried business luncheon. (14) I _____ (not, want) to work with that company anymore.

B. (15) Job security _____ (value). (16) People _____ (not, expect) to move from company to company or from city to city. (17) If people _____ (do) their work and _____ (maintain) a good relationship with the boss, they _____ (move) up within the organization. (18) The boss _____ (be) always the boss.
(19) He _____ (become) the group's leader because of his past successes.
(20) He _____ (act) as a father to all of the workers.

Perspective 1: (21) My career _____ (be) very important to me.
(22) I _____ (work) for three different companies in four different cities over the past 15 years. (23) Every time I _____ (change) jobs, I _____ (get) a better paying job. (24) Right now I _____ (work) at a small company, but I _____ (think) about changing companies again because I _____ (not, promote) in three years. (25) I _____ (*modal of possibility*) _____ (apply) for a job in a larger company. However, the job (26) _____ (involve) a move to another city. (27) It used to be easier to move, but now that I _____ (marry), I _____ (*modal of necessity*)

174   UNIT 8 *Work*

think about my husband. (28) _____ he _____ (*modal of ability*) find a good job in another city?

Perspective 2: (29) When I _____ (retire) next month, I _____ (work) at this same company for 45 years. (30) Perhaps I _____ (*modal of unfulfilled possibility*) _____ (make) more money in a different company, but I _____ (never, think) about applying for another job. (31) I _____ (be) a part of this company and the company _____ (be) good to me.

(32) I _____ (miss) my co-workers when I _____ (retire) next month. (33) My wife and I _____ (take) a trip. (34) It _____ (be) the first three-week vacation I _____ (ever, take). (35) I _____ (not, know) what I _____ (do) when I _____ (get) back from my vacation. (36) I _____ (*modal of possibility*) be very bored.

C. (37) The country _____ (become) a "credential" society.

(38) It _____ (be) very important to have a college degree as one's ticket to a job interview. (39) Professional people _____ (respect) more than other workers in business.

Perspective 1: (40) In my country, a self-employed man _____ more highly _____ (respect) than a professional who _____ (work) for someone else. (41) I _____ just _____ (finish) my college degree but I _____ (not, plan) to get a job in a company. (42) I _____ (open) my own restaurant in the next year.

(*Continued on the next page*)

UNIT 8 Review

Perspective 2: (43) My father _____ (own) his own business and he _____ (want) me to take over for him when he _____ (retire). (44) I _____ (work) summers in the business since I _____ (be) 16. (45) I _____ (start) in the lowest job and now I _____ (know) every employee. (46) But I _____ (graduate) from college in two years and I _____ (decide) that I _____ (not, want) to work in my father's business. (47) I _____ (*preference*) go to law school. (48) I _____ (know) my father _____ (be) upset when I _____ (talk) to him about this, but I _____ (hope) he _____ (understand).

3.5 Talk It Over and Optional Writing

Choose one of these questions to discuss with your classmates. Then write a composition about your ideas.

1. What have been your most rewarding work experiences?
2. What have been your worst work experiences?
3. What kind of job do you hope to have in the future?
4. What can companies do to help workers balance the requirements of family and work?

4 TROUBLE SPOTS: *DO* VERSUS *MAKE*; ARTICLES

Do and *make* are often confusing. In general, we *do* actions, especially routine activities and chores, and we *make* or produce things. However, there are many expressions with *do* and *make* which must be memorized.	(a) I **did** the assignment, but I **made** lots of mistakes. (b) Teachers **make** assignments; students **do** homework. (c) I **did** the housework and **made** my bed. make a trip do me a favor make it clear do your work make an effort do well make a choice / decision
Use *the* with different kinds of communication.	**the** radio **the** phone **the** fax (Note: TV is commonly used without *the*: What's on TV tonight?)
Don't use *the* with languages except with the word *language*.	English **the** English language Thai **the** Thai language Arabic **the** Arabic language

4.1 *Do* or *Make*?

Complete the phrase with the correct verb, *do* or *make*.

1. _____ the cooking
2. _____ a trip
3. _____ it in pencil
4. _____ an apology
5. _____ the bed
6. _____ your work
7. _____ well
8. _____ a decision
9. _____ someone cry
10. _____ dinner
11. _____ the TV clearer
12. _____ it clear enough to understand
13. _____ me a favor
14. _____ the laundry
15. _____ my work more difficult
16. _____ more money
17. _____ an effort
18. _____ a cup of coffee

4.2 Articles

Complete the sentences with *a*, *an*, *the*, or an X for no article.

1. Could you get _____ phone? It's ringing.
2. We need _____ phone in the garage. I can't hear calls when I am working out there.
3. I heard _____ news on _____ radio last night.
4. We have recently purchased _____ short-wave radio.
5. Now we can listen to _____ news from my country in _____ Spanish.
6. The French government has _____ organization which tries to keep foreign words out of _____ French language.
7. Did you see what was on _____ TV last night?
8. If _____ desks are too close together, people sometimes get on each other's nerves.
9. When was _____ fax machine invented? How did we ever get along without _____ faxes?

5 PREPOSITIONS AND PHRASAL VERBS

Prepositions of Logical Relationships

of	used for geographic locations and institutions	the center **of** town the University **of** Washington
	parts of a whole; possession	the heart **of** the matter the leg **of** the table
except	used to show that something is not included	(a) All of the states, **except** Alaska and Hawaii, are in the continental United States. (b) Everyone, **except** Jerome, must work overtime.
with, by	show who or what does something	**with** your help **with** our teacher made **by** hand written **by** Hemingway **by** car **by** bus
without	not having	**without** your cooperation

178   UNIT 8 Work

Adjectives + *of*	Many adjectives are followed by *of*.	afraid **of**, aware **of**, capable **of**, careful **of**, confident **of**, conscious **of**, critical **of**, full **of**, glad **of**, ignorant **of**, positive **of**, proud **of**, uncertain **of**
Phrasal Verbs		(c) I need to **take care of** that matter before it gets worse. *(look after)* (d) They **checked out of** the hotel by 10:00 a.m. *(officially leave)* (e) There is still time to **get / back out of** this deal. *(escape, leave a commitment)* (f) They didn't want to **move out of** the neighborhood. *(leave an area)* (g) We're **out of** time. We'll continue this tomorrow. *(have no more)*

5.1 Practice with Prepositions

With a partner, ask and answer the questions.

1. What weren't you capable of doing when you were younger?
2. What are you most positive of at this time in your life?
3. What do you do when you're out of money?
4. How did you get here today?
5. Who was *Hamlet* written by?
6. What are you most uncertain of?
7. What can you do without?
8. What are you most afraid of: hurricanes or fire?
9. What time do you usually have to check out of hotels?
10. What was the last place you moved out of?
11. What are you most proud of at this point in your life?
12. Are there some things children should remain ignorant of?
13. When you were growing up, what were your parents most critical of about you?
14. When you talk in front of a group, what are you most conscious of?

LISTENING TEST

Listen and circle the letter of the statement which best describes the situation.

1. a. I have worked all my life.
   b. I always work hard.
   c. I worked harder than usual.

2. a. I think they were wrong when they didn't call us.
   b. They called us.
   c. They were not late.

3. a. It is optional.
   b. It is required.
   c. We prefer it.

4. a. I know who repaired the machine.
   b. The machine keeps breaking down.
   c. I repaired the machine two times.

5. a. You haven't finished the job yet.
   b. You finished the job.
   c. You haven't started the job yet.

6. a. Someone gave him instructions.
   b. He gave the instructions.
   c. The instructions were confusing.

7. a. They finished the project before I worked there.
   b. They were still working on the project.
   c. They have finished the project now.

8. a. We don't expect any difficulty.
   b. It isn't any trouble.
   c. We didn't have any problems.

9. a. I got everything done last night.
   b. I haven't done my homework yet.
   c. I did my homework this morning.

10. a. I know it's fine to borrow his car.
    b. It may be possible to borrow his car.
    c. I borrowed his car last week.

QUIZ YOURSELF

Circle the letter of the best answer to complete each sentence.

1. Small business owners _____ take risks to own and manage their own businesses.
   a. must have
   b. have to
   c. could have

2. If you are not a highly motivated person, you _____ happy working for yourself.
   a. should not be
   b. could not have been
   c. may not be

3. The government _____ support small businesses. This is essential for their success.
   a. must
   b. had to
   c. ought

4. He _____ a job in a large, successful company, but he wanted to try to make it on his own.
   a. could have been getting
   b. could get
   c. could have gotten

5. That company _____ for several years by one family. We call that a family-influenced firm.
   a. has been controlled
   b. has been controlling
   c. being controlled

6. One of the big differences between self-employed business people and managers is that the self-employed must work long hours. However, they decide when those hours _____.
   a. will be
   b. will have been
   c. will had been

7. If you _____ a family business, you will have more job security and a bigger share of the profits.
   a. have been
   b. are having
   c. have

8. A disadvantage of working in a family-run business is that if you _____, you may not be promoted.
   a. have not related
   b. do not relate
   c. are not related

9. There were fewer problems in their business because early on they _____ a plan for control in the future. It was based on the quality of work rather than family relationship.
   a. had developed
   b. have developed
   c. have been developed

10. Children of small business owners _____ to be more successful small business owners than people who simply have a business administration degree.
    a. have found
    b. have been found
    c. are finding

UNIT 8 Review

UNIT 9

Infinitives

Travel

1 INFINITIVES AND GERUNDS

FORM	An **infinitive** is *to* + the base form of the verb.	(a) I'd like **to travel** with you.
	A **gerund** is the *-ing* form of the verb used as a noun.	(b) I enjoy **traveling**.
USE	Both **infinitives** and **gerunds** are used: • as the complement of a verb • as the subject of a sentence Infinitives are used with the false subject *it*.	(c) I decided **to take** my vacation in June. (d) They considered **going** to India. (e) **Flying** is a lot faster. (f) **To fly** is a lot faster. *(less common)* (g) **It** is interesting **to travel** by train.
	Infinitives are commonly used after an adjective, adverb, or noun.	(h) I'm *afraid* **to fly**. (i) He doesn't know *where* **to stay**. (j) I don't have *enough* money **to stay** at the Ritz. (k) A travel agent is the *person* **to ask**.
	Gerunds are commonly used as the objects of prepositions.	(l) I'm afraid *of* **flying**. (m) She worried *about* **traveling** alone. (n) I'm going to insist *on* **having** a window seat.

Note: Sometimes it is difficult to know whether to use the infinitive or the gerund. The uses of each are explained in detail in this unit on infinitives and in the next on gerunds.

1.1 Get in Motion: Infinitives and Gerunds

A. Underline the gerunds and infinitives in this conversation.

KAREN: So how was your trip?

LIZ: Oh, it was all right.

KAREN: Just all right?

LIZ: Well, John and I have different ideas about how to travel.

KAREN: Really?

LIZ: Yes! He likes running around, seeing everything, visiting all the museums and historic places. I hate being busy from day to night! I just want to relax. I like to sit on a beach or around a pool, go shopping, eat in nice restaurants. He hates to do that!

KAREN: Well, what about doing different things? Have breakfast together and decide where to meet for dinner.

LIZ: Oh, he wants me to go with him. It's not very much fun to explore all by yourself.

KAREN: Well, yes, this does seem to be a problem. Maybe it would be a good idea to talk to John about this.

LIZ: Talking doesn't seem to help.

B. Answer these questions.

1. What do you like to do when you travel? Are you like Liz or like her husband?

2. Is there any activity you hate doing on a trip?

3. Do you like traveling alone or do you usually want someone to go with you?

4. What advice would you give to Liz and John?
   I would advise Liz to . . .
   I would advise John to . . .

5. Have you ever gone on a trip with someone who had very different ideas about how to spend time? Describe this experience.

UNIT 9 Infinitives

2 VERB + INFINITIVE

The most common use of **infinitives** is to complement (complete) verbs.	(a) I **want to go** to Canada this summer. (b) He **promised to take** her to Europe for their tenth anniversary. (c) They **struggled to get** their clothes into their small suitcases. (d) He **hesitated to make** the plane reservations so many months in advance.
The **negative form** of the infinitive is **not to** + base form of the verb.	(e) We decided **not to go** away.
If there are two or more infinitives connected by **and** or **but**, it is not necessary to repeat the **to**.	(f) They wanted **to get away and see** the world. (g) They wanted **to get away, see** the world, **but not spend** a lot of money.
Many verbs that take infinitives have a **future sense**. The infinitive action often has not happened yet, or, if the verb is in the past, had not happened at the time of the main verb.	(h) Please ask her **to call** me. (i) They offered **to help**.
Common verbs which may **take an infinitive**:	agree endeavor plan* wait appear expect prefer* want arrange fail pretend attempt* hate* promise bother hesitate refuse claim hope say consent intend* seem decide learn struggle decline like* threaten demand love* try* deserve* offer venture
*These verbs may also take a gerund.	
See Appendix E for more verbs which take infinitives.	

UNIT 9 Travel

2.1 Get in Motion: Verb + Infinitive

What advice would you give to a friend who is going to another country for the first time? Be sure to include an infinitive.

1. Try . . .
2. Before you leave, arrange . . .
3. Don't hesitate . . .
4. Wait . . .
5. Remember . . .
6. While I'm in the train (airplane / bus / car), I always attempt . . .
7. If you have any problems with your hotels, demand . . .

2.2 Listening: Going to Disney World

Listen to the conversation. Are the following statements true, false, or unknown? Write T, F, or U.

_____ 1. Mary intends to go to Disney World with her family.

_____ 2. Antonio has been to Disney World.

_____ 3. Antonio intends to go to Disney World next year.

_____ 4. Mary has decided not to visit Epcot.

_____ 5. Mary is planning to spend five days at Disney World.

_____ 6. Mary's children don't really want to go to Disney World.

2.3 Infinitives

Complete the sentence to go with the picture. Use an infinitive in your answer.

1. Mary and her family planned

2. Unfortunately, she waited too long

(Continued on the next page)

UNIT 9 Infinitives   185

3. So she decided

4. They attempted

5. Unfortunately, she had forgotten

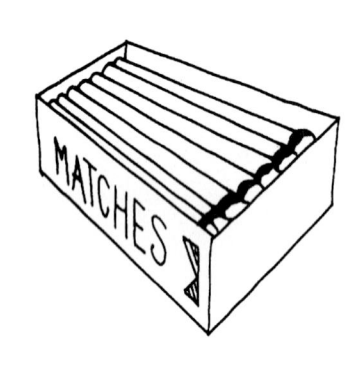

6. Luckily, other people offered

7. The weather threatened

8. Mary decided she didn't like

186   UNIT 9   Travel

3 VERB + NOUN PHRASE + INFINITIVE

Some verbs may be followed by a **noun phrase** or **pronoun** + **infinitive**.	(a) I **asked my brother to make** a reservation through his travel agent. (b) His books **motivated Janet to travel** to faraway places. (c) Did they **invite you to go** with them?
Common verbs which take a noun phrase + infinitive:	advise forbid promise allow force remind ask get require call on hire send cause instruct teach caution invite tell choose lead train convince motivate trust dare need urge direct order want drive permit warn encourage persuade wish expect prepare
These verbs are often used in the **passive voice**.	(d) She **was motivated to travel** to faraway places. (e) He **was told to wait** at the airport.

See Appendix E for more verbs which take a noun phrase / pronoun + an infinitive.

3.1 Get in Motion: Verb + Noun Phrase + Infinitive

A friend's parents are coming to visit your city. Your friend has written to ask your advice about where to stay and what to do. Use verbs from the list as infinitives. You may use a verb more than once. Sometimes you will need to add a noun phrase or a pronoun, such as *them* or *me*. You may need to make some infinitives negative.

bring	contact	go	join	look for	make
mention	pay	phone	reserve	see	spend
stay	take				

Dear _____,
         (your idea)

(1) Please ask your parents _____ when they arrive. I will be expecting their call. (2) I would advise _____ at the _____ Hotel. It's
                                                                                                   (your idea)
the nicest hotel in the city. (3) However, if they don't want _____ a lot of money on a hotel, tell them _____ a room at the _____ Hotel.
                                                                                                                                                                        (your idea)

(Continued on the next page)

It's not as expensive, but it's still very nice. (4) Would they like _____ their reservations for them?

I'd be happy to do that if they tell me which hotel they want. (5) I'd like _____ me for dinner the first night they get here. (6) I plan _____ them to the

_____ Restaurant. It's a great restaurant and I'm looking forward to taking them
  (your idea)

there. (7) I hope they will allow _____ for dinner. Your parents have treated me to dinner so many times!

(8) I know your parents don't really like sports, but they really should see _____
                                                                                (your idea)

It's very famous here, so I will try to convince them _____ with me to see it.

(9) I would caution them _____ because people dress casually here.

(10) Anyway, I'll expect _____ me when they arrive. (11) Can't wait _____ them! Wish you were going to be here too! (12) I almost forgot _____ the weather. (13) The weather is sometimes _____,
                                                                        (your idea)

so remind _____ a/an _____.
                              (your idea)

(14) When they drive here from _____, there's a wonderful
                                 (your idea)

_____. Tell _____ it! Also, I haven't seen photographs
  (your idea)   (your idea)

of your family in a long time. (15) Please get _____ some recent photographs!

3.2 Noun Phrase or Not?

Ask a classmate questions using these phrases. Add a noun or pronoun before the infinitive if necessary.

EXAMPLE
what countries / want / visit
What countries do you want to visit?

1. need / rent a car / when / travel
2. intend / take any trips in the next year
3. how much / import laws / allow / bring back from another country
4. what / import laws / forbid / bring into the country
5. what / friends / advise / not / do / when you travel
6. what / tour guides / warn / never / do
7. hesitate / travel / to any countries
8. your friends / tell / visit / anyplace

4 CAUSATIVES AND VERBS OF PERCEPTION

There are two groups of verbs that may be followed by a noun phrase / pronoun + base form of the verb.

Causatives	make, let, help, have	(a) They **made** him **show** his passport. (b) Did they **have** you **open** your suitcase?
Verbs of Perception	watch, look at, observe, feel, see, hear, listen to, notice	(c) We **saw** him **enter** the museum without paying. (d) Did you **listen to** him **talk** about his trip to Brazil?

Note: Verbs of perception may also be followed by a noun phrase / pronoun + gerund. See Unit 10, page 204.

4.1 Get in Motion: Causatives and Verbs of Perception

Complete the sentences with the correct causative or verb of perception and an infinitive without *to*. Be sure to put the main verb in the appropriate verb tense.

1. (bring, carry, have, make)

    Geun Kim went camping on a school trip. The teacher _____ each boy _____ part of the food. He _____ one person _____ rice, another *kim-chi*, and another vegetables.

2. (change, help, put up, notice)

    The sun was shining as they started their hike. However, as they neared their campsite, they _____ the weather _____. It began to rain, so the teacher _____ the boys _____ the tent next to a beautiful small river.

3. (go, fall, feel, make)

    Unfortunately, one of the boys had dropped the bag of rice. The teacher was angry and _____ the boys _____ to sleep without any food. In the middle of the night, Geun Kim _____ something _____ on his face. It was water. The tent had sprung a leak.

(Continued on the next page)

UNIT 9 Infinitives

4. (begin, feel, hear, shout)

The boys _____ the tent _____ to move.

They looked out and realized that their tent was surrounded by water. The teacher woke up when he _____ the boys _____.

5. (hear, help, say, swim)

The teacher _____ them _____ to the side of the river. When Geun Kim reached dry land, he collapsed. He woke up when he _____ his brother _____ his name.

He was in a hospital.

4.2 Serial Story and Optional Writing

A. In a group, take turns making up sentences in a story about terrible or wonderful events that happened on a trip you took. Use the verbs listed here. Begin with:

| helped | noticed | made | overheard |
| had | listen to | felt | saw |

The other day we took a trip to _____. On the way, _____ noticed . . .

B. Write a composition on one of these topics. Use the words above if possible.

1. Describe your worst travel experience.
2. What was the most interesting trip you ever took? Why?
3. What is the most popular honeymoon destination in your country?
4. Where do tourists go to see traditional culture in your country?
5. What country would you most like to travel to? Why?

5 INFINITIVES AS SUBJECTS

Infinitives may also be used as subjects in sentences but this is not very common in English.	(a) **To travel** alone is sometimes boring.
We usually use the false subject *it* to introduce the infinitive subject.	(b) ***It*** is sometimes boring **to travel** alone.
For is generally used to indicate the subject of an infinitive phrase.	(c) ***For her* to travel** alone was rare. (d) It was rare ***for her* to travel** alone.

190   UNIT 9 *Travel*

5.1 Get in Motion: Infinitives as Subjects

Decide which of the two choices fits your opinion. Make a complete sentence. Use the false subject *it*.

EXAMPLE
a good idea   make reservations for a hotel before you travel
wait to get a hotel when you arrive
It's a good idea to make reservations for a hotel before you travel.

1. a good idea
   - change some money before you get to a foreign country
   - wait to see what the exchange rates are

   _____

2. a mistake
   - John didn't ask the airline about the baggage allowance
   - Sally weighed her luggage at home

   _____

3. the law
   - hide your purchases when you come back through customs
   - declare your purchases at customs

   _____

4. smart
   - the customs agent didn't believe Alicia hadn't bought her camera on her trip
   - Walter registered his expensive cameras with customs before he left on his trip

   _____

5. a good idea
   - mail some gifts from abroad to your family
   - bring everything home with you

   _____

6. wise
   - imagine you won't get sick on a trip
   - find out what vaccinations are necessary before you leave

   _____

7. smart
   - carry a photocopy of your passport
   - keep the photocopy in your passport

   _____

8. a good idea
   - Ahmed has copies of prescriptions of his medicine
   - Nancy isn't worried about getting sick

   _____

9. advisable
   - not check on what gifts you can take into a country
   - find out what items cannot be taken into a country before you buy gifts for people you will be visiting

   _____

10. not a good idea
    - Carlos did not carry cash
    - Sonya did not carry traveler's checks

    _____

UNIT 9 Infinitives   191

5.2 Listening: A Resort for Everyone?

A. Look at the interests of these people who are planning to take a vacation.

Fred
has a limited budget
loves to ski

Martha
likes swimming pools
likes to shop and sightsee
is able to afford a luxury hotel

Alex
likes to golf
likes to gamble
likes to stay in luxurious hotels

B. Listen to the advertisements and take notes about each hotel.

C. Work with a partner to decide which hotel is best for each person.

It's (cheaper / more expensive) for (name) to stay at the _____ Hotel.

It's better for (name) to go to the _____ Hotel because it's possible for him / her . . .

The _____ Hotel is not the best place for (name) because . . .

5.3 Decisions, Decisions

Your group is going on a nine-day trip to another country together. You all have good jobs, so you have fairly good incomes. However, you are not wealthy. Try to reach a consensus in your group about the following decisions. Whenever possible, use the false subject *it* with infinitives in your discussions.

1. Is it better to stay in elegant hotels or in average-priced hotels?

2. You are going to Jamaica. Is it more important to have an opportunity to relax or to see as much as possible of the country? Is it better to stay in Kingston, the big city, or in a beach resort?

3. Is it more enjoyable to travel independently or to be part of a tour group?

4. You have a stop in London for six hours. You can do two of these things. Which two would you choose? Why?

   go to the Tower of London
   visit Parliament
   go to a museum
   see a play
   walk along the Thames River
   watch the Changing of the Guard at Buckingham Palace

5.4 Talk It Over and Optional Writing

Discuss this question with a group of classmates. Then write a paragraph giving your opinion.

Is it possible for people on limited incomes to travel? What are some ideas to keep travel expenses low?

6 FORMS OF INFINITIVES

Simple	(a) He was a wanderer. His dream was never **to stay** in any one place for more than two years.
Perfect	(b) She was happy **to have lived** abroad when she was young.
Continuous	(c) He wanted **to be traveling** throughout the summer months.
Passive	(d) It was hard **to be tied down** with a family.
	(e) It was upsetting **to have been treated** so badly in Customs.
Negative	(f) To marry someone in another country meant **not to see** her family for long periods of time.

6.1 Get in Motion: Recognizing Infinitive Forms

Underline the infinitives and decide if they are simple, continuous, perfect, passive, or negative constructions.

1. One hot summer when I was traveling to Germany, we were forced to stay in New York for 72 hours.
2. The delay was necessary because the engine of the airplane had to be replaced.
3. The worst part was from time to time we were taken from the hotel to the airplane to be served our meals.
4. Each time we expected to be leaving any minute.
5. It was not possible to go sightseeing because we never knew when we were going to take off.
6. We had to be waiting at the hotel for a call and could not even explore New York. At one point I felt so depressed that I wanted to cancel my trip and just be flown back home.
7. Although our group was not allowed to leave, similar flights each day took off for Germany.
8. They decided not to make three groups of 300 people unhappy, but rather to make our group very unhappy.

(Continued on the next page)

9. It was terrible for everyone to have been treated this way but one couple in our group was particularly unhappy.

10. They had only a few days of vacation to celebrate their marriage. What a way to spend a honeymoon!

6.2 Forms of Infinitives

Complete the sentences with the correct form of the infinitive. Be careful. Some sentences need the perfect infinitive form.

EXAMPLE
By the time he retires, he hopes ____to have saved____ (save) enough money to travel quite a bit.

1. He hoped _____ (never, see) looking like a tourist. He always tried _____ (dress) like the local people.

2. They recognized the tourists easily. The locals didn't need _____ (get) a tan and the visitors wanted _____ (sunbathe) from morning to night.

3. It was good _____ (travel) a lot when she was young and single because once she got married she had _____ (watch) after children whenever they were on vacation.

4. All she needed was a good tour book _____ (explore) a new city but her husband couldn't manage _____ (get) around without being in an organized group.

5. She was embarrassed _____ (live) in many countries without bothering _____ (learn) the local languages.

6. They agreed _____ (not, distract) by the expensive hotels and _____ (satisfy) with a simple, less expensive tourist lifestyle.

7. She wanted _____ (visit) museums while her friends were shopping.

8. Their idea of a vacation was _____ (volunteer) on an archeological dig.

9. He is said _____ (offend) nearly everyone in the hotel with his loud voice and cultural insensitivity.

10. She was wise _____ (not, drink) the water and _____ (order) no ice in her drinks. Everyone else got sick.

194   UNIT 9 *Travel*

6.3 Forms of Infinitives

A. Complete the sentences with the correct form of the infinitive. Be careful. Some sentences require the passive infinitive form.

1. (develop, protect, provide)

    Tourism is both good and bad for the local community. It challenges the government _____ adequate facilities, yet still _____ the environment. Adequate housing, transportation, and food need _____ for tourists.

2. (disturb, not disturb, respect)

    Tourist activities cause wildlife, water, and soil _____. Therefore, the government must educate tourists _____ local customs and _____ the environment.

3. (establish, manage)

    Tourism motivates local people _____ businesses but it also overloads services, such as water, garbage, and roads. The growth of tourism needs _____ so that there isn't an increase in prices, traffic, and noise.

4. (buy, die, revive)

    Today tourists in Canada are eager _____ native art. Their interest has caused the traditional art of Canada's Inuits _____. The art of making soapstone carvings was beginning _____ before the tourists renewed interest in it.

5. (be, hunt and fish, support)

    Native people hunt and fish _____ themselves. Sometimes this causes problems between them and tourists, who also want _____, but for recreation. As a result, tourists are urged by the government _____ sensitive to the local culture as well as to the environment.

6. (not disturb, feed, not feed)

    Tourists are asked _____ the wild animals even though the animals want _____. Tourists are also urged _____ the nests of birds.

B. Discuss these questions with a partner.

1. What are some missed tourism sites which your country could develop? Why would they be interesting?
2. Describe how tourism has had a negative effect on an area you are familiar with.

6.4 Active or Passive?

Complete the sentences with the active or passive form of the infinitive.

EXAMPLE
He hates ___to be awakened___ (awaken) early when he's on vacation.

1. Dorothy and Joe Thomas like _____ (spend) their vacations relaxing at a resort.
2. Joe has a lot of energy and he likes _____ (be) up early.
3. It is common for him _____ (find) on the golf course by 6 a.m. on vacations.
4. Dorothy's ideal vacation is _____ (treat) like a queen.
5. She loves _____ (serve) breakfast in bed on vacations.
6. She also likes the bed _____ (make) and the room _____ (clean) by someone other than her!
7. At night, she likes the bed _____ (turn down) and chocolates _____ (leave) on the pillow.
8. In the afternoon, Joe sometimes urges Dorothy _____ (join) him on a sightseeing or shopping expedition.
9. However, Dorothy hates _____ (force) to do anything on vacation, so he sometimes goes alone.
10. One year Joe suggested a camping trip to Dorothy, but she refused _____ (go).
11. She said, "Imagine all the dishes that would need _____ (wash) and no dishwasher _____ (find) for miles and miles!"
12. "And there wouldn't be any restaurants! Every meal would need _____ (prepare)! That's certainly not my idea of a vacation."
13. Joe did not offer _____ (prepare) all the meals and wash all the dishes himself.
14. They decided _____ (go) to a resort instead.

196 UNIT 9 *Travel*

7 INFINITIVES WITH *TOO* OR *ENOUGH*

Infinitives are often used with *too* or *enough*.

too = more than what is good or necessary	before adjectives and adverbs	(a) It is **too cold to tour** the city today. (b) They worked **too hard not to get** more vacation time.
enough = as much as necessary	after adjectives and adverbs	(c) It was **hot enough to swim** in the sea. (d) They worked **hard enough to afford** a trip to Europe.
	before or in some cases after nouns	(e) We don't have **enough money to get** a taxi. (f) We don't have **money enough to get** a taxi.

7.1 Get in Motion: Infinitives with *Too* or *Enough*

These people had problems when traveling. Explain why, using *too* or *enough*.

EXAMPLE
My French isn't very good. I thought the room cost 375 francs, but it cost 675 francs.
Her French wasn't good __*good enough for her to understand*__ the price.

1. Helen invited her friends in Spain for dinner at 6:00 p.m. They didn't arrive until 9:00, the normal hour for dinner in Spain.

   6:00 was _____ dinner in Spain.

2. At a restaurant in France, Carl thought the dinner was over after dessert and he stood up to leave. Everyone else was waiting for coffee.

   It was _____ to leave the table.

3. Françoise expected to negotiate a deal with the Japanese company in one visit to Japan. The Japanese were surprised that she was trying to finalize things before they had established a relationship.

   She didn't allow _____ to establish a business relationship.

4. The Japanese visitors went to a bar. The waitress was very friendly until they paid for their first drinks and gave her a 5 percent tip. She was slow to wait on them after that.

   A 5 percent tip was _____. The waitress was insulted.

5. Sylvia gave her hostess a very expensive present. It was embarrassing for her hostess to receive such a gift.

   The gift was _____ her hostess.

7.2 Talk It Over

Discuss these questions with a group of classmates.

1. Have you had any embarrassing experiences while traveling because of differences in customs?
2. When you see tourists in your hometown, what surprises you about them? What do they do that is different from what the local people do?

8 TROUBLE SPOTS: WORD CHOICE; ARTICLES

of or *for*	Both *of* and *for* are used after an adjective and before the noun and infinitive in a false subject *it* sentence. These are often adjectives which express an opinion or a feeling. Use *of* to comment on the person or organization who performed the action expressed in the infinitive. Use *for* to comment on the action.	(a) It was **generous of you to translate** for them. *(You were being generous to translate for them.)* (b) It was **interesting for us to visit** another country. *(Our visiting another country was interesting for us.)*
Reduced Infinitives	When a sentence with an infinitive is reduced, the *to* remains.	(c) He wanted **to smoke** on the plane but the attendant asked him **not to**.
Articles	We do not use *the* for names of beaches, falls, parks, squares, religious places, businesses, holidays, days of the week, or direction words.	Laguna Beach Texaco Niagara Falls Christmas Eve Central Park Sunday Roosevelt Square north heaven BUT: **the** Boeing Company **the** Proctor & Gamble Company **the** West **the** Northeast **the** Fourth of July

8.1 Prepositions *of* / *for* and False Subject *It*

Combine these to make sentences with the false subject *it*. Decide if *of* or *for* is correct.

EXAMPLE
(exciting)   You won a free airplane ticket to anywhere in the world.
It was exciting for you to win a free airplane ticket to anywhere in the world.

1. (smart)   You packed your bag light.
2. (good)   He took his sunscreen with him.
3. (typical)   He was rude to the local people when he was traveling.
4. (rude)   He didn't tip the waitress.
5. (funny)   They saw so many tourists.
6. (usual)   They charged the tourists money when the tourists took their pictures.
7. (unkind)   They laughed at the romantic folk dances.
8. (good)   You brought some cool drinks down to the pool.
9. (thoughtful)   She asked permission to take a picture of their holy place.
10. (embarrassing) She saw no women in the bar.

8.2 Articles

In a small group, see if you can match the description with the names of these places. Complete the phrases with the correct article or leave blank, if appropriate.

Waikiki	Yellowstone	Amazon	hell	south
Victoria	Everest	New Year's	Ottoman	Pacific
Revolution	Time		Southwest	Caspian

1. falls in Zimbabwe / Zambia: _____ Falls

2. period in history when industry began rapid development:
   _____ Industrial _____

3. famous beach in Honolulu: _____ Beach

4. largest ocean in the world: _____ Ocean

5. tallest mountain in the world: _____ Mt. _____

6. famous national park with geysers and boiling hot springs in Wyoming:
   _____ National Park

7. large sea north of Iran: _____ Sea

8. area where the states of Arizona and New Mexico are located: _____

9. longest river in the world: _____ River

(Continued on the next page)

10. large areas of North Africa, the Middle East, Central Europe, and Mediterranean countries ruled by the Turks from 1300 to 1922: _____ Empire

11. holiday on January 1: _____ Day

12. according to religion, place where sinful people go after death: _____

13. weekly news magazine with largest circulation in the United States: _____ magazine

14. direction of Antarctica: _____

9 PREPOSITIONS AND PHRASAL EXPRESSIONS

down

down the road, up and **down**, **down** the stairs, **down** under the house

Phrasal Expressions with *Down*

(a) If the engine **breaks down,** we'll have to get rid of this car. *(stop working)*
(b) The house **burned down** in spite of the firefighters' efforts. *(destroy by fire)*
(c) They **closed down** the hotel during the remodeling. *(stop operation)*
(d) The exchange rate has been **kept down** by government intervention. *(control)*
(e) How could I **turn down** a free trip to Mexico? *(refuse)*
(f) The airport workers' strike has caused a **slowdown** in air traffic. *(slowed operations—noun)*
(g) They **backed down** from confronting the customs' officials. *(yield)*
(h) When the airfares **go down,** we'll purchase our tickets. *(decrease)*

See Appendix D for definitions of phrasal verbs.

9.1 Down, Under, Below

Complete the phrases with the appropriate preposition: *down*, *under*, or *below*.

1. _____ to Texas
2. _____ the covers
3. _____ from the shelf
4. _____ the age of eight
5. _____ the hill from our house
6. in the paragraph _____
7. _____ the circumstances (in this situation)
8. _____ the Equator
9. _____ sea level
10. _____ on the floor

9.2 Up or Down?

Complete the sentences with *up* or *down*. See Appendix D for help with phrasal verbs.

1. The car broke _____ two hours into the trip.
2. I burned _____ all of his pictures once the relationship was over.
3. They closed _____ that resort because tourism has slowed _____ so much.
4. If those pictures turn _____, I'd love to see them. I hope you haven't lost them.
5. Parties in Spain rarely break _____ before midnight.
6. Don't back _____! Hold your position no matter what.
7. If the airline prices keep going _____, we'll be able to take that vacation.
8. There was a lot of fog so air traffic was slowed _____ for several hours.
9. When he was backing _____, he severely damaged the car behind him.
10. Keep _____ your lessons. Some day you will be able to speak Spanish like a native.
11. The hotel that burned _____ was extremely rundown so the insurance didn't pay very much after the fire.

UNIT 9 Infinitives   201

LISTENING TEST

Listen and circle the letter of the statement that has the same meaning.

1. a. I traveled alone.
   b. I couldn't travel alone.
   c. I was advised not to travel by myself.

2. a. They did not go to Paris.
   b. They may go to Paris.
   c. They went to Paris.

3. a. It's a good idea.
   b. It takes a long time.
   c. It's not cheap.

4. a. He traveled quite a bit when he was younger.
   b. He still travels quite a lot.
   c. He wishes that he had traveled more.

5. a. She was supposed to clean the house.
   b. She is expecting to clean the house later.
   c. She thought the house was going to be cleaned.

6. a. He usually doesn't travel by train.
   b. People typically don't travel by train.
   c. Train travel is unpopular.

7. a. We were forced to wait at customs.
   b. There was a long line at customs.
   c. Everyone except us had to wait at customs.

8. a. I'm not considering going to the restaurant.
   b. The restaurant is too expensive for me.
   c. I wonder if the restaurant has a good reputation.

9. a. I think we should go now.
   b. We'd better walk.
   c. We may need to take a bus.

10. a. Everyone thought it was a good idea to go there.
    b. A lot of people thought about going there.
    c. People didn't think we should go there.

QUIZ YOURSELF

In each passage, circle the letter of the underlined words or phrases that are incorrect.

1. My best vacation was an unplanned one I took in the 1960s as a foreign student in Germany. A friend, Anna, (a) <u>persuaded</u> me at 9 p.m. one night to catch an evening train to the coast of Italy, where we (b) <u>expected to find</u> an inexpensive fishing village (c) <u>to be lived in</u>.

2. We (a) <u>decided to take</u> a local train from Genoa and travel until we saw a town we considered (b) <u>to have been</u> interesting. Having U.S. dollars (c) <u>enabled us to live</u> cheaply—a room in a *pensione* near the beach and two meals a day only cost us $2.00.

3. I could never have planned such a fun vacation. I trusted my friend, who spoke four languages, (a) <u>to be handled</u> the language, and (b) <u>to lead</u> me in adventures. We proceeded (c) <u>to explore</u> the village, islands, and meet the local people.

4. Our days were leisurely. There was no need (a) <u>to have gotten up early or gone</u> to bed early. While I sunbathed on the beach, Anna preferred (b) <u>to go swimming</u> in the Mediterranean and (c) <u>to be invited</u> onto yachts.

5. Every evening the townspeople liked (a) <u>to walk</u> along the shore and it (b) <u>proved to be</u> good exercise after a large meal. We also went to discotheques to dance and (c) <u>to have met</u> people.

6. Once we managed (a) <u>to have become acquainted</u> with some locals, we were taken from shop to shop (b) <u>to meet</u> cousins and cousins of cousins. Everyone in the town seemed (c) <u>to be related</u>.

7. We had decided (a) <u>to get away</u> from our everyday lives with fellow Americans living abroad. So when we saw other Americans, we (b) <u>pretended us to be</u> foreigners. One of Anna's languages was Czech and she (c) <u>taught me to reply</u> with a simple yes or no to anything she said.

8. We were never awake (a) <u>to see</u> the fishermen leave in the morning, but people (b) <u>encouraged to go</u> to the beach to welcome their return. We were there (c) <u>to relax</u> and we felt the pace of their lives without it bothering ours.

9. We had intended (a) <u>to stay</u> only one week but our lives were so involved with the town that we refused (b) <u>to return</u> from our university holiday. We resolved (c) <u>to have suffered</u> the consequences of missing one week of classes.

10. I had forgotten (a) <u>to have notified</u> the director of our program that we had left the country so I sent him a postcard. I didn't want him (b) <u>to be worrying</u> about us. I wrote him (c) <u>not to worry</u> for we were having a good time and added, "Wish you were here!"

UNIT 9 Infinitives

UNIT 10

Gerunds

Recreation

1 VERB + GERUND

Gerunds are the *-ing* form of the verb.	(a) I like **skiing** downhill better than **skiing** cross-country. (b) They enjoyed **going** to the mountains in the evening for night **skiing**. (c) My nephew suggested **snowboarding** and I'm considering **trying** it. (d) If it keeps on **snowing**, I recommend **snow-shoeing** this weekend.
The negative form of the gerund is *not* + gerund.	(e) They recommend **not hiking** in the mountains this weekend because of avalanche danger. (f) We discussed **not enrolling** in a ski school but taking private ski lessons instead.
Gerunds are used as complements of certain verbs:	admit include appreciate keep (on) avoid mind (object to) can't help miss consider postpone deny put off discuss quit enjoy recommend finish risk give up suggest imagine

See Appendix E for a more complete list of verbs that are followed by gerunds.

1.1 Get in Motion: Gerunds as Verb Complements

Complete these sentences about yourself.

1. On a typical weekday, I spend most of my time _____, but on the weekends, I can most often be found _____.

2. My favorite recreational activities include _____, _____, and _____. These activities require / don't require _____ a lot of energy. They do / don't require _____.

3. On the weekdays, I don't mind _____, but on weekends, I _____.

4. I try to postpone _____ for as long as I can.

5. I enjoy _____, but I try to avoid _____ for as long as possible.

6. Every time I go _____, I can't avoid _____.

1.2 Infinitive or Gerund?

Complete the sentence with the correct form of the verb in parentheses.

1. Many people enjoy _____ (participate) in outdoor activities in their leisure time. They want _____ (get) away from work and household responsibilities.

2. The outdoor recreation industry is growing rapidly. If people plan _____ (ski), _____ (canoe), _____ (sail), or _____ (bike), they need _____ (have) equipment and appropriate facilities.

3. Once they begin a sport, most people can't help _____ (buy) all of the equipment which companies say is required _____ (do) the activity well.

4. About 25 percent of all Canadians admit _____ (own) adult bicycles, camping equipment, and cross-country skis.

(Continued on the next page)

UNIT 10 Gerunds   205

5. We suggest _____ (visit) the provincial parks in Canada if you are interested in beautiful scenery as well as recreational opportunities. One of my favorite parks _____ (visit) is in the Canadian Rockies.

6. Developers are willing _____ (fulfill) the interests of conservationists. However, the government is willing to risk _____ (harm) the environment.

7. Many people would like _____ (participate) in a sport but they don't get _____ (try) it because they lack time, money, or proper equipment.

8. They also put off _____ (do) the sport if they don't have a partner, if the facilities are too far away, or if the weather is bad.

9. They would rather wait for the weather _____ (get) better so they postpone _____ (hike) or _____ (jog).

10. If you intend _____ (learn) _____ (ski), it's good _____ (start) with weekly lessons.

11. When bad knees forced him _____ (give up) _____ (play) tennis, he decided _____ (take up) golf.

12. Some people try _____ (buy) all the equipment they need _____ (participate) in a sport. However, they should consider _____ (rent) first.

13. I decided _____ (avoid) _____ (go) skiing on weekends because of the crowds.

Canoeing

Cross-country skiing

UNIT 10 *Recreation*

2 VERBS THAT TAKE INFINITIVES OR GERUNDS

Some verbs may be followed by either an **infinitive** or a **gerund** with little or no change in meaning:	attempt be begin bother can't bear continue deserve	dislike dread fear go hate intend like	love neglect plan practice prefer can't stand start	(a) I like **to ski**. (b) I like **skiing**.
These verbs take an infinitive if the infinitive has a subject; otherwise, they take a gerund:	advise allow encourage forbid require teach permit		(c) My friend **advised** me **to stretch** before I started to run. (d) Experts **advise stretching** before you start to exercise. (e) He **taught** his daughter **to ski**. (f) He **taught skiing** at a nearby resort.	

See Appendix E for a more complete list of verbs which are followed by gerunds or infinitives.

2.1 Get in Motion: Listening

Listen to the conversation between Martina and Frances and complete the sentences below.

1. Martina is planning _____ this weekend.

2. At one time, Martina couldn't bear _____ because she was afraid of tilting sideways on the sailboat.

(Continued on the next page)

UNIT 10 Gerunds   207

3. Martina met a man at a party whose job was to teach _____.

4. Martina signed up for sailing classes so that man would teach _____.

5. Frances is envious because Martina's husband likes _____.

6. Frances's husband likes _____.

7. Frances tries to encourage _____, but _____.

8. Martina thinks someone should forbid _____.

9. Frances isn't optimistic about this because the people who choose TV programs love _____.

2.2 Talk It Over and Optional Writing

A. Discuss these questions with a classmate.

1. Are there any recreational activities you hate?
2. Why did you start doing the activities you like?
3. Which of these ideas would you recommend to Frances, whose husband watches sports shows on TV all the time?

   _____ forbid watching TV during the daytime

   _____ require him to spend time with her

   _____ shut off the electricity

   _____ join him and pretend to enjoy watching sports

   _____ (your ideas)

   _____

   _____

4. Do you think it's a problem when partners enjoy doing different things? Is it important to encourage sharing activities?

B. Write a letter to Frances, giving her advice. Use five of these verbs in your answer:

advise	keep on	discuss
suggest	quit	want
avoid	try	encourage

208   UNIT 10 Recreation

3 VERBS THAT TAKE INFINITIVES OR GERUNDS BUT CHANGE IN MEANING

remember	+ infinitive = not forget	(a) I always **remember to take** mosquito repellent.
	+ gerund = have a memory of	(b) I **remember getting** very sore muscles on that hike.
forget	+ infinitive = not remember to do something that you intended or that was expected	(c) I **forgot to bring** the insect repellent.
	+ gerund = not remember the experience	(d) I won't ever **forget taking** this beautiful hike. (e) I must have been tired last night. I **forgot your calling** me.
regret	+ infinitive = be sorry (used in formal or written English to introduce bad news)	(f) I **regret to tell** you the campground is already full for that weekend.
	+ gerund = be sorry about a decision made in the past (often followed by a negative gerund)	(g) I **regret coming** to this campground; it is crowded and noisy. (h) I **regret not going** to a different campground.
stop	+ infinitive = start the activity described by the infinitive verb	(i) Let's **stop** here **to rest** for a few minutes.
	+ gerund = stop the activity described by the gerund verb	(j) Let's **stop walking**. (k) I **stopped smoking** to improve my health.
mean	+ infinitive = intend	(l) I didn't **mean to hike** so far, but it was such a beautiful day.
	+ gerund = result in	(m) Taking the detour **meant going** ten extra miles.
try	+ infinitive = make an effort	(n) Let's **try to walk** ten miles a day.
	+ gerund = experiment with an activity	(o) Let's **try speed-walking**. It's supposed to be better for you than jogging.

UNIT 10 Gerunds

3.1 Get in Motion

Complete the sentences with a gerund or infinitive. Add a noun or pronoun, if necessary.

1. I have always regretted _____ (not, take) gymnastics as a child.
2. I have always wanted _____ (do) gymnastics.
3. When I was 35, I decided _____ (start) _____ (do) gymnastics.
4. A friend advised _____ (not, start) gymnastics at my age.
5. Later I would regret _____ (not, listen) to her.
6. I would have preferred _____ (be) in a class with people my age, but of course very few 35-year-olds begin _____ (take) gymnastics, so I had to take a course with university students.
7. At the beginning of the first class, the teacher taught us _____ (do) handstands. She showed us the technique and said, "OK. Now you try _____ (do) it."
8. Everyone else in the class did it easily, but every time I tried _____ (do) it, my arms wouldn't hold me up.
9. The teacher advised _____ (do) it a different way.
10. She said, "If you mean _____ (do) gymnastics, you have to visualize the movement."
11. I must have forgotten _____ (visualize) the whole movement because I finally got up into the handstand just fine. However, when I came down, I hurt a muscle.
12. I will never forget _____ (feel) that pain.
13. Not only did I have to stop _____ (take) gymnastics, I could hardly walk for three weeks!
14. I think this wouldn't have happened if the teacher had required _____ (warm) up our muscles before we started _____ (perform) the gymnastics.
15. I suppose if I had stopped _____ (think) about it, I wouldn't have started _____ (take) gymnastics at my age.
16. However, that would have meant _____ (admit) I was getting old, and I certainly didn't mean _____ (do) that at 35!

17. I can't bear _____ (not, exercise), so I started a yoga class as soon as my muscle healed.

18. Yoga is supposed _____ (be) much kinder to older muscles!

3.2 Infinitives or Gerunds?

Complete these sentences using a gerund or infinitive in the first blank and an appropriate word in the second. Keep the subject related to recreational activities.

EXAMPLE
I remembered ___*to shower*___ before I went ___*swimming*___.
I quit ___*skiing*___ after I broke ___*my leg twice*___.

1. I remember _____ when I am _____.
2. Don't try _____ when you are _____.
3. I tried _____ when I went _____.
4. I regret not _____ when I was _____.
5. Experts advise _____ when you are _____.
6. A friend of mine started _____ after he finished _____.
7. People deserve _____ after they have gone _____.
8. Stop _____ when you are _____.
9. I stopped _____ after I got through _____.
10. I sometimes forget _____ before I start _____.
11. I quit _____ after I had been _____.
12. Imagine _____ when you are _____.
13. Exercising every day means _____.
14. I always mean _____.
15. I will never forget _____.
16. We recommend _____ before starting _____.
17. Don't miss _____ when you go _____.
18. They suggest _____ before you try _____.

4 GERUNDS AS NOUNS

Gerunds are more commonly **subjects** in a sentence than infinitives are.	(a) **Jogging** is her favorite sport but it is hard for her to jog since she hurt her hip.
Gerunds are also used as **objects of prepositions**.	(b) I am tired *of* **hiking**. Let's think *about* **setting** up our camp for the night.

4.1 Get in Motion

Discuss these questions with a classmate.

1. What is more beneficial for children, doing an individual sport like gymnastics or a team sport like soccer? Why?

2. What is better exercise, playing golf or playing tennis?

3. How important is exercising to you? Prioritize these activities in your life:

    _____ Working

    _____ Seeing friends

    _____ Exercising

    _____ Watching TV

    _____ Studying

    _____ Taking care of your family

    _____ Reading

    _____ _____
    (other activity)

4. Do you think people who exercise all their lives are smart or crazy? Why?

5. How are young people and older people different in their attitudes about exercise? What are young people concerned about? What are older people worried about or afraid of?

4.2 Listening: Exercising

A. Listen to the information about Jane, Marge, and Ron, who all decided to start exercising. Write notes with information about the three.

Jane _____

_____

Marge _____

_____

Ron _____

_____

B. Compare your notes and discuss these questions with a classmate.

1. From what you know about exercise, which person's approach to exercise would be recommended by medical experts? Why? Use these phrases in your discussion:

   Doctors recommend . . .
   Experts warn against . . .
   Doctors encourage . . .
   . . . is safer than . . .

2. How are these people's exercise routines similar to or different from yours?

4.3 Preposition and Verb Form Practice

Complete the sentences with the correct form of the verb in parentheses. Then underline the correct preposition.

1. In the 1990s many people _____ (turn) (into / to) _____ (ride) mountain bikes to get aerobic exercise.

2. Because (of / that) _____ (see) too many "overuse" injuries in the '80s, sports medicine specialists _____ (recommend) less demanding exercise programs.

3. In recent years heart doctors _____ (accuse) the exercise craze of the '80s (in / of) _____ (promote) too much exercise and these doctors _____ (argue) (for / in) _____ (not / exercise) so much.

4. However, there is a widespread acceptance (of / to) _____ (exercise) as an important factor (for / in) _____ (prevent) heart disease.

(Continued on the next page)

UNIT 10 *Gerunds*   213

5. A 20-minute period of aerobic exercise three times a week is adequate (from / for) _____ (improve) your strength and _____ (use) your heart and lungs efficiently.

6. If you aren't agreeable (for / to) _____ (set) aside exercise periods, at least consider _____ (walk) 30–40 minutes total in a week.

7. Doctors approve (in / of) _____ (engage) in low-impact exercise workouts.

8. Although people complain (about / in) _____ (be) too tired to exercise, exercising actually _____ (give) the body energy.

9. If you dream (about / in) _____ (have) a healthy-looking body, you must go (for / without) a lot of fat in your diet and see (about / in) ways to add more aerobic activity.

10. Don't let the expense of some sports get in the way (for / of) _____ (improve) your health. Brisk walking is a cheap and safe exercise, suitable (for / in) different ages and lifestyles.

11. Listen (for / to) the advice of doctors and don't _____ (overexercise).

12. People may laugh (about / in) it, but _____ (do) housework and gardening can be low-impact exercise.

13. People who participate (in / to) _____ (exercise) regularly live longer.

14. If you are resistant (for / to) _____ (exercise) regularly, look (for / into) _____ (intersperse) your day with five-minute walks.

15. Even elderly people benefit (from / to) _____ (get) regular exercise. Doctors say that _____ (lift) moderate weights helps older people _____ (stay) in better physical condition.

16. It's not easy (for / to) _____ (keep) (on / up) _____ (exercise) regularly. It takes determination.

4.4 Talk It Over and Optional Writing

Discuss these questions with a group of classmates. Then write a paragraph about a decision you made.

1. Do you think women should be allowed to participate in the same sports that men do? Should they be allowed to play on men's teams?

2. Do you know people who take exercising too seriously? Explain what they do and why you think it is not healthy.

5 MODIFYING GERUNDS

Traditionally, we use the **possessive** form of a noun or pronoun to modify a gerund.	(a) I really appreciate **your taking** the time to help with this. (b) Her parents worried about **Sally's losing** so much weight.
Because the possessive form is more formal, it is more common in writing than in speaking. The possessive form is not used as much in speaking.	(c) I don't mind **you going** to the party without me. (d) My parents are opposed to **me getting** an apartment. (e) They are worried about **Sally jogging** after dark.
Sometimes gerunds have **objects**.	(f) **Winning the game** was very exciting.

5.1 Get in Motion

Respond to these situations by completing the sentences.

EXAMPLE
Your sister wants to go to Antarctica for vacation.
I can't understand *her wanting to go there.*

1. I gave you information about traveling to Hawaii.
   I really appreciate . . .

2. Salespeople call you on the phone to try to sell you something.
   I'm opposed to . . .

3. You live next to a tennis court and people have been playing tennis at midnight.
   I'm calling to complain about . . .

4. Carl did not remember your tennis date.
   I'm angry about . . .

5. Susan's father is in the hospital.
   I'm sorry about . . .

6. Your brother wants to move to another city.
   I can't understand . . .

7. Your little sister called you. She is going to New York by herself.
   I'm worried about . . .

8. They are going on vacation for four weeks.
   I'm envious of . . .

9. Your friend would like to borrow your car.
   I don't mind . . .

10. They did not tell you their plans.
    I'm angry about . . .

6 FORMS OF GERUNDS

Simple	(a) **Running** in a marathon was her dream.
Perfect	(b) **Having done** 20 laps exhausted her.
Passive	(c) They appreciated **being informed** about the problem.
Perfect Passive	(d) They liked his **having been chosen** captain of the team.
Negative	(e) **Not winning** didn't matter; only the challenge was important.

6.1 Get in Motion

Complete these sentences with the correct form of the verb in parentheses. Look out for passive and perfect gerund forms!

1. _____ (exercise) is also a good way of _____ (socialize).

2. Some people exercise because they like _____ (challenge) physically or _____ (be) healthy.

3. There is a sense of accomplishment which comes from _____ (work) hard to do well in a sport.

4. _____ (attend) sports events is recreation for many people.

5. On Sundays our family enjoyed _____ (walk), _____ (go) for a drive, or _____ (have) a picnic.

6. Because she had roller-skated for years, she thought it would be easy to take up _____ (ice-skate).

7. _____ (go) to concerts, plays, and restaurants is not as popular as _____ (watch) movies in leisure time.

8. _____ (visit) by friends is her favorite pastime. She loves _____ (cook) and hates _____ (not, have) company on the weekend.

9. _____ (give) a year's membership in the health club made her more willing to exercise.

10. I don't recall _____ (go) there, but they all say that I did.

Snowboarding   Skateboarding   Windsurfing

11. _____ (snowboard) and _____ (skateboard) are sports that appeal to young people.

12. _____ (challenge) individually and physically is what makes sports such as _____ (windsurf) interesting.

13. In the army, he had to experience _____ (parachute) by _____ (push) out of an airplane, so _____ (skydive) as recreation has never appealed to him.

14. Some people believe Bungee _____ (jump) is an example of a death wish activity.

15. _____ (rock climb) is becoming an indoor as well as an outdoor activity due to the growth of rock climbing facilities in urban areas. _____ (live) near the mountains is no longer a reason for city dwellers to miss _____ (increase) their climbing skills.

16. _____ (elect) the Most Valuable Player by his teammates was the highlight of the baseball season.

17. A runner's _____ (warm up) enough can result in injured muscles.

18. Already _____ (learn) to ski made it easier for him to catch on to _____ (snowboard).

UNIT 10 Gerunds   217

7 TROUBLE SPOTS: WORD CHOICE; PARALLELISM; ARTICLES

have expressions + gerund *spend / waste time* + gerund	Expressions with *have* (*have a good / bad time, have fun, have trouble / a problem*), and those with *spend / waste time* can be followed by a gerund.	(a) Did you **have a good time backpacking**? (b) He **had a problem reserving** a room for us. (c) I am **having trouble finding** good equipment. (d) Are you **spending a lot of time preparing** for the camping trip?
to + gerund	Sometimes *to* is not followed by the base form of the verb. This commonly happens with these expressions:	*accustomed to* *introduce to* (e) Snowboarding is *adapt to* *the key to* **preferable to** *adjust to* *limit to* **skiing.** *agreeable to* *look forward to* (f) They were *alternative to* *pay attention to* **resistant to** *change from* *preferable to* **changing** their *(gerund) to* *put a stop to* plans. *(gerund)* *resistant to* *in contrast to* *similar to* *dedicated to* *solution to* *equal to* *submit to* *essential to* *get around to*
remember, remind	*Remember* means "not forget." *Remind* means "**cause** to remember."	(g) **Remember** to get your skis waxed. (h) **Remind me** to get my skis waxed. (i) Do you **remember** the fun we had on our trip to Aspen? (j) That **reminded me** of my ski trip to Aspen.
like	Don't confuse *like*, the conjunction meaning "as," with *like*, the verb meaning "enjoy."	(k) He is **like** a fish in the water. (l) He **likes** to swim.
Parallelism	Make sure items in a series are in **parallel** form.	(m) **Swimming, boating,** and **waterskiing** are his favorite activities. (n) It was fun **to swim, boat,** and **waterski** most of the summer.
Articles	Don't use the article *the* for games, sports, or diseases.	soccer waterskiing basketball swimming AIDS cancer EXCEPTIONS: **the** measles, **the** mumps, **the** flu

218   UNIT 10 Recreation

7.1 Speaking Practice

Ask your partner these questions. Answer in complete sentences.

1. What sports did you have trouble learning?
2. When did you have a good time participating in a sport?
3. What outdoor activity do you like the most? What is this activity like?
4. What indoor activity do you have a good time doing?
5. What kind of activity are you most resistant to?
6. What sports do you find boring?
7. What kinds of physical problems can a person get from exercising?
8. What was your favorite indoor game as a child?
9. What can happen if you are outdoors in cold weather without warm clothing on?
10. If I came to your country, what outdoor activity would you want to introduce me to?
11. What's a healthy alternative to jogging?
12. What's the key to healthy exercising?
13. What does snow remind you of?
14. What do you remember the most about childhood outside activities?

7.2 Editing Practice

Correct the error in each sentence, if any. There may be more than one mistake.

1. He reminded me of going to the sport store to get some biking shorts that are on sale.
2. Snowboarding likes skiing but there is only one wide board to stand on.
3. He was diagnosed with the cancer.
4. The hiking is a great way to exercise and also seeing beautiful scenery.
5. When you are going to do a lot of hiking, it is essential to buy good boots.
6. I have been having a difficult time to find good hiking boots.
7. Remember buying good socks for hiking or your feet will be terribly blistered.
8. The baseball game will be over by 7:00 because they don't have a lighted field.
9. Did you get around to try skydiving?
10. I am like an elephant when I try to ice-skate.

7.3 Talk It Over and Optional Writing

Discuss these questions with a classmate. Then write a composition about one of the topics you discussed.

1. What have been the positive and negative aspects of the fitness craze of the last 25 years?
2. Have you ever belonged to a health club? What were the benefits of this membership?
3. Walking is the most popular physical activity in the United States. Gardening is the second most popular. Why do you feel these activities are so popular?
4. Choose a recreational activity. Explain to a friend why this is a worthwhile activity and (if appropriate) how your friend can start doing it.

8 PREPOSITIONS AND PHRASAL VERBS

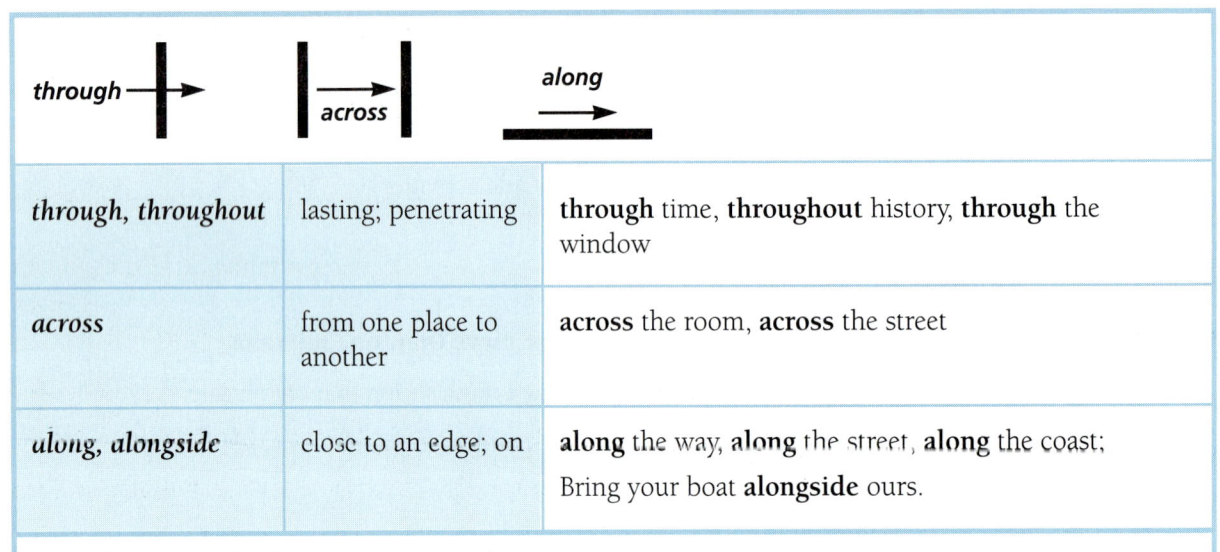

through, throughout	lasting; penetrating	**through** time, **throughout** history, **through** the window
across	from one place to another	**across** the room, **across** the street
along, alongside	close to an edge; on	**along** the way, **along** the street, **along** the coast; Bring your boat **alongside** ours.

Phrasal Verbs with Through, Across, Along

(a) This money will **see me through** the month. (*continue to support*)
(b) Let's **run through** these steps one more time. (*go over*)
(c) Our plans **fell through** this time. (*not work out*)
(d) We're **through** with this exercise. (*be finished*)
(e) If you **come across / run across** any old pictures, save them for me. (*find*)
(f) Gardening as a pastime **cuts across** all ages and socioeconomic backgrounds. (*touch*)
(g) It's hard **to get across** the dangers of skateboarding to young enthusiasts. (*communicate*)
(h) They **get along** very well when they are playing outside. (*be congenial*)
(i) **Come along** with us on Sunday. We are going hiking. (*accompany*)
(j) I can **go along** with them only so far. (*support*)

8.1 Through, Across, Along, Alongside

Complete the sentences with the appropriate preposition: *through*, *across*, *along*, or *alongside*.

1. We danced all _____ the night and then fell asleep exhausted.
2. News of the games traveled quickly _____ Western Europe and on into Eastern Europe.
3. The festival will last _____ Sunday.
4. The children ran _____ beside the parade as it wound _____ the city.
5. The sun is trying to peak _____ the clouds.
6. We could hear their TV _____ the walls. It was very annoying!
7. I knew that they were staring at me _____ the restaurant, but I didn't know why.
8. I've been thinking of you _____ the miles.
9. We lost him somewhere _____ the way. He's a very slow hiker.
10. I would love to have a house _____ that river, but I would worry about floods.

8.2 In Other Words

Circle the letter of the expression which has the same meaning as the underlined words.

1. I can <u>see you through</u> these difficult times.
   a. help you look at
   b. provide you with support
   c. help you realize

2. What kind of impression is he trying to <u>get across</u>?
   a. communicate
   b. understand
   c. reach

3. <u>How did you get along</u> on that trip?
   a. How did you go on the trip?
   b. How was the trip?
   c. How did you avoid each other on the trip?

4. We are going to <u>run along</u> now. See you.
   a. leave
   b. jog
   c. practice

5. Could you help me <u>run through</u> my lines for the play?
   a. crash into
   b. find
   c. practice

6. <u>Come along</u> on Sunday. It should be fun.
   a. happen
   b. join us
   c. follow

7. If you <u>run across</u> that ad, I'd like to see it.
   a. find accidentally
   b. meet
   c. jog into

8. Let's <u>cut through</u> the red tape.
   a. reduce
   b. take a short cut
   c. bring down

UNIT 10 Gerunds

LISTENING TEST

Listen and circle the letter of the statement that has the same meaning.

1. a. I forgot to go to that restaurant.
   b. I didn't remind you to go to the restaurant.
   c. I have forgotten about going to that restaurant.

2. a. Understanding is important.
   b. Variety is important.
   c. Exercise is important.

3. a. I taught him to swim.
   b. He led her swimming classes.
   c. He didn't like to swim.

4. a. I like to watch TV and read.
   b. I like watching TV more than reading.
   c. I prefer reading to watching TV.

5. a. I want to tell you something.
   b. I was unhappy speaking openly.
   c. I'm sure it's OK to speak openly.

6. a. Students don't have to take gym classes.
   b. They require taking gym classes.
   c. The high school has never required students to take gym class.

7. a. I plan to exercise more.
   b. I exercised a lot.
   c. I didn't exercise very much.

8. a. I think it's important to make an effort.
   b. I'm interested in whether you have had that experience.
   c. I think you have done that before.

9. a. I'm not going to get excited about class next week.
   b. I'm happy that we don't have class next week.
   c. I'm unhappy about classes next week.

10. a. Nancy went skiing.
    b. I went skiing.
    c. Nancy didn't think about going skiing.

2.2 Interview with Adjective Clauses

Interview a classmate. Use these expressions in your questions and answers.

1. you / a person / likes to eat everything
2. you / a person / is careful about eating healthy food
3. what / a food / you love
4. what / a food / you hate
5. who / the best cook / you know

2.3 Sentence Combining

Combine these sentences in as many ways as possible.

EXAMPLE
McDonald's trademark is golden arches.
People recognize these arches all over the world.
McDonald's trademark is golden arches, which people recognize all over the world.
McDonald's golden arches are a trademark that people recognize all over the world.
People recognize McDonald's trademark, golden arches, all over the world.

1. Outside of Los Angeles in 1937, the McDonald brothers opened the hamburger drive-in.
   The hamburger drive-in would become the first McDonald's.

2. Successful businesses often sell "franchises."
   Franchises are owned independently but are part of the restaurant chain.

3. McDonald's was the first fast-food franchiser.
   This franchiser became successful in the United States.

(Continued on the next page)

UNIT 11 Adjective Clauses

4. In the 1960s McDonald's introduced playground equipment.
   Families could enjoy this equipment.

   _____

5. Thirty percent of all hamburgers are sold at McDonald's.
   Hamburgers are sold in the United States.

   _____

6. There are centralized shipping points.
   These shipping points prepare the portions and pre-cook the food.
   The food is assembled by workers at the fast-food restaurants.

   _____

7. McDonald's introduced a low-fat hamburger substitute.
   The public did not like the low-fat hamburger substitute.

   _____

8. When fast-food chains open in foreign countries, they often make changes in their menu.
   The changes in the menu reflect the culture of the country.

   _____

9. An example of this is a green-tea ice cream.
   This ice cream is marketed by Baskin-Robbins in Japan.

   _____

10. Restaurants hire consultants.
    Consultants help them decide about changes.
    They need to make changes.

    _____

2.4 Talk It Over and Optional Writing

Discuss these questions with a classmate. Then write a composition about one of the topics you discussed.

1. What were your happiest or worst memories of food in your childhood?
2. Describe a typical evening meal scene with your family as a child.
3. Do you think children should learn to eat all kinds of food, or should they only be served the food they like?
4. What are the attitudes in your family or culture about people who are picky eaters—that is, people who refuse to eat certain foods?
5. From your point of view, what is considered good service in a restaurant?
6. Would you want to own a restaurant? Why or why not?

UNIT 11 Eating

3 REPLACING THE OBJECT OF THE PREPOSITION IN AN ADJECTIVE CLAUSE

The pronouns **which** or **that** replace the object of a preposition when it refers to a **thing**.	(a) I have never been to the restaurant. Everyone is talking **about the restaurant.** (b) I have never been to the restaurant **which** everyone is talking **about**. (c) I have never been to the restaurant **that** everyone is talking **about**.
Whom or **that** replaces the object of a preposition when it refers to **people**.	(d) Some people are vegetarians. I spend a lot of time **with these people.** (e) Some people **who(m)** I spend a lot of time **with** are vegetarians. (f) Some people **that** I spend a lot of time **with** are vegetarians.
It is also possible to **omit the relative pronoun** in these sentences when it is not the subject in the adjective clause.	(g) I have never been to the restaurant everyone is talking **about**. (h) Some people I spend a lot of time **with** are vegetarians.
In formal English, you "front" the preposition. If the preposition is fronted, you cannot use the word *that*. You also cannot omit the relative pronoun.	(i) I have never been to the restaurant **about which** everyone is talking. (j) Some people **with whom** I spend a lot of time are vegetarians.

3.1 Editing Practice

Correct any errors in these sentences.

1. The restaurant about that I was telling you has gone out of business.
2. Who was the man whom you were having dinner with him?
3. That's the place whom I was telling you about.
4. The people with who I spend the most time are wonderful cooks.
5. Garlic has a very strong taste that some people don't like it.
6. That is an interesting restaurant that everyone is talking about it.
7. People own restaurants have long work days.
8. It is hard to find managers which you can trust to take care of the restaurant for you.
9. The restaurant about you told me was excellent!
10. I saw the waitress I know her.

3.2 Listening: Restaurant Recommendation

A. A friend has been to a restaurant that you are planning to go to. Listen to his advice about the restaurant. Circle or cross out things in the illustration according to his recommendation.

B. Share your answers with a classmate by describing what you plan to do when you go to the restaurant.

I'm going to sit at the table that is . . .

230 UNIT 11 Eating

6 ADJECTIVE CLAUSES THAT GIVE ADDITIONAL INFORMATION

So far, all the clauses you have studied have given information that was **necessary** to identify the noun. If the clauses restrict the noun referred to, you do not use a comma.	(a) The coffee **which they drink in Turkey** is very strong. *(which coffee?)* (b) Tea is a beverage **which originated in the area of Tibet, Western China, and part of Northern India.** *(which beverage?)*
If the clause just gives **additional information** about the noun (the noun is restricted enough), use a comma.	(c) The coffee, **which we served in small glasses**, was very strong.
The commas are important. They often change the meaning of the sentence.	(d) The visitors **who wanted coffee** sat at the table. *(Not all the visitors sat at the table. The ones who wanted coffee sat there.)* (e) The visitors, **who wanted coffee**, sat at the table. *(All the visitors sat at the table and all of them wanted coffee.)*
Proper nouns are usually restricted enough. They need commas when additional information is given in a clause.	(f) Turkish coffee, **which I really enjoy**, is quite strong. (g) The Japanese tea ceremony, **which takes years to master**, is a work of art. (h) Shen-Nung, **who was a Chinese emperor in 2737 B.C.**, is supposed to have accidentally invented tea when leaves fell into his hot water.
If you are giving information about the **whole sentence**, you must use a comma.	(i) We sat outside to have coffee, **which was delightful**. *(The whole experience was delightful, not just the coffee.)* (j) Coca-Cola was originally sold to relieve mental and physical exhaustion, **which means it was sold as a medicine**. *(the reason it was sold, not just the exhaustion)*
That may **not** be used to introduce an "additional information" clause and you **cannot omit the pronoun.**	(k) There is still a question about whether the original Coke recipe contained cocaine, **which is a highly addictive drug**. (l) NOT: The original Coke might have contained cocaine, **that is a highly addictive drug**. (m) NOT: The original Coke might have contained cocaine, **is a highly addictive drug**.

UNIT 11 Adjective Clauses

6.1 Get in Motion

Put commas in these sentences, if necessary.

1. The coffee I drank this morning was Italian.
2. Coffee, which I love to drink, is getting expensive.
3. The host, who was very nice, showed us to our table.
4. The waitress who brought us coffee was very nice.
5. Espresso coffee, which I often drink, is very common in Italy and France.
6. I had coffee this morning, which is something I rarely do.
7. I bought Italian coffee, which was unusual for me.
8. Italian coffee, which I like to drink, is hard to buy in the supermarket.
9. The Italian coffee which I drank yesterday was delicious.
10. My neighbor, who comes over for coffee every morning, tells me all the neighborhood news.

6.2 Commas or Not?

Put commas in these sentences, if necessary.

1. Tea is the most popular beverage in the world after coffee, which is the most profitable.
2. Most cultures have rules that limit how much and when people may drink alcoholic beverages.
3. Coffeehouses and teahouses have traditionally been places where people socialize around the drinking of a beverage.
4. Some religions prohibit their members from drinking beverages which contain caffeine or alcohol.
5. When people come to our house, we invite them to have a cup of coffee or a soft drink, which is mainly a sign of our hospitality.
6. Tea time, which is between 5:00 and 6:00 p.m. in England, is a pleasurable social pastime.
7. Drinking alcohol, which is often prohibited among young people, can be a symbol of rebellion.
8. Some people only drink wine with meals, which means they don't consider wine drinking to be pleasurable if there is no food.
9. In the summer, iced tea, which is often served with a piece of mint, is very popular in the United States.
10. In some countries tea which is hot is considered a better drink in hot weather because the hot drink will make you feel cooler.

6.3 Contrast the Meaning

Are the statements that follow each sentence true or false? Write T or F.

1. In the 1980s, mineral water, most of which was imported from Europe, became very popular.

   _____ Only mineral water from Europe was popular.

2. Mineral water which was carbonated was the most popular.

   _____ Not all mineral water was carbonated.

3. People who drank mineral water thought that this was a healthy thing to do.

   _____ Everyone thought this was healthy.

4. Perrier, which was imported from France, became the most famous brand of mineral water.

   _____ Some Perrier was imported from other countries.

5. In 1990, people were shocked to find out that benzene, which is a carcinogen, was found in Perrier.

   _____ Only some of the benzene is a carcinogen.

6. Perrier officials who spoke with the public said that this was very unusual.

   _____ All Perrier officials spoke with the public.

7. In Vergeze, France, where Perrier is bottled, water filters which normally take benzene out of the water showed high levels of benzene.

   _____ All water filters are used to take benzene out of the water.

8. Perrier replaced the water filters, which seemed to solve the problem.

   _____ The water filters solved the problem.

   _____ Replacing the water filters solved the problem.

7 EXPRESSIONS OF QUANTITY IN ADJECTIVE CLAUSES

Adjective clauses may begin with **expressions of quantity**. Because the relative pronoun is an object of the preposition *of*, only **which** or **whom** may be used. These clauses give additional information, so you need to use a comma.	(a) The restaurant industry, **40 percent of which** is fast food, is a very large part of the American economy. (b) Of the children interviewed, **most of whom** were very young children, 90 percent reported pizza was their favorite food.
Either of which / whom and *neither of which / whom* are also common expressions used in these adjective clauses that give additional information.	(c) They serve fish and chicken there, **either of which** is fine with me. (d) I went to the Star Café with Ann and Jody, **neither of whom** had been there before.

7.1 Get in Motion: Expressions of Quantity

Underline the best choice to complete each sentence.

1. Our diet, most of (which / whom) consists of rice and vegetables, is very healthy.
2. My friends, many of (which / whom) eat meat, don't care what they eat.
3. Prepared foods, many (which / of which) contain chemicals, are not good for you.
4. Chicken or fish, (either / many) of which is easy to prepare, has less fat than red meat.
5. My children, (either / neither) of whom like green vegetables, are hard to please.
6. The menu, (most / none) of which was vegetarian, listed a couple of meat dishes.
7. The people at the party, most of (who / whom) were vegetarians, left the meat untouched.
8. My three roommates, (all / either) of whom hate to cook, go out to eat a lot.
9. The restaurants, (which many / many of which) are inexpensive, are listed in the directory.
10. The food manufacturers, 40 percent (which / whom / of which / of whom) are located near large cities, depend on farmers outside the city for their supplies.

UNIT 11 Eating

7.2 Listening: Eating Disorders

A. Look at the definitions of *bulimia* and *anorexia*. Discuss the questions with your teacher.

Bulimia: An eating disorder in which a person binges and purges.

Anorexia: An eating disorder in which a person severely limits the amount of food he / she eats.

1. What word in the definitions means "to overeat"?
2. What word in the definitions means "to eliminate everything you have eaten"?
3. Karen sometimes eats two boxes of cookies and then throws up. Is she bulimic or anorexic?
4. Rhonda is extremely thin. She hardly eats anything. Is she bulimic or anorexic?

B. Listen and fill in the statistics in this chart.

1. Percentage of eating disorders that affect women:	_____
2. Average number of calories a teenager takes in every day:	_____
3. Number of calories a person may eat in a short binge:	_____
4. Possible length of a short binge:	_____
5. Possible length of a long binge:	_____
6. Number of calories a person may eat in a long binge:	_____
7. Number of calories a person who has anorexia may eat in a day:	_____
8. Age when most eating disorders happen:	_____

7.3 Completing Expressions of Quantity

Complete the sentences with an expression of quantity.

1. People with eating disorders, most _____ are women, often have low self-esteem.

2. Cases of bulimia, 10,000 _____ were reported in one year, are increasing.

3. Doctors questioned 3,000 children, 20 percent _____ were overweight.

4. The doctors were surprised at the answers, 40 percent _____ indicated that the children thought they were overweight.

5. The media images make thinness attractive, all _____ makes it difficult to feel all right about not being thin.

6. People with anorexia, many _____ also show symptoms of bulimia, have

UNIT 11 *Adjective Clauses*

7.4 Talk It Over and Optional Writing

A. Discuss this question with a group of classmates.

"You can never be too rich or too thin." Do you agree or disagree with this quote?

B. Now write a paragraph about your opinion on this topic. Use at least three adjective clauses in your paragraph.

8 REDUCTIONS

Adjective clauses may be **reduced** in two ways.	
Drop the **pronoun + be** if the pronoun is *who*, *which*, or *that*.	(a) Caffeine, **which is a drug**, is present in most soft drinks. (b) Caffeine, **a drug**, is present in most soft drinks. (c) A baby **who was exposed to caffeine** has a chance of birth defects. (d) A baby **exposed to caffeine** has a chance of birth defects.
If there is **no be** in the clause, change the verb to the present participle.	(e) A pregnant woman **who drinks caffeine** exposes her unborn child to birth defects. (f) A pregnant woman **drinking caffeine** exposes her unborn child to birth defects.

8.1 Get in Motion: Reductions

Underline the reduced adjective clause that describes a noun in each sentence. Circle the noun it modifies. State the full adjective clause.

EXAMPLE

(Laura,) having heard that garlic has a strong taste, was surprised at the sweet taste of baked (garlic,) served as a vegetable in Italian restaurants.

who had heard that garlic has a strong taste
which is served as a vegetable in Italian restaurants

1. A friend of mine named Alice loves garlic.

2. However, Alice, realizing that many people in the United States don't like the smell of garlic, doesn't eat garlic very often.

3. Alice, not wanting to offend people, only eats garlic during her vacations, at which time she eats as much garlic as possible.

4. Many people, considering garlic good for the health, eat garlic every day.

5. Garlic, considered by many people as medicinal, is now sold in pill form.

6. The pills, consisting of dried garlic, are not supposed to give people garlic breath.
7. People eating garlic together will not notice the smell of garlic on each other's breath.
8. The secretary, the only one who hadn't eaten garlic at lunch, knew they had eaten garlic as soon as they walked back into the office.
9. *Tzatziki,* a famous Greek dish, is made with garlic.
10. *Kim chee,* made with garlic and cabbage, is a famous Korean dish.
11. Dishes containing uncooked garlic leave a strong smell and taste of garlic in the mouth.

8.2 Reductions

With a partner reduce these adjective clauses or participial phrases in as many ways as possible, if possible.

EXAMPLE
Tom, who is a true coffee-lover, spends a lot of money at the coffee shop which is in his building.
Tom, a true coffee-lover, spends a lot of money at the coffee shop in his building.

1. We know that caffeine, which is a drug which affects the central nervous system, causes nervousness.
2. Some drugs which are used as pain relievers have large quantities of caffeine per capsule.
3. Since 1985 soft drinks which have large amounts of caffeine have become very popular in the United States.
4. People who are concerned about the harmful effects of caffeine have other beverage choices.
5. Decaffeinated drinks, which are an alternative to drinks with caffeine, have been shown to have negative effects on health as well, even causing cancer in laboratory animals.
6. Other foods which contain caffeine are chocolate, some puddings and gelatins, and some candy.
7. The number of people who drink milk has decreased in the past 20 years, whereas the number who consume soft drinks has nearly doubled.
8. Coffee consumption in the United States was the highest in 1962 when 75 percent of all Americans drank it.
9. The number of cups of coffee which are consumed per person per day has also declined.
10. People who are between 20 and 40 are more likely to drink soft drinks than coffee.

8.3 Talk It Over

Discuss these questions with your classmates.

1. How do you feel about the taste and smell of garlic?
2. Do you know of other famous dishes made with uncooked garlic?
3. Sarah and Roberto share an office. Sarah loves to eat Greek food and often comes back from lunch smelling of garlic. Roberto hates the smell of garlic.
   a. Do you think Roberto should say anything to Sarah?
   b. If so, how can he express himself so that he will not hurt Sarah's feelings?
   c. Should Sarah stop eating food with garlic?

9 TROUBLE SPOTS: WORD CHOICE

one of the, the only one	**One of the** and **the only one** take a singular verb.	(a) **One of those restaurants is** closing. (b) **The only food** that I dislike **is** lima beans. (c) **The only one** in our family who **eats** meat is my father. *(The relative clause refers to one, so the verb is singular.)*
	However, in an adjective clause following **one of the**, the verb refers to the noun that follows **one of**, so the verb in the adjective clause is plural.	(d) **One of the restaurants** that **are** open for breakfast is the Sunshine Café. *(The adjective clause refers to **restaurants**, which is plural, so the verb is plural.)*
	In spoken English, however, most people use the singular verb in the relative clause following **one of the**.	(e) **One of the restaurants** that is open for breakfast is the Sunshine Café.
all of, whole	Although **all** and **whole** can have the same meaning (everyone or everything), **all of** is an expression of quantity, like **half of the . . . , part of the . . .** **Whole** is an adjective.	(f) **All of the meal** was appropriate for vegetarians. (g) **The whole meal** was appropriate for vegetarians.

9.1 Editing Practice

Underline any errors in these sentences.

1. One of the dietary laws which has survived in Judaism and Islam is not eating pork.
2. The whole of them were very strict about not drinking alcohol.
3. The Bangkok Café is one of the restaurant that I go to a lot.
4. The only food not to avoid are plants.
5. The all vegetables are very healthy, high in vitamins and low in fat.
6. All the thing was a big problem.
7. One of the dish was broken when the waiter dropped the tray.
8. Kathy is the only one of my friends who hate to cook.
9. My brother is one of the chefs who teach at the cooking school.
10. One of the ingredients in that dish is very difficult to find.

10 PREPOSITIONS AND PHRASAL EXPRESSIONS

Prepositions of Location

before	indicates a relationship in time or place	**before** midnight	**before** the judge
after	indicates a relationship in time	**after** midnight	**after** the meeting
between	location in relation to two things	**between** the two buildings	
among	location in relation to more than two things or people	**among** friends	**among** the books on the shelf
ahead, beyond	in front / further in front of the speaker	the car **ahead** of us / **beyond** me	**ahead** of me in school / **beyond** my knowledge
in back of, behind	away from the front	**in back of** me / **behind** my house	

Phrasal Verbs with *After, Between, Behind, Ahead, Back*

(a) It's hard to **look after** so many kids at one time. *(take care of)*
(b) I hope you don't let this problem **stand / come between** you. *(cause problems)*
(c) Don't **fall / get behind** in your work. If you **are behind** already, get a tutor. *(lag)*
(d) A good education is the key to **getting ahead**. *(succeed)*
(e) **Go ahead** and finish that page. I'll check it when I **get / come back**. *(begin) (return)*
(f) **Looking ahead**, I plan to **go back** to my country in June. *(plan) (return)*
(g) I'll **pay** you **back** when he **gives** me my checkbook **back**. *(pay something owed) (return)*
(h) It is not easy to **look back** at the mistakes one has made. *(remember)*
(i) **Put** it **back** right now! *(return)*

See Appendix D for more phrasal verbs.

UNIT 11 Adjective Clauses

10.1 Preposition Practice

With a partner, decide which preposition would be logical: *between, among, ahead, beyond, back,* or *behind*.

1. Let's just keep this _____ you and me. It'll be our secret.
2. They kept going _____ and forth _____ the two ideas.
3. She knew how to read before kindergarten. She was really _____ of the game.
4. They were tired, but they kept on walking because they knew that the house was just _____ the trees in front of them.
5. We're out of gas. We'll have to stop at the gas station _____.
6. _____ to the drawing board! We've got to start all over again.
7. They've been talking about her _____ her back again.
8. If you get that work done _____ of time, we can leave early today.
9. It's _____ words. I just can't believe it.
10. There is quite a distance _____ Los Angeles and San Francisco.
11. When you look _____ the scenes, you can see what really goes on.
12. They shared their profits _____ the three of them.
13. Quiet times alone in that family were few and far _____.
14. Why he behaved that way is _____ my understanding. I just don't get it
15. They are a little _____ the times. They only recently bought a color TV.
16. You shouldn't eat a lot _____ meals. It will ruin your appetite for dinner.

10.2 Prepositions and Phrasal Expressions

Ask your partner these questions. Answer in complete sentences.
1. How do you plan to get ahead in life?
2. What could stand between you and your plans for a successful life?
3. When did you get back from school / work yesterday?
4. What do you look ahead to for the future?
5. What is something someone forgot to give back to you?
6. Are you getting behind in your school work?
7. Is there anyone you have to look after?
8. When you look back on this time in your life, what will be your strongest memory?
9. What will you do after dinner?
10. What do you do before breakfast?

LISTENING TEST

Listen and circle the letter of the statement that has the same meaning.

1. a. All pizza is made that way.
   b. I like only certain kinds of pizza.
   c. I don't like fast food very much.

2. a. Forty percent of the students went to the Thai restaurant.
   b. All of the students were from Thailand.
   c. Four of the students were from Thailand.

3. a. She needed more things to cook the dish.
   b. She was at the grocery.
   c. She was probably cooking a Mexican dish.

4. a. The man sent me a letter.
   b. I have met the man many times in San Francisco.
   c. I sent a man a letter.

5. a. We had several visitors.
   b. We had one visitor.
   c. We had three visits.

6. a. We went to a neighbor's house.
   b. We want to sell our car.
   c. A neighbor came to see us.

7. a. They didn't stay at a hotel.
   b. The place is a hotel.
   c. They didn't want to stay at the place.

8. a. I get things done, but not in the morning.
   b. I get more done in the morning.
   c. This morning I got nothing done.

9. a. The mother didn't want to embarrass the boy.
   b. The boy told his mother something embarrassing.
   c. The boy didn't want to be embarrassed.

10. a. Having dinner out made us late.
    b. The restaurant made us late.
    c. The service at the restaurant was very good.

UNIT 11 Eating

QUIZ YOURSELF

Circle the letter of the error in each passage.

1. Considering world cooking, perhaps the greatest contribution (a) that the Chinese have made has been the wok. The Chinese (b), concerned about limited fuel, designed the wok to quickly cook meat and vegetables (c), cutting in very small pieces.

2. Because many Indians don't eat meat, they have developed a cuisine (a) who uses many spices, (b) giving vegetables variety. Curries are a good example of dishes (c) which are highly spiced.

3. One of the contributions of Native Americans was corn (a), that was first grown in North America. The Europeans (b) who immigrated here adapted it into their diet. Nowadays, corn on the cob (c), which is a summer dish, is considered as American as apple pie.

4. Greek, Turkish, and Arabic cooking uses a lot of olive oil, (a) which is a very healthy vegetable oil. Food (b) which is kept in olive oil can be preserved for several days even at room temperature. When you drive through these regions, you will see fields of olive trees (c), many of them are hundreds of years old.

5. It is difficult to say which Italian dish (a), spaghetti or pizza, is most popular in the world. Most countries (b), borrowing these dishes, created their own variations (c), relying on local ingredients.

6. Thai restaurants (a), being a new arrival on the ethnic food scene, have become very popular in recent years. Thai cooking (b), which is well-known for its interesting flavors and hot spices, is exotic to most Americans (c), whose Americans like to eat a less spicy diet.

7. Count Rumford (a), an American-born physicist, is said to have designed the first cooking range (b), provided an even cooking temperature, and (c) influencing the future of cooking.

8. American cooking inventions (a), microwave ovens and Teflon pans, have probably had more influence on cooking than actual dishes or ingredients. The goal of many of these inventions has been to make cooking more convenient (b), which freeing the cook from the kitchen, and (c) allowed women to spend more time outside of the home.

9. Anthropologists now believe that primitive man (a), who provided protein for his family, must have eaten the bone marrow of animals (b), who other animals had already killed and eaten on. Primitive man (c), like a scavenger, would descend on the kill before any other hungry animals came into the area.

10. Our ancient ancestors (a), who mainly ate plants and very lean meat, were healthier than we (b), who eat so much fat, are today. It is different, however, from one culture to another. The culture (c) which we live influences us to eat food rich in fat.

4   WH- QUESTION NOUN CLAUSES

Wh- questions are introduced in noun clauses with **who(m), whose, what, which, when, where, why,** or **how**.	(a) The newspaper told us **who won the tournament**. (b) I don't know **whose magazine this is**. (c) Do you know **where I can buy a newspaper?** (d) **Why they say that** is hard to understand.
Wh- noun clauses may be **reduced to infinitives** if the subject of the main clause and that of the noun clause are the same. The infinitive often expresses the idea of obligation, necessity, or ability and replaces **should, need, can,** or **could**.	(e) I don't know **where I should pay for this paper**. (f) I don't know **where *to pay* for this paper**. (g) Do you know **where you can get that?** (h) Do you know **where *to get* that?**

4.1 Get in Motion

Use the noun clauses on the right to complete the sentences for numbers 1 through 7. Then fill in your own opinion in 8 and 9.

EXAMPLE
The **business** section explains *what businesses are doing*.

1. The **TV** section lists _____.

2. _____ is a subject in the **home** section.

3. The **people in the news** section is interesting because it tells us _____.

4. People read the **obituary** section to find out _____.

what is happening in the world

what famous people are doing

which houses are for sale

what programs are on TV

when you should plant a garden

which companies are good investments

who has died

254   UNIT 12 In the News

5. Real estate agencies advertise in the **home** section because they want people to know _____.

6. _____ is usually on the **front page** of a newspaper.

7. I am interested in investing. I read the **business** section because I want to know _____.

8. My favorite section is the _____ section because I like to know _____.

9. I never read the _____ section because _____ is boring to me.

4.2 Question Words

Work with a partner. Complete these conversations with noun clauses.

Conversation 1

CINDY: I can't find the TV section. Have you seen it?

MARCO: No. I don't know where (1) _____.

CINDY: I wanted to find out what time (2) _____ (include a movie name). Do you know?

MARCO: No, sorry. I have no idea when (3) _____.

Conversation 2

MARI: Let's go see a movie tonight.

TOMO: That's a good idea. Do you have any idea what (4) _____ at the Cinemax?

MARI: No, I haven't heard what (5) _____.

TOMO: Today's paper will tell us (6) _____.

MARI: That's true. Do you know where (7) _____?

TOMO: Yes, it's over there.

MARI: OK. Here's the movie section. Have you heard which (8) _____?

TOMO: This one is supposed to be good. It's at the Star Cinema. I don't remember where (9) _____.

MARI: Let's call and ask them how (10) _____.

UNIT 12 Noun Clauses and Indirect Speech

4.3 Clauses and Infinitives

Change these sentences from a noun clause to an infinitive, if possible.

1. I'm trying to decide which movie I should see.
2. I don't know how many tickets I need to buy.
3. I don't know how many tickets Frank brought.
4. I never know how much time I need to allow to get to the airport.
5. I wonder where I can find a newspaper.
6. Mark is trying to decide which apartments he wants to look at.
7. Graciella is looking in the paper to decide which house she should go to see.
8. The advertisements in the travel section show which airlines fly to different places.
9. I am trying to decide which airline I should fly to Mexico on.
10. Do you know how I can get to the airport?

4.4 Noun Clauses

Complete these sentences with the information given.

EXAMPLE
A murder occurred last night.
The police report stated __(that) a murder occurred last night__.

1. Who was the murder victim?
   The police have not announced _____.

2. He was a 60 year old man.
   They have only said _____.

3. Was he shot or stabbed?
   They have not said whether _____.

4. Have they found the murder weapon?
   Reporters have asked the police if _____.

5. The murder took place in a wealthy neighborhood.
   Reporters know where _____.

6. The murder took place in an exclusive neighborhood.
   The fact that _____ is surprising.

7. "We have just started our investigation."

   The police spokesperson said that they _____.

8. What was the motive for the murder?

   No one mentioned _____.

4.5 Listening: Mystery

A. Underline the stressed syllable in these words. Practice the pronunciation of these words and use them in the sentences below. Be careful of the verb forms.

alibi	investigate	motive	neighbor
exclusive	investigation	murder	neighborhood
	investigator	murderer	weapon

1. A gun was the murder _____.

2. Who _____ the man? Who was the _____?

3. A police _____ is leading the _____ into the murder.

4. Why would anyone kill him? What could be the _____?

5. They were very wealthy and lived in a _____ that was quite _____.

6. His wife couldn't have killed him. She has a(n) _____. She was at the hairdresser's.

UNIT 12 Noun Clauses and Indirect Speech   257

B. Listen and complete the sentences below using noun clauses.

1. Police are not saying . . .
2. They don't know . . .
3. The neighbor can't imagine . . .
4. She is worried about . . .
5. As for Mrs. North, the police have not said . . .
6. Aaron Jaffee wanted to know . . .

4.6 Investigation

A. In a group, each person takes one number between 1 and 5. Turn to the files in Appendix G. Student 1, look at File 7. Student 2, File 9. Student 3, File 11. Student 4, File 17. Student 5, File 20. It does not matter if you have more than one file number or if two students have the same file number.

Look at the file for your number and memorize the information.

B. Now go around from classmate to classmate and ask your question:

Do you know if / whether / who / where / how . . . ?

C. Get in a group with at least one person who had each number (1 through 5). Report on the information you learned. Figure out who could have murdered Mr. North. Who had a motive? Who had an alibi?

5 -EVER WORDS TO INTRODUCE CLAUSES

Use *wh-* question words with *-ever* to introduce clauses which mean **any time / place / one / way.**	(a) **Whatever you do** is OK with me.	anything
	(b) Tell **whoever calls** that I'm busy.	anyone
	(c) Tell **whomever you talk to** that I'm out.	anyone
	(d) I'll come **whenever you want.**	anytime
	(e) **Whichever one you buy** is fine with me.	any of the choices
	(f) I can go **wherever you want.**	anyplace
	(g) They get by financially **however they can.**	any way

258   UNIT 12 *In the News*

5.1 Get in Motion

Complete these sentences with *whenever, whatever, whoever, wherever,* or *whichever.*

1. A: When do you want to leave?
   B: I don't care. _____ you want to go is fine with me. On the 5:00 news they said there could be a parking problem, though.

2. A: Where do you want to eat dinner?
   B: It doesn't matter. _____ restaurant isn't too expensive is OK with me. Choose _____ one you want to go to. Here's a list in the entertainment guide.

3. _____ wrote that article did not do enough research.

4. A: Did they take everything in the store?
   B: No, they took _____ they could sell easily. At least that's what the newspaper said.

5. Tell _____ asks that I'm in a meeting.

6. _____ I go for lunch is always terribly crowded.

7. _____ reason he gave she believed. She never knew when he was lying.

8. _____ you talk to will tell you the same thing.

9. According to the travel section, all the resorts there are wonderful. You'll like _____ one you choose.

10. I'm flexible. _____ you decide is fine with me.

5.2 -ever Clauses

Angel North is under arrest for the murder of his father. He is in shock and is leaving most of the decision-making to other people. Complete his responses to these questions his mother asks him.

1. Angel, how could you do such a thing?
   Don't believe what they are saying about me. _____ they say is untrue!

2. Who do you think did it?
   I don't know, but I sure hope they catch _____ did it fast!

3. Which lawyer do you think we should hire?
   _____ lawyer is going to prove me innocent! Hire _____ you think is best.

(Continued on the next page)

4. Are you going to say you are innocent or insane?

   I will use _____ defense the lawyer advises me to, but I am, of course, innocent.

5. Do you think we have enough money to pay a lawyer?

   I have _____ much Dad left me in his will.

6. Angel, when do you want to talk with a lawyer?

   I don't care. _____ you say is fine with me.

7. What time do you want to see the lawyer?

   _____ time is convenient for the lawyer is fine with me. I'm not going anywhere.

8. Where do you want me to put these letters from your friends?

   Put them _____ you want. I'm too upset to read them.

9. What should I tell your friends?

   _____ you say is all right with me.

10. I think I'm going to call a press conference. What do you think about that?

    You can do _____ you think is best. I don't mind.

11. You can have two visitors tomorrow. Who do you want to see?

    I'll see _____ you ask to come.

12. I'll have to go soon. Is that all right with you?

    _____ you have to go is fine with me.

5.3 Sentence Completions

Complete the sentences.

1. I spend a lot of time in / at . . .

   I go there whenever . . .

2. My ideal place to live would be wherever . . .

3. It's important that whichever place I live in has / is . . .

4. However long I live, I hope . . .

5. I usually listen to . . . radio station.

   I usually like whoever / whatever . . .

UNIT 12 *In the News*

6 REPORTED SPEECH

Many noun clauses report what someone else said. The noun clause is the object of the reporting verb in these sentences. You may omit *that*.	(a) "I love the performance," he said. *(actual quoted words)* (b) He said **(that) he loved the performance.** *(reported speech)* (c) "We want tickets to the ballet," they said. (d) Did they say **(that) they wanted tickets** to the ballet?

Use the formal sequence of tenses to indicate that it is reported speech, not direct quotation. That is, shift back in time.

(e) "It **starts** at 8."	He said that it **started** at 8.
(f) "It**'s starting** now."	He said that it **was starting** then.
(g) "It **has** already **started**."	He said that it **had** already **started**.
(h) "It **started**."	He said that it **had started**.
(i) "It **was starting**."	He said that it **had been starting**.
(j) "It **will start** soon."	He said it **would start** soon.
(k) "It **can start** soon."	He said it **could start** soon.
(l) "It **may start** soon." *(possibility)*	He said it **might start** soon.
(m) "You **may start** soon." *(permission)*	He said that I **could start** soon.
(n) "It **has to start** soon."	He said it **had to start** soon.
(o) "It **must start** soon."	He said it **had to start** soon.
(p) "**Start** now!"	He said **to start** then!
(q) "**Don't start** now!"	He said **not to start** yet.

You do not need to follow the sequence of tenses:

• when the speech has just been spoken	(r) "The program **has** just **started**."
	(s) He said the program **has** just **started**.
• when it is a general fact or truth	(t) She said that the studio **is** open from 9:00 to 9:00 every day.
• when the reporting verb is in the present tense	(u) She says that she **will come** at 5:00 P.M.
• when making the modal perfect would change the meaning	(v) "He **should be** here on time," she said.
	(w) She said he **should be** there on time. (NOT: She said he **should have been** there on time.)
• when the noun clause in the quoted speech is in the past perfect or past perfect continuous tense	(x) "He **had been trying** to do it," she said.
	(y) She said that he **had been trying** to do it.

Adverbs and pronouns must also change in reported speech.	(z) "**We had** a lot of fun dancing **here last night**." (aa) They said that **they had had** a lot of fun dancing **there the night before**.

UNIT 12 Noun Clauses and Indirect Speech

6.1 Get in Motion

Change the quotes into reported speech.

EXAMPLE
I hate to dance.
She says that ___she hates to dance___.

1. "Why do you hate to dance?"
   I asked her why _____.

2. "My mother taught dance classes when I was young."
   She told me that _____.

3. "I had to dance, so I always hated it."
   She said that she _____.

4. "I will never force my children to dance."
   She promised that _____.

5. "What time does the performance start?"
   I asked what time _____.

6. "It starts at 8:00."
   They told me that _____, so let's hurry!

7. "Call me later because I have to get ready for the performance."
   He told me _____.

8. "Don't forget the tickets!"
   He said _____.

9. "I won't forget them."
   I told him _____.

10. "Be careful driving! It may be icy tonight."
    She told me _____ because _____
    _____.

11. "There must be enough room for the dancers to change costumes here."
    They said that _____.

12. "Why didn't we just stay at home? The crowds are terrible!"
    I hate to go to a performance with her. She's always asking me why _____.

6.2 Talk It Over and Report

A. Discuss these quotes with a classmate. Which one do you agree with? Why?

"No man in his senses will dance."—Cicero
"To dance is to live."—Snoopy

B. Report on your conversation to the class.

6.3 Reported Speech

Jean Martin just interviewed a famous dancer. Read the interview transcript and complete the article below.

JM: How did you get involved in dancing?
D: Well, my family lived in an apartment building next to the practice hall for the National Dance Company, so I spent a lot of time watching them. That got me interested in dancing.
JM: Do you have any advice for young dancers starting out now?
D: Don't give up your dreams!
JM: Do you think fewer people are going into dance now than in the past?
D: Yes, that's definitely true. People are too practical now. They want a guaranteed paycheck and aren't willing to sacrifice for their talent. That's why I've started this scholarship program, Dance Forever, to support young people who have an interest in dancing.
JM: Do you have any plans to retire?
D: I won't ever really retire from dancing. However, I may get involved in dancing in a different way, as a teacher for example.
JM: Well, thank you very much.

Last week, in my interview with this famous dancer, I asked him how (1) _____

in this kind of dancing. He told me that as a youth he (2) _____ next to the

National Dance practice hall and that he (3) _____ a lot of time watching them.

When I asked him (4) _____ for young dancers, he told them

(5) _____ dreams.

As for the reasons why fewer people are going into dance now, he feels that

(6) _____ practical. To encourage more young people to go into dance, he told

me (7) _____. When I asked him (8) _____ to retire,

he answered (9) _____ retire from dancing. However, he thought

(10) _____ involved in a different way, perhaps as a teacher.

UNIT 12 Noun Clauses and Indirect Speech   263

6.4 Talk It Over and Optional Writing

A. In a group, add different kinds of dancing you are familiar with to this list.

| square dancing | line dancing | break dancing | folk | tango |
| polka | waltz | ballet | tap | |

_____   _____   _____

_____   _____   _____

_____   _____   _____

B. Discuss which kinds of dances you have seen. Tried? Like to watch? Like to do? Have difficult / easy steps? Have slow / quick rhythm?

C. Summarize your discussion using these verbs.

| reported that | denied that | said that | told me that | stated that |

7 NOUN CLAUSES WITH EXPRESSIONS OF URGENCY

When a noun clause follows an expression of urgency, such as **a request, order,** or **strong suggestion,** it is followed by the **simple form** of the verb. This happens because there is an unreal quality: Something is urgently requested because it is not happening now.	(a) It was *necessary* that she **be** here early. (b) I *asked* that he **not waste** his money gambling.
These words trigger the simple form: • nouns such as *advice, proposal, recommendation, requirement*	(c) My *advice* is that he **not gamble** anymore.
• verbs such as *ask, advise, command, demand, desire, direct, insist, order, prefer, propose, recommend, require, suggest, urge*	(d) She *advised* that he **not gamble** anymore.
• adjectives such as *advisable, anxious, desirous, essential, imperative, important, indispensable, necessary, urgent*	(e) It is *advisable* that he **not gamble** anymore.

264 UNIT 12 *In the News*

In informal English, it is OK to use *should* in sentences with *advise* and *suggest*.	(f) I *suggested* that he **should see** a counselor about his gambling addiction.
Some native speakers prefer to use an infinitive rather than a noun clause with *ask, advise, command, direct, order, require,* and *urge*.	(g) I *advised* him **to take** that class. (h) Did you *ask* me **to do** that? (i) You should *urge* them **to sign up** for it. (j) Are we *required* **to take** that? (k) They *directed / commanded* him **to go**.
Note the difference in meaning:	(l) She insisted **that I be on time.** *(She ordered me to be prompt in the future.)* (m) She insisted **that I had been on time.** *(She firmly stated that I had been prompt in the past.)*

Homeless People Face Freezing Weather

Yesterday, the coldest day of the year, homeless people sought shelter in subw
stations and the doorways of buildings as the temperature dropp

7.1 Get in Motion

Sometimes in the newspaper you read reports about people who have problems. Complete these sentences with your ideas about these problems.

EXAMPLE
GOVERNMENT TRIES TO CUT SPENDING
Finally! Citizens have been urging that government cut spending for years!

1. NURSE STEALS MONEY FROM ELDERLY PATIENT!

   That's terrible! I would insist that the nurse . . .

2. FIRE STARTED BY CHILD PLAYING WITH MATCHES

   Isn't that terrible? It's absolutely essential that parents . . .

3. ACCIDENT CAUSED BY DRUNK DRIVER

   What a shame! The judge should require that that person . . .

4. CHILD HURT IN AUTOMOBILE ACCIDENT!

   I bet the child wasn't wearing a seatbelt. Parents should insist that . . .

(Continued on the next page)

5. FIRE IN MOVIE THEATER CAUSES INJURIES AS PEOPLE FIND EXITS LOCKED!

    Can you believe that? I'm sure it's a regulation that all emergency exits . . .

6. CHILD SWALLOWS SMALL TOY.

    How terrible! It's so important that parents . . .

7. SIXTH ACCIDENT AT DANGEROUS INTERSECTION

    Why don't they put in a traffic light? I am going to write a letter to suggest . . .

8. BANKER TAKES MILLIONS FROM CUSTOMERS

    The judge should require that this person . . .

9. BRIDGE CLOSED FOR REPAIRS

    It is recommended that drivers . . .

10. GARBAGE COLLECTORS GO ON STRIKE FOR HIGHER PAY!

    Garbage collectors demand that the city . . .

7.2 Expressing Urgency

Complete the sentences with a noun clause.

EXAMPLE
In a war, the government does not tell the public the truth.
The people who oppose the war demand ____*that the government tell the public*____ the truth.

1. The government wants to keep the truth hidden from the other side.

    The government feels that it is important _____.

2. "Mr. President, don't tell the media the number of people who have died."

    The president's advisors recommended _____
    the media the number of people who had died.

3. The government doesn't want to stop fighting yet.

    If the public knew how many people were dying, they would insist _____
    fighting immediately.

4. The government doesn't want journalists to enter the war zone.

    The government demands _____ the war zone.

5. Journalists, on the other hand, want the government to let them into the war zone.

    Journalists insist _____ into the war zone.

6. The government hopes that journalists will cover different stories.

    The government prefers that _____.

266   UNIT 12 *In the News*

7.3 Talk It Over and Optional Writing

Discuss this situation and the questions below with your classmates. Write a report about one part of the conversation.

Martina Lutz is a reporter for a large newspaper. While investigating a crime, she interviewed a person who admitted that he had committed a murder. However, Martina would not tell a judge the name of the person she interviewed. She went to jail for 90 days because she refused to tell the person's name.

1. Do reporters have to tell the names of the people they interview in your country?
2. What difficulties will reporters have if they tell the names of their "sources"?
3. What would you have done if you had learned about a murderer while you were doing an interview?
4. How do you feel about freedom of the press?
5. Do newspapers have a responsibility to give all groups equal news coverage, even if they represent a very violent point of view, for example, hate groups?
6. Do you believe newspapers have the right to invade people's privacy in order to get news about them to the general public? For example, does the public have a right to know about the private lives of politicians?
7. Do you believe newspaper editors choose news items in order to influence how we feel about our world? That is, do they "set the agenda" so that we are concerned about some causes and ignore others?

8 TROUBLE SPOTS: WORD CHOICE

tell, say	*Tell* must be followed by a noun or pronoun which refers to a person. *Say* may be followed by the information that is being reported. *Say* is not followed by an indirect object.	(a) He **told me** that dancing was an important part of rural African life. (b) He **said** that dancers often wore bright masks or face and body paint.
whom	Although in everyday conversation people do not pay very much attention to the *who / whom* distinction, in more formal English *whom* is used to introduce a noun clause when that clause has a subject.	(c) I asked **who** wanted to dance. (d) I asked **whom** he wanted to dance with. (e) I knew **that that** was not the case.
that that	Some sentences will have *that* together twice.	

UNIT 12 Noun Clauses and Indirect Speech

8.1 Sentence Completions

Complete the sentences with words from Box 8. Follow the formal rules for *who / whom*.

1. She gives dance classes in nursing homes as a kind of therapy.
   I don't know _____ she teaches dance to in those homes.

2. Prehistoric people danced 20,000 years ago.
   We know that _____ is the case from cave drawings.

3. Tap dancing grew out of African, Irish, and English dance steps.
   He _____ that these were the steps which influenced tap dancing.

4. I like to watch musicals, such as "West Side Story," which have great dance scenes in them.
   She _____ me that she likes to watch musicals because of the dancing.

5. Flamenco dancing of Spain is believed to be a combination of Indian, Arabic, gypsy, and Sephardic Jewish influences.
   _____ could have guessed that this dance form had such a variety of influences?

6. When the waltz was introduced in the 1800s, it was considered sinful because the dancers were too close together.
   I read that _____ is not unusual when new dances are created.

7. Some classical dancing of Asian countries employs pantomime and puppets.
   I know _____ that is true in Thailand and Indonesia.

8. My brother went to his first dance last night. He _____ me _____ was there, but he wouldn't tell me _____ he danced with.

9. Dancing is great exercise.
   She _____ that dancing is great exercise.

10. I went to the ballet last night. I can't remember _____ directed it, but it was wonderful.

9 PREPOSITIONS AND PHRASAL VERBS

Prepositions

out of • from • away from

out of, from	indicate a source	**out of** love, **out of** wood, **from** Africa, **from** memory
away from	indicates a direction from the speaker	**away from** here, **away from** that idea

Phrasal Verbs with *Away from, Away, Out of, Out*

(a) I **came away from** there exhausted. *(leave)*
(b) You should always carefully **put away** the game pieces after playing. *(store)*
(c) Don't **throw** those directions **away**! *(discard)*
(d) He's been **working away at** that for hours. *(continuously make an effort)*
(e) I **gave** my backgammon set **away** and I wish I hadn't. *(donate)*
(f) I just can't **figure** this game **out**. *(understand)*
(g) Did you **find out** how to play it? *(discover)*
(h) The banker **hands out** the money in Monopoly. *(distribute)*
(i) Let's **try** this new game **out**. *(test)*
(j) We have **run out of** money. *(deplete, use up)*
(k) There is still time to **back out**. We don't have to **carry out** those plans. *(leave a commitment) (fulfill)*

See Appendix D for more phrasal verbs.

9.1 Practice with Prepositions

Ask your partner the following questions. Answer with complete sentences.

1. When was the last time you were away on vacation?
2. What do people sometimes do out of love? out of loneliness?
3. What do you sometimes want to get away from?
4. What is your desk made out of?
5. What is paper made from?
6. What can you cook from scratch?
7. From your point of view, what is the hardest part of learning English?
8. What are some words in English that are from your language?

9.2 Practice with Phrasal Verbs

Review the definitions in Box 9. With a partner, write the phrasal verbs that match these definitions.

1. discover: _____
2. return to its storage place: _____
3. fail to complete: _____
4. left: _____
5. discard: _____
6. understand: _____
7. no longer have any: _____
8. experiment with: _____
9. complete: _____
10. give up ownership: _____
11. continuously make an effort: _____
12. give; distribute: _____

LISTENING TEST

Listen and circle the letter of the statement that has the same meaning.

1. a. I want to know where to buy a newspaper.
   b. I want to know how much it costs.
   c. I want to know if you have a newspaper.

2. a. Whether they told us the truth or not is not important.
   b. It is clear that they told us the truth.
   c. We think it's important that they not lie to us.

3. a. I have strong feelings about the decision.
   b. I am willing to do whatever you want.
   c. You can decide what time we go.

4. a. They did not talk to reporters.
   b. They talked to reporters.
   c. Whether they talked to reporters or not is not clear.

5. a. We should wait to do anything.
   b. We should make our decision quickly.
   c. We can't talk to them now.

6. a. They wanted us to wait there.
   b. They told us they couldn't wait.
   c. They suggested that we go somewhere else.

7. a. I am asking when we need to go.
   b. I am asking if we need to go.
   c. I am asking where we need to go.

8. a. They don't know how it happened.
   b. They don't know anything about it.
   c. They aren't sure when it happened.

9. a. He is going to meet us tomorrow.
   b. He might meet us tomorrow.
   c. He said he couldn't meet us tomorrow.

10. a. I'm not sure about where they are going to stay.
    b. I'm not sure about how they are going to get here.
    c. I'm not sure about the time they plan to arrive.

QUIZ YOURSELF

Circle the letter of the best answer to complete each sentence.

1. _____ animal you choose is your decision, but dogs require more care than cats.
   a. However
   b. Whoever
   c. Whichever

2. According to the article, most of the people answering the survey felt _____ their animals provided companionship and pleasurable entertainment.
   a. which
   b. _____ (nothing)
   c. whatever

3. They reported _____ the San Diego Zoo has one of the largest collections of animals in the world.
   a. that
   b. what
   c. which

4. It is crucial that that butterfly _____ carefully preserved or it will become extinct.
   a. is
   b. be
   c. was

5. _____ zoos try to educate the public as well as to entertain is clear. Their research and conservation are sometimes less obvious.
   a. _____ (nothing)
   b. That
   c. What

6. She advised that I _____ the National Air and Space Museum while I am in Washington, D.C.
   a. do not miss
   b. am not missing
   c. not miss

7. I hope I _____ to Williamsburg to see how colonial Americans lived.
   a. could go
   b. can go
   c. may go

8. The Louvre is probably the most well-known art museum in the world but do you know how man miles of galleries _____? Eight!
   a. has it
   b. it has
   c. does it have

9. I don't know where _____ a map of the museum.
   a. can I get
   b. I can get
   c. can get I

10. Do you know _____ the British Museum is open today?
    a. that
    b. _____ (nothing)
    c. whether

UNIT 13

Adverb Clauses and Related Connectors

Courtship, Marriage, and Divorce

1 SEQUENTIAL TIME

Adverb clauses of sequential time answer the question **when** something happens and indicate the sequence of events. They are always connected to a main clause. They are introduced by subordinate conjunctions, such as **before, after, as soon as, once, until,** and **since.**

The adverb clause may go at the **beginning** of the sentence, **medially,** or at the **end.** Medial position is less common. If the adverb clause is at the beginning, use a comma to separate it from the main clause.	(a) **Before they got married**, they dated for several years. (b) A woman's main duty **after she got married** was to have a son. (c) A woman doesn't have to change her last name to her husband's last name **after she marries.**
Use the **present** or **present perfect** tense to express the future in a time clause.	(d) They'll make their wedding plans **after they get their parents' approval.** (e) They'll make their wedding plans **after they have gotten their parents' approval.**
As soon as shows that immediately after one event happens, another event happens.	(f) **As soon as they decided to get married**, their parents started objecting.
Once indicates that the second event comes soon.	(g) He was nervous about the wedding. **Once he arrived at the church**, he felt much better.

274

Until indicates that the event or situation in the main clause stopped when the event or situation in the time clause occurred.	(h) They fought about their wedding plans **until they got married.** *(Then they didn't fight about them anymore.)*
Until often indicates a negative / positive relationship.	(i) He believed that she would marry him **until she announced her marriage to someone else.** *(Then he didn't believe it anymore.)*
Since indicates when something began to happen. Use the **present perfect** tense to show that an action began in the past and is continuing now, is still important, or may happen again.	(j) They **have intended** to get married **since they first met.**

1.1 Get in Motion

Complete these sentences with your own ideas.

1. Before a man gets married,_____.

2. Until a woman gets married, _____.

3. Once a couple gets married, _____.

4. People should have children _____.

5. People shouldn't have children _____.

6. After a woman has children, _____.

7. Ever since the world began, _____.

8. Until I get / got married, _____.

9. As soon as a woman gets married, _____.

10. After a couple has children, _____.

1.2 Sentence Combining

Use these connectors to combine ideas in A and B. You may need to use the connector in the initial position.

EXAMPLE
Women with careers sometimes wait to have children *until after* they are established in their field.

| before | after | as soon as | once | since | until |

A
- in some countries a man did not ask a woman to marry him
- women have started going to college
- it was acceptable for women to go to college
- in some countries, women stop working
- in my country, women with jobs work
- men rarely get married
- women with careers sometimes wait to have children
- love at first sight means that you fall in love

B
- they get jobs
- they get married at later ages
- he had bought or built a house for her to live in
- they get married
- they used to get married when they were teenagers
- they are established in their field
- you see someone
- they have children

2 OTHER WAYS TO EXPRESS SEQUENTIAL TIME

Use **a preposition + a noun phrase** to show sequential relationships and give your sentences variety.	(a) **until** the birth of her son (b) **prior to** her marriage (c) **before** her wedding (d) **since** her wedding day
Use **adverbial transitions** to indicate the sequence of events. Unlike subordinate conjunctions, these transition words connect main clauses. They often begin a clause, sometimes interrupt it for emphasis, and occasionally appear at the end.	(e) **In the past**, the bride's family had to pay for the wedding. (f) The marriage law went into effect in 1980; **after that**, couples could have only one child. (g) Daughters were considered to be a burden to their families **at that time**.
Adverbial transitions need **strong punctuation**: a semicolon (;) or a period (.).	(h) They got married; **after that**, she moved in with him. (i) They got married. **After that**, she moved in with him.

See Appendix F for more sequential time connecting words.

A bride in pre-Communist China

A bride in Communist China

2.1 Get in Motion

Complete the sentence with the best connector.

1. (Since, After that, Prior to)

   _____ its Communist Revolution, China had had a patriarchal system for 2,000 years.

2. (In the past, Until, Since)

   _____ the patriarchal system ended, daughters were considered to be a burden to their families.

3. (At that time, Prior to, In the past)

   _____ in history, a woman's main function was to provide a son.

4. (Since, After that, Once)

   A woman lived with her own family until she got married. _____, she moved into her husband's family's house.

5. (After that, Prior to, After)

   _____ marrying, she did not live with her own family any more.

6. (At that time, After, After that)

   _____ the death of her husband, a woman could not remarry.

7. (after, prior to, at that time)

   It was not unusual for a childless wife to commit suicide _____ her husband died.

8. (Before that, Before, Until)

   The Marriage Law of 1950 made dowries illegal. _____, families of the brides were required to provide huge dowries.

UNIT 13 *Adverb Clauses and Related Connectors* 277

3 SIMULTANEOUS TIME

When introduces a specific event time clause.	(a) **When he asked her to marry him,** she said "yes."
Whenever also introduces a specific event time clause. It means "any time."	(b) **Whenever they discussed the wedding,** she felt nervous.
So long as and *as long as* are used when an event happens only if another event does.	(c) **So long as their daughter seemed happy,** they didn't want to criticize her husband.
While indicates events that happen at the same time and often indicates the longer event.	(d) **While they have lived together,** they have been very happy.
During cannot introduce a time clause. It must be followed by a noun phrase.	(e) They have been very happy **during their marriage.**
Transitions also show simultaneous time. Use strong punctuation with these.	(f) They planned to get married. **In the meantime,** they lived with their parents. (g) Their parents, **at the same time,** were trying to convince them not to get married.

See Appendix F for more sequential time connecting words.

3.1 Get in Motion: Listening

A. Listen to the conversation between two friends. Then decide what happened first in each group. Put a ✓ next to the event that happened first. Some events happened at the same time. If this is so, put a check next to both of them.

1. _____ Arlene went to high school

   ✓ Arlene met Gregory for the first time

2. _____ Arlene's brother went to basketball practice

   _____ Arlene's brother got a ride with Gregory

3. _____ Gregory almost ran into Arlene with his car

   _____ Arlene was coming home

   _____ Gregory and Arlene's brother were going out

278   UNIT 13 *Courtship, Marriage, and Divorce*

4. _____ Arlene graduated from high school

   _____ Arlene got a job at a company

5. _____ Arlene got a job at the same company where Gregory worked

   _____ Gregory asked Arlene out

   _____ Arlene and Gregory have been together

B. Can you retell the story? Use time transitions and conjunctions to combine sentences.

3.2 Connectors versus Transitions

A. In this dialogue, five international students are discussing courtship and marriage customs in their countries. Underline the correct subordinate conjunction or adverbial transitions to complete the dialogue. If necessary, look at Appendix F for information about these connectors.

CHANTAL: I would never, ever marry someone my parents chose for me. I think arranged marriages sound terrible!

YOKO: There are some advantages to them, though. Think how long it takes to meet someone who is right for you. In my country, (while / nowadays / whenever) a lot of young men and women still go to a matchmaker who introduces them to possible mates.

MARIA: I suppose it's not so different from placing a personal ad in a newspaper. Those ads are a modern way to meet someone.

AHMED: (Since / When / As long as) I return to my country, my parents will have selected a girl for me to marry.

CHANTAL: But what if you don't like her? It would be a nightmare to marry someone and (after / afterwards / once) realize you didn't like her.

AHMED: I'll have a chance to meet her a few times with her family around. She won't be a total stranger (at the moment when / when / during) we get married.

PING: My parents had an arranged marriage. It was very common in my country (in the past / beforehand / before that).

YOKO: Would you say they are happily married?

PING: My mom said she didn't know my father (beforehand / previously / before) the wedding day but over the years he was very kind to her. She respected him. She says (when / during / every time that) you live with a man for a long time, you can learn to love him.

YOKO: I think I would like to be in love and (later / after / prior to) get married.

CHANTAL: I couldn't marry someone I didn't love. For me, there would have to be some romance.

MARIA: Aren't there some situations (while / when / at the moment when) you would marry someone without being in love? I mean, practical situations. For instance, would you marry someone to get ahead socially? Would you marry for money or for a chance to live in another country? (Ever since / So long as / Soon after that) you benefited in some way, would you agree to a non-romantic marriage?

CHANTAL: Not me! It would have to be a really deep, romantic love.

B. Which courtship and marriage customs are common in your culture? Which student do you most identify with?

A bride and groom in Saudi Arabia

3.3 Talk It Over: Discussing Engagement and Marriage Traditions

A. List the engagement and marriage traditions in your culture. For example: Who gives presents to the bride and groom? Does the groom pay a bride price? Do engagements have to be made public? Who pays for the wedding and the honeymoon? Can the groom see the bride in her wedding dress before the wedding ceremony?

Engagement Customs:

_____ 1. _____
_____ 2. _____
_____ 3. _____
_____ 4. _____
_____ 5. _____

Marriage Customs:

_____ 1. _____
_____ 2. _____
_____ 3. _____
_____ 4. _____
_____ 5. _____

B. Put an L next to the customs you like. Discuss them with a partner. Use time clauses and transitions.

EXAMPLE
When a couple becomes engaged, . . .
Whenever there is a marriage in our family, . . .

C. Choose one of the following topics to write a composition about.

1. You have been given one million dollars for a fantastic wedding and honeymoon. Plan the extravaganza. In writing, report how the two-week event will progress. Use the clauses and expressions you have studied in this unit.

2. Describe the engagement and wedding customs in your country. Which ones do you like and which do you not like?

4 PLACE

Use *where* to introduce clauses of place.	(a) **Where they live**, there are not many families with children.
Wherever and *everywhere* mean "in any place."	(b) They take their children with them **wherever they go**. (c) **Everywhere they go**, they take their children with them.

See Appendix F for more place connecting words.

4.1 Get in Motion

Match the main clause to a logical *where* clause. Then discuss how these customs differ from wedding customs in your culture.

1. There are often flowers _____.
2. Before the ceremony, the bride waits _____.
3. During the ceremony, the couple stands _____.
4. After the ceremony, guests wait _____.
5. In contrast to the wedding location, the reception is often _____.
6. Couples often honeymoon _____.

where the marriage ceremony takes place

where people can dance

where no one can find them

where the minister is

where the groom can't see her

where they can congratulate the bride and groom

4.2 Time and Place Connectors

Complete the sentence with the best connecting word.

1. (once, since, until)

    I won't get married _____ I meet a woman I love.

2. (At that time, While, Wherever)

    _____ mothers, most Japanese women do not work outside the home.

3. (Where, As soon as, While)

    _____ unmarried, most young Colombian adults live with their parents.

4. (Everywhere that, Prior to, In the meantime)

    _____ men were the breadwinners in the family, women were the full-time housekeepers and mothers.

5. (while, at the same time, during)

    Most people had marriages with traditional roles _____ my grandparents' lifetimes.

6. (After that, Wherever, Before)

    In pioneer America, women had no choice about where the family lived. _____ the pioneer husband wanted to move, the pioneer family moved.

7. (after, since, as soon as)

    In a patriarchal society, a woman is treated with great respect _____ the birth of a son.

8. (prior to, after, once)

    In ancient Rome, _____ a woman was ready to get married, she dedicated her childhood clothes to the gods of her family.

The family tree of Joseph Gutierrez Barker

282   UNIT 13 *Courtship, Marriage, and Divorce*

4.3 Review of Time and Place Clauses

Combine the sentences below using the words in parentheses. Do not change the meaning or verb tense. Use pronouns to avoid repetition. Use appropriate punctuation.

EXAMPLE
A Vietnamese woman gets married.
A Vietnamese woman does not change her last name.
(when)
When a Vietnamese woman gets married, she does not change her last name.

1. Our names indicate which families we belong to.
   They may also show our religious or cultural traditions.
   (at the same time)

2. Spanish is spoken.
   Children are given names of saints from the Catholic church.
   (wherever)

3. You become a mother in an Arab country.
   You are known as the "mother of . . ."
   (after)

4. In Turkey, on the second day of a baby's life, the father takes it in his arms.
   The father whispers three times the name it will have.
   (then)

5. In some places families are more traditional.
   Names are given according to a strict genealogical chart.
   (where)

(Continued on the next page)

6. A person in a family dies.
   A newborn baby cannot be given that person's name because that would be bad luck.
   (after)

   _____
   _____

7. Husbands and wives address each other.
   They use words of endearment such as "honey," "sweetheart," or "dear" rather than their given or first names.
   (whenever)

   _____
   _____

8. In the United States, women traditionally took their husband's last name after marrying.
   Many women keep their last name.
   (nowadays)

   _____
   _____

4.4 Talk It Over and Optional Writing

Choose one of these questions to discuss and report on to your classmates. Then write a paragraph about one of these topics.

1. Are there any traditions for naming children in your culture or family? For example, when are the children given names? Who gives the name? Is there a special ceremony or celebration?

2. Why were you given the name you have? Does it have a meaning? How many names does a person have in your culture?

3. In some cultures, spouses do not call each other by their given or first names. They use words of endearment: "honey," "sweetheart," or "dear." Do your parents call each other by their given names? If you are married, how do you address your spouse?

4. Is it all right to name a child for a deceased ancestor, for example, a grandmother or grandfather? Is it bad luck to name a child for a deceased brother or sister?

5. Do women in your culture change their names when they marry?

6. Do you believe names affect our personalities? That is, do names give us characteristics? Are some names considered bad luck in your culture? Are some names, for example, the names for God, never given to children?

7. Are certain names repeated in each generation in your family? If you have children, what names will you give them?

5 CONTRAST

Use **while** and **whereas** to show **direct opposition** in adverb clauses.	(a) **Whereas divorced women historically had custody of their children**, today many divorced parents share the care. (b) Some people marry for love **while others do so for financial reasons.**
Although, even though, though, even if, and **no matter what / where** are concession subordinate conjunctions. These conjunctions show that you accept the information that they introduce, but you have some doubts about it. They also suggest that what is in the main clause was not expected.	(c) **Although a divorce was easy to get**, it was a very difficult step to take. (d) She wanted to remain friends **even though they got a divorce.** (e) **Even if he wanted to remain friends after the divorce**, she didn't. (f) **No matter what happened to the marriage**, they wanted to remain friends.
The contrast words **despite** and **in spite of** introduce noun phrases. If you add **the fact that** to these expressions, an adverb clause must follow.	(g) **Despite their mother's wishes**, the children went to live with their father. (h) **In spite of their mother's wishes**, the children went to live with their father. (i) **In spite of the fact that it was against their mother's wishes**, they went to live with their father.
These are contrast transition expressions: nonetheless in contrast / comparison but and yet however whatever happens in either case Transition words need strong punctuation.	(j) They had a terrible divorce; **however**, their children came out of it in good shape. (k) They had a difficult marriage; **in contrast**, they had a very easy divorce. (l) **Whatever happens**, they will stay married.
On the contrary indicates the opposite is true. **On the other hand** introduces an alternative, not an opposite.	(m) In Islamic countries, divorce is not frequent. **On the contrary**, it is very rare. (n) Children usually hate to have their parents divorce. **On the other hand**, if their parents are always fighting, divorce can be a relief for the children.

Note: **Anyhow, anyway,** and **after all** are only used in spoken English. **But** can begin a sentence in spoken English but should not begin a sentence in formal writing.

See Appendix F for more contrast connecting words.

UNIT 13 Adverb Clauses and Related Connectors

5.1 Get in Motion

Circle the letter of the most logical way to complete the sentences.

1. While Grant wants to get married, _____.
    a. he is looking for a wife.
    b. he hasn't met the right person yet

2. Louisa has always gone out with a lot of different boys, whereas _____.
    a. her sister has gone out with many different people
    b. her sister has always had the same boyfriend

3. In contrast to _____, Hans and his wife take separate vacations.
    a. most married couples
    b. most married couple do

4. Hans likes to go fishing _____ his wife likes to go shopping.
    a. however
    b. whereas

5. When they were first married, Maria used to pretend to like fishing; _____, she really hated it.
    a. however
    b. despite

6. Their independent vacations, despite _____, are very satisfying for each person.
    a. they are unusual
    b. being unusual

7. In spite of _____, Hans and Maria are very happy together.
    a. their differences
    b. they are very different

8. Although _____, the children adjusted to it in time.
    a. their parents got a divorce
    b. their parents' divorce

5.2 Contrast Connectors

Underline the best connecting word.

Michelle and her parents have very different ideas about the kind of person she should marry. (1) (While / On the contrary) Michelle's parents want her to marry someone from a similar background, this does not matter to Michelle at all. (2) (However / In contrast), she seems to go out of her way to meet people who are different from her family. (3) (While / But) Michelle's parents did not worry about her unusual assortment of friends when she was younger, now that she is in her twenties, they are getting concerned. (4) They do not want to criticize her friends, (and yet / in contrast) they are afraid she will make the wrong decision. (5) They hope, (where / however), that Michelle will meet someone she likes whom they will approve of also.

286   UNIT 13 *Courtship, Marriage, and Divorce*

Michelle's friend Susanna is in a different situation. Susanna's parents are very happy with the man who wants to marry her. (6) (While / In contrast), Susanna, (though / whereas) interested in this man, is not convinced that she should marry him. (7) She cares about him, (but / while) she's not wildly in love with him. (8) (While / However) it would be easy to agree to marry him, Susanna is not sure that she will be happy with him forever. (9) She would hate to end her relationship with him, (and yet / in contrast) she thinks there may be another more exciting relationship in her future.

(10) (In comparison / However) to Michelle and Susanna, Toby is not even thinking about getting married yet. (11) (Although / On the other hand) planning to get married at some point, Toby doesn't think she has met the right person yet. She knows a lot of people. (12) (Nonetheless / In spite of), none of them seem to be possibilities. Toby believes that it is just as easy to fall in love with a rich person as a poor one. So far, she hasn't met very many wealthy people. (13) (However / While), she's still optimistic.

5.3 Contrast

Read each situation and then complete the sentences about non-traditional living situations.

Situation A: Mary, a 40-year-old single woman, owns a large house with five bedrooms. She rents space in her house to four other people, two men and two women. They are all graduate students or people with jobs. Everyone has a part of the house that he or she is responsible for keeping clean and each person cooks for the whole group one night a week. When someone moves out, Mary advertises for a new housemate. Everyone in the house interviews the applicants and chooses the new housemate. Most people enjoy this "cooperative" living situation and live there for several years. Surprisingly, none of Mary's housemates have ever become romantically involved with each other.

1. Although most 40-year-old women are married, Mary . . .
2. Whereas most single women live in small apartments, . . .
3. Some people might expect the housemates to become involved with each other romantically. On the contrary, . . .
4. Though it is somewhat unusual, this living situation . . .

Situation B: Alice and Susan are both single parents. They share a three-bedroom apartment. Their two young daughters share one of the rooms. They share expenses and take turns shopping, cooking, and cleaning.

5. Most single parents live alone. In contrast, . . .
6. Alice and Susan's daughters feel like sisters even though . . .
7. This living situation, although _____, is very practical for Alice and Susan.
8. The two children are quite happy in spite of . . .

5.4 Talk It Over and Optional Writing

A. Which of the following is most important in deciding who to marry? Rank them, starting with 1 for the most important.

_____ Your family's approval   _____ Financial situation

_____ Love and romance   _____ Similar educational backgrounds

_____ Social position   _____ Religion

_____ _____ (your choice)

UNIT 13 Adverb Clauses and Related Connectors   **287**

B. Discuss your ideas with your classmates. Try to reach a consensus and report to the rest of the class.

C. Write a composition giving your opinion on this statement: It is just as easy to fall in love with a rich person as a poor one. Use five contrast expressions in your composition.

5.5 Combining Ideas

A. Use the words in parentheses to combine these ideas.

1. Ann and Phil have been involved for years / they have no plans to get married (although)
2. their strong feelings against marriage / they act like every other married couple (in spite of)
3. Phil's parents were unhappy about the situation at first / they got used to it (nonetheless)
4. this situation has gone on for years / Ann's parents have never gotten used to it (even though)
5. not wanting to lose touch with Ann / they refuse to talk to Phil (while)
6. Ann / wanting to see her parents / will not visit them without Phil (despite)
7. Ann's mother telephones Ann / she won't visit her (though)
8. the situation / difficult / is not terribly unusual (although)

B. What do you think about this situation? Give your opinion, using concession clauses or expressions.

In spite of the fact that . . .
I think that . . . even though . . .

5.6 Talk It Over and Optional Writing

Discuss advantages and disadvantages in the following situations. Be specific and use contrast conjunctions and transitions. Choose one topic to write a composition about.

1. What are the advantages and disadvantages of arranged marriages?
   While people in arranged marriages . . .
   In spite of the fact that . . .

2. Many newspapers today carry personal ads—notices by men or women to meet someone to date or marry. What are the advantages or disadvantages of meeting people this way?

3. Many people are having babies as teenagers nowadays. What are the advantages and disadvantages of having babies when you are this young?

4. Conversely, many married couples, especially two-career couples, are waiting until they are in their middle to late thirties to have children. What are the advantages and disadvantages of having babies when you are this old?

6 CAUSE AND RESULT

Because and *since* introduce the reason or purpose behind an action.	(a) **Because they were getting divorced,** they sold the house. (b) The divorce surprised their friends **since they didn't seem unhappy.**	
Now that means "because now" and must be followed by a present or present perfect tense.	(c) **Now that they are divorced,** they are happier. (d) **Now that they have gotten divorced,** they get along much better.	
So . . . that and *such (a) . . . that* introduce the result clause for an action.	**so + adjective / adverb + *that***	(e) Their marriage was **so bad that** their divorce came as no surprise. (f) They fought **so often that** everyone expected a divorce.
	so much / little + non-count noun + *that*	(g) There was **so little happiness** in their relationship **that** divorce looked very attractive.
	so many / few + count noun + *that*	(h) There were **so many problems** in their marriage **that** they didn't know where to begin.
	such + adjective + plural count noun or non-count noun + *that*	(i) They had **such cultural differences** between them **that** they decided not to get married. (j) The marriage counselor gave them **such bad advice that** they didn't return to talk to her.
	such a + adjective + singular count noun + *that*	(k) Their relationship was in **such a mess that** no one expected it to last.
Because of, due to, on account of, and *as a result of* must be followed by a noun phrase. If you add *the fact that* to these expressions, you need to have an adverb clause follow.	(l) **Because of the divorce,** the children did not see very much of their father. (m) The children did not see very much of their father **due to the divorce.** (n) The children did not see very much of their father **due to the fact that they lived with their mother.**	

(Continued on the next page)

UNIT 13 *Adverb Clauses and Related Connectors*

So that and *in order that / to* show that the action in the main clause is done for a specific purpose. *So that* and *in order that* are usually followed by *would, should, could, may,* or *might*. *In order (not) to* is followed by the simple form of the verb.	(o) They waited to get divorced **so that they wouldn't upset the children.** (p) They waited to tell the children about the divorce **so that they could prepare them for the shock.** (q) **In order not to disturb** the children's lives, the couple tried to stay together.
These transition expressions show cause, result, or purpose: *so, therefore, consequently, as a result, as a consequence, with this in mind, for this reason* Transition expressions need strong punctuation.	(r) They didn't want to hurt the children. **Therefore,** they didn't get a divorce. (s) He fell in love with another woman; **consequently,** they got a divorce.

See Appendix F for more cause and result connecting words.

6.1 Get in Motion

Complete the statements using the information given.

1. They were too young. They shouldn't have gotten married.
   I don't think they should have gotten married because . . .
   They had problems because of . . .

2. However, they shouldn't get divorced. They have children.
   I don't think they should get divorced now that . . .

3. A lot of people stay together in unhappy relationships because they don't want to hurt their children.
   A lot of people stay married so that . . .
   A lot of people stay married in order not to . . .

4. Everyone was surprised when they decided to get divorced. They seemed so happy.
   They seemed so happy . . .
   They appeared to be very happy together, so everyone . . .
   They appeared to be very happy together. Consequently, . . .
   Everyone was surprised since . . .

5. She wanted to leave him but she didn't know how she would support herself.
   She stayed with him since . . .
   She didn't have any money of her own, so . . .

6. They traveled for their jobs. They rarely saw each other.
   They rarely saw each other because of . . .
   They traveled so much that . . .

6.2 Listening: Divorce in Islam

A. Before you listen, complete these sentences. Use the words below:

Islam	Islamic	pregnant	pronouncement
revocable	irrevocable	marriage contract	support

1. Before a couple marries, their families agree to the terms of the _____.
2. A formal, verbal statement is a _____.
3. One of the major religions of the world is _____.
4. _____ laws are different from civil laws.
5. When a woman is going to have a baby, she is _____.
6. After a divorce, the husband must provide financial help or _____ for his ex-wife.
7. When something can be canceled, it is _____. When it cannot be canceled, we say it is _____.

B. Listen to this information about divorce in Islam. Are these statements true or false, according to the listening? Write T or F.

_____ 1. Since Islamic divorce is easy to do, it is not taken seriously.

_____ 2. The divorce pronouncement immediately ends the marriage.

_____ 3. Every woman automatically has the right to announce she is divorcing her husband since it is part of the marriage contract.

_____ 4. They must wait to remarry.

_____ 5. The father provides for the children's support wherever they live.

_____ 6. There is a two-month waiting period before the divorce is final.

_____ 7. The second divorce is revocable.

_____ 8. The husband may remarry but the wife may not.

_____ 9. After a divorce, all of the children stay with the mother.

_____ 10. A husband may reconsider the divorce pronouncement during the waiting period.

6.3 Cause and Result

Combine each pair of sentences in two ways. Use the connectors in parentheses. Be careful about punctuation.

EXAMPLE
There is a three-month waiting period.
Many couples reconsider getting a divorce.

(because)
Because there is a three-month waiting period, many couples reconsider getting a divorce.

(consequently)
There is a three-month waiting period; consequently, many couples reconsider getting a divorce.

1. Islamic divorce sounds very simple compared to a Western divorce.
   People think it is common.
   (as a consequence)

   _____

   (because)

   _____

2. She is not mentally healthy.
   She does not have custody of her children.
   (as a result)

   _____

   (because of)

   _____

3. They cannot work out their problems.
   They have called on two family members to help them with their problems.
   (now that)

   _____

   (since)

   _____

4. Their parents have tried to stay polite to each other during the divorce.
   The children feel comfortable with both parents.
   (on account of)

   _____

   (so)

   _____

6.4 Cause-and-Result Connectors

Combine the following sentences using the words in parentheses with the underlined part. Use pronouns to avoid repetition. Use appropriate punctuation.

EXAMPLE

In the United States around two million children's lives are affected yearly.
Their parents divorce each other.
(due to)

In the United States around two million children's lives are affected yearly *due to their parents' divorcing each other.*

1. Children are not prepared for divorce.
   They must quickly learn to be more independent.
   (since)

2. Many fathers don't pay child support.
   Governments have intervened to make fathers financially more responsible.
   (therefore)

3. Parents are often damaged by the effects of divorce.
   Children's needs may be neglected during the first difficult years.
   (because)

4. For some children, their parents' unhappy marriage made family life miserable.
   They are happier living with one parent.
   (so . . . that)

5. Remarriage may mean a child's economic and emotional environment will be more stable.
   Children may be happier.
   (as a consequence)

6. Divorced men and women are optimistic.
   Their remarriage rate is very high.
   (due to + *noun phrase*)

7. Divorce rates in Canada are not as high as in the United States.
   Canada has a high number of Roman Catholics who do not believe in divorce.
   (such a . . . that)

8. Many men remarry younger women.
   The age gap between a child and his or her step-mother may be uncomfortably narrow.
   (therefore)

UNIT 13 *Adverb Clauses and Related Connectors*

6.5 Cause and Effect

Discuss the following in a small group and then report to the class using cause-and-result and contrast clauses.

What effects does divorce have on children? Consider these aspects:

1. absence of one of the parents
2. loss of standard of living
3. addition of new family members through remarriage (step-brothers / sisters, half-brothers / sisters, step-parents)

6.6 Talk It Over

Discuss these questions with your classmates.

1. How common is divorce in your culture? Do women who get a divorce usually remarry?
2. Who gets custody of the children after a divorce?
3. Is there a problem of fathers not paying child support?
4. When people marry in your country, do they make a promise to be married forever? In many wedding ceremonies in the United States, those who marry vow to be faithful "as long as we both shall live" or "until death do us part." Do you have a similar vow?

7 REDUCED ADVERB CLAUSES

If the subject in the adverb clause and the main clause are the same, the adverb clause may be reduced. This is one way to give your sentences more variety.

To reduce, **drop the subject and the verb be** in the adverb clause.	(a) I ran into my ex-husband **while I was shopping**. (b) I ran into my ex-husband **while shopping**. (c) **Although she was a good mother**, she had to give up her children. (d) **Although a good mother**, she had to give up her children.
If there is no *be* verb, **change** the adverb clause verb **to the present participle**.	(e) **Since she had a son**, she has been treated better by her in-laws. (f) **Since having a son**, she has been treated better by her in-laws.
You may **drop** the subordinate **conjunction** with simultaneous actions.	(g) **While shopping**, I ran into my ex-husband. (h) **Shopping**, I ran into my ex-husband.
Because is always **dropped** in reduced clauses.	(i) **Because she is divorced**, she has gone back to her birth last name. (j) **Being divorced**, she has gone back to her birth last name. (k) **Because she got married** when she was young, she has never experienced living on her own. (l) **Having gotten married** when she was young, she has never experienced living on her own.
You may also **omit** *being* in the reduced clause.	(m) **Being divorced**, he is afraid to get involved again. (n) **Divorced**, he is afraid to get involved again.
Make sure the reduced clause is near the word it refers to.	(o) **Being divorced**, he is afraid to get involved with her. (NOT: He is afraid to get involved with her, being divorced.)

7.1 Get in Motion: Reductions of Adverb Clauses

Reduce the following sentences, where possible.

1. A woman, after she marries, may make her family name her new middle name.
2. They fought a lot until they agreed on the wedding plans.
3. Once his wife could not bear a son, a husband could take additional wives.
4. Whenever it is possible, couples should discuss finances before they get married.
5. While she is married, a woman's property belongs to her husband.
6. Though she is a good mother, Frances had to give up her children.
7. While it sounds easy, divorce in Islam is not taken lightly.
8. Because states have changed to no-fault divorce, many women and children have become poorer.
9. Because she is terribly unhappy in her marriage, Margo has decided to file for divorce.
10. Since they have gotten divorced, they have gotten along better.

7.2 Editing Practice

Correct the error in each sentence. Remember that not all sentences can be reduced. If they can't be reduced, make the sentence complete.

1. While they mothers, most Japanese women do not work outside the home.
2. Although divorce, they were still friends.
3. Because being divorced, they rarely saw each other except when one of them was picking up the children.
4. Wherever the guests looking, there were flowers.
5. Because not caring any more about his appearance, he never cut his hair.
6. Since getting divorced, the children spend most of their time with their mother.
7. Women answered that their free-choice marriages were better than arranged marriages, when interviewed.
8. When arranged marriages, parents often mismatch young people.
9. Women considered their lives to be more difficult after having got marrying.
10. Although they being happy, they went to a marriage counselor to make their marriage even better.

8 TROUBLE SPOTS: WORD CHOICE

After cannot connect two main clauses. Use *after that* as a transition expression.	(a) They got married; **after that**, they had a huge reception. (b) **After** they got married, they had a huge reception.
When in fact connects two main clauses by discrediting the first clause. It always introduces the second clause.	(c) It sounds like he is happy since the divorce **when in fact** he is quite miserable.
Regardless of means "in spite of."	(d) **Regardless** of the outcome, they want to remain friends.
Instead is a transition word, whereas *instead of* is followed by a noun phrase.	(e) They didn't divorce. **Instead**, they stayed together and worked on their marriage. (f) They stayed together **instead of divorcing**.
Rather than may be followed by a noun phrase or by the simple form of the verb.	(g) **Rather than a divorce**, they decided on a separation. (h) **Rather than divorce**, they decided to work on their marriage.

8.1 Editing Practice

Correct the error in each sentence, where necessary.

1. He was very faithful to his wife rather than disturbs the trust they had built up.
2. Regardless of he was a manager of a large bank, his wife handled the finances at home.
3. They called off the wedding. After, they had to contact all the guests to tell them.
4. She was in love again regardless being hurt so many times before.
5. He appeared calm during the wedding ceremony; when in fact, he was so nervous that he had forgotten to bring the rings.
6. Regardless of they were angry, they were able to discuss what had happened.
7. She didn't like to go fishing with her husband. Instead of, she stayed in the cabin and read a good book.
8. Rather have his wife be a homemaker, he encouraged her to work.
9. She froze meals before she went away instead her leaving nothing for her husband to eat.
10. They stopped watching TV during dinner. After they communicated with each other more.
11. Rather than have his wife works, he wanted her to stay home.

UNIT 13 Adverb Clauses and Related Connectors

9 PREPOSITIONS AND PHRASAL VERBS

about, on	with a topic	**about** marriage; **on** the topic
about, around	approximate	**about** 20 people; **around** 40 degrees
in	for money, languages, a condition	**in** yen, **in** English, **in** good repair, **in** color
against	touching; in conflict or opposition	**against** the wall; two **against** one; **against** the divorce
by, near, beyond	with time	**by** 10:00; **near** noon; **beyond** 8:30

Phrasal Verbs with about, on, by

(a) They need to **think about** that more. They haven't **talked about** it enough. *(consider) (discuss)*
(b) They haven't **told** us **about** having any problems in their marriage. *(inform)*
(c) Be sure to **look in on** Grandma when you're in her neighborhood. *(check)*
(d) You can **drop in on** her. You don't have to phone ahead. *(visit, usually without notice)*
(e) Her family **looked down on** him because he was from a lower social class. *(scorn)*
(f) We **cut down on** expenses by going out for dinner less. *(reduce)*
(g) Their friends didn't **pick up on** the fact that they weren't getting on well. *(notice, understand)*
(h) She **stood by** her husband no matter what. *(support)*
(i) My parents **lived by** a very strict moral code. *(follow)*
(j) If you **go by** a store on your way home, pick us up some milk. *(pass)*

See Appendix D for more phrasal verbs.

9.1 Preposition Practice

Complete the sentences with *about, on, in, around, against, by, near,* or *beyond.*

1. Did I tell you _____ the lecture we attended yesterday? The professor was speaking _____ the topic of divorce customs in different cultures.

2. I am not _____ divorce; sometimes it is very necessary. However, if more people lived _____ the rules, there would be less unhappiness _____ marriage. Couples should make a commitment to stand _____ each other through thick and thin.

3. If we are going to cut down _____ the number of divorces, we are going to have to think _____ ways to help people make better marriage choices.

4. Their divorce cost about $10,000 _____ German marks.

5. _____ the time their child was born, they knew their marriage was _____ bad shape.

6. There were _____ 30 people in the reception line, so we decided to congratulate the bride and groom later.

7. I used to look down _____ the idea of arranged marriages, but now I realize that they have some benefits.

8. Although her parents were _____ the marriage, they supported her decision.

9.2 Practice with Phrasal Verbs

Supply the missing preposition.

1. Treating others as you would like to be treated is a good rule to live _____.
2. My parents taught me not to look down _____ people who were less fortunate than we were.
3. Please feel free to drop in _____ us any time you're in the neighborhood.
4. Why are you telling me _____ this now? I should have heard of this much earlier.
5. He never picks up _____ her self-centeredness. He thinks she's a very generous person.
6. "Stand _____ Your Man" was a very popular song about giving your husband emotional support.
7. Could you look in _____ the children? They have been quiet for a long time and I'm wondering what they're up to.
8. Let's talk with your father _____ it before we make a decision.
9. If we cut down _____ fat intake, we'll be a lot healthier.

UNIT 13 Adverb Clauses and Related Connectors

LISTENING TEST

Listen and circle the letter of the statement which best describes the situation.

1. a. I stayed home.
   b. I went to a movie.
   c. I studied.

2. a. I had a terrible time because I got sick.
   b. I couldn't go on the trip because I got sick.
   c. The trip was fine even though I got sick.

3. a. Tom wanted to tell her the truth even though it might hurt her feelings.
   b. Tom decided not to tell her the truth because it might hurt her feelings.
   c. Tom didn't think it would hurt her feelings to tell the truth.

4. a. I had a car once.
   b. Having a car allowed me to go away on weekends.
   c. I went away for weekends even without having a car.

5. a. It was impossible to look for it.
   b. We knew where to look.
   c. We looked everywhere for it.

6. a. They haven't decided where they want to have the wedding.
   b. They decided on a place but it wasn't available for the wedding.
   c. They are going to have the wedding at the place they decided on.

7. a. Their parents made the wedding a fine ceremony.
   b. Not everyone was happy about the marriage.
   c. The wedding wasn't sad because everyone was there.

8. a. Everyone expected their fighting to last.
   b. Their fighting surprised everyone.
   c. People expected their fighting to cause their marriage to fail.

9. a. Because of the divorce they will see little of their father.
   b. The custody arrangement means that they will see both parents equally.
   c. Unless their parents agree on custody, they will not see both of them a lot.

10. a. They expected to have a wonderful time.
    b. They were surprised that they had a wonderful time.
    c. They felt very bad.

UNIT 13 Courtship, Marriage, and Divorce

QUIZ YOURSELF

Circle the letter of the expression which has the same meaning as the underlined words.

1. Due to so many women working outside the home, family life has changed dramatically.
   a. Because   b. Since   c. Because of

2. When a wife works, men are relieved of the sole responsibility of breadwinning so that they can focus on working less and enjoying life more.
   a. for   b. As a result,   c. so long as

3. Though men and women are different, their roles in the home may be the same.
   a. Therefore,   b. Wherever   c. Although

4. When both the husband and wife work, more household chores need to be shared.
   a. Concurrently,   b. At the same time,   c. As long as

5. It is possible for a man to be happy even though his wife makes more money than he does.
   a. Nonetheless,   b. whereas   c. in spite of the fact that

6. Frank's wife got a better job in a different city. As a result, he gave up his job and followed her.
   a. Furthermore   b. So that   c. Therefore

7. Whenever their son became sick, Patty and Mike took turns staying home from work to care for him.
   a. As long as   b. While   c. Every time that

8. As soon as they got married, they combined all of their finances.
   a. Until   b. Once   c. After that,

9. While Mary liked classical music, her husband preferred country and western.
   a. Even though   b. Due to   c. Despite

10. Because of their constant fighting, they went to a marriage counselor to get help for their marriage.
    a. Until   b. Due to   c. Since

UNIT 14

Conditionals

Alternatives

1 REAL CONDITIONS

Real conditional clauses show results that are possible in the present or future or were possible or habitual in the past.

Present	(a) If women **work** outside the home, family life **changes**.
	(b) If you **live** near his folks, your marriage **may change**.
Future Use the present or present perfect tense in a future *if*-clause.	(c) If they **get** married, they **will have** a big wedding.
	(d) We **will read** about it if things **change / have changed**.
Past	(e) In more traditional times, if people **loved** each other, they **got** married.
	(f) If they **wanted** children, they **got** married.
	(g) They **had** to work hard if they **were supporting** large families.

302

1.1 Get in Motion: Real Conditionals

Complete these sentences about what happened in the past and now in your country / culture. Use the correct form of the verb in parentheses.

EXAMPLE
(get)   In the past if a woman ___got___ married, her property or money *became her husband's*.

Today if she ___gets___ married, her property or money *is still her husband's*. OR: *remains hers*.

1. (die, go)   Formerly, if the husband _____ before his wife, the marriage property _____ to . . .

   Now if he _____ before her, the joint property _____ to . . .

2. (break)   Years ago if someone _____ an engagement, . . .

   Nowadays, if someone _____ an engagement, . . .

3. (be)   In my grandmother's day if a woman _____ unhappily married, . . .

   Presently, if a woman _____ unhappy in her marriage, . . .

4. (find)   It used to be that if a husband _____ that his wife had been unfaithful to him, . . .

   Currently, if he _____ that she has been unfaithful to him, . . .

5. (discover)   Past times if a wife _____ that her husband had been unfaithful to her, . . .

   These days if a wife _____ that her husband has been unfaithful to her, . . .

6. (want)   In the past, if a couple in my culture _____ to live together without being married, . . .

   If a couple _____ to live together without being married today, . . .

7. (have)   Some time ago, if an unmarried woman in my culture _____ a baby, . . .

   If an unmarried woman in my culture _____ a baby today, . . .

UNIT 14 *Conditionals*

1.2 Present, Future, Past

Complete the sentences with information about your country. Use the correct form of the verb in parentheses.

1. In _____, if a woman _____ (be) married and
   (country)
   _____ (have) children, she usually _____
   (work / not work).

2. If she _____ (not have) children, a married woman usually
   _____ (work / not work).

3. When my parents were young, a woman _____ (work / not work) if she
   _____ (be) married. If she _____ (have)
   children, she _____ (work / not work).

4. I expect that my daughter _____ (work / not work) if she
   _____ (get) married. If she _____ (have)
   children, she _____ (work / not work).

5. In general, if both parents _____ (work) today, children
   _____ (benefit / not benefit) because . . .

6. Nowadays if children _____ (stay) home with their mother, children
   _____ (benefit / not benefit) because . . .

7. When I was a child, . . . _____ (take) care of me. If my parents
   _____ (want) to go out at night, . . .

1.3 Present, Future, Past

Discuss the possibilities.

EXAMPLE
You may never get married.
If I never get married, I may be very lonely when I am old and no longer working.

1. You may live to be 100.
   If I live to be 100, . . .

2. When Alicia gets married, she wants her husband to share everything 50–50.
   If he does, . . .
   If he doesn't help her, . . .

3. In more traditional times, people were expected to get married.
   If people didn't get married, . . .
   If a woman wasn't married by age 25, . . .

304   UNIT 14 *Alternatives*

4. Divorce is difficult for children, but so is an unhappy marriage.
   If a couple stays together because of the children, . . .
   If a child's parents get divorced, . . .

5. You may not be able to have children.
   If I am not able to have children, . . .

6. Most parents expect their children to get married.
   If their children don't get married, . . .

7. When Mrs. Franklin gets old, she expects to live with her children.
   If they take her into their house, . . .
   If they don't take her in, . . .

8. In some countries, the oldest son takes care of his parents when they get old.
   When my parents get old, . . .
   If I take care of them, . . .
   If I don't take care of them, . . .

2 UNREAL CONDITIONS: PRESENT AND FUTURE

Unreal conditional clauses talk about a world that does not exist. But if it did, these would be the results.

Use the **past form** of the verb to show that a present or future condition is not true. Use **would** in the result clause to show that the result is not true. **Could** and **might** are also possible.	(a) If she **loved** you, she **would marry** you. (But she doesn't love you.) (b) She **would marry** him if he **agreed** to have children. (But he hasn't agreed to.) (c) If you **knew** him better, you **might like** him more. (You don't know him very well. It's not definite that you will like him more, but it is possible.) (d) We **could see** a lot more of each other if we **lived** closer. (We don't live close to each other. We would have the ability to see each other more if we did.)
Were is the only form of the verb **be** that is used in a present unreal conditional clause.	(e) He is single. If he **were** married, he **would need** a larger apartment. (f) If I **were** you, I **would talk** to your parents about this situation.

2.1 Verbs in Conditionals

Underline the correct form of the verb in parentheses.

1. If they (decide / decided) to get married, we will give a big party for them.
2. If you want, I (will / would) change the date.
3. If they (are / were) happy together, would they be thinking about a divorce?
4. What (will / would) you do if you had to make this decision today?
5. I (will have / would never have) children if I weren't married.
6. Who gets custody of the children if a couple (gets / got) divorced?
7. If he (did not ask / doesn't ask) me to marry him, I will ask him.
8. If we (have / had) enough money, my wife wouldn't work.
9. If they have the wedding nearby, we (will / would) go.
10. We (won't / wouldn't) go if they had the wedding in New York.

2.2 Real or Unreal?

Are these conditions real or unreal? State the fact or possibility.

EXAMPLE
If I were married, I would want to have children.
Unreal. I am not married.

If I get married next year, I won't be able to have a big wedding.
Real. I may get married.

1. If Juan and Anna decide to get married, their parents will be very pleased.

   _____

2. If they weren't so different from each other, they wouldn't argue so much.

   _____

3. If women wait a long time to have children, they may have difficulties.

   _____

4. If I have children now, I might not be able to have a career.

   _____

5. If she won't marry him, he should try to find someone else.

   _____

6. If my parents argued, they went into a different room where we couldn't hear them.

   _____

7. If couples have a large wedding, it costs a huge amount of money.
   _____

8. If they had a big wedding, they would have to borrow money to pay for it.
   _____

9. If they were planning to get married, their parents would be delighted.
   _____

10. If my mother wasn't at home, she always had a baby-sitter for me.
    _____

2.3 Get in Motion

Eduardo is from Peru and his wife is from Australia. His parents live in Peru, but he and his wife live in Australia. Write unreal conditional sentences with the ideas below.

EXAMPLE
Eduardo's wife has a high-paying job in Australia. They do not live in Peru.
If Eduardo's wife ___didn't have___ a high-paying job in Australia, they ___would live___ in Peru.

1. Eduardo and Hannah are married. Eduardo's parents want them to have children.
   If they _____ married, his parents _____ them to have children.

2. Eduardo and Hannah are young. They don't want to have children now.
   If they _____ older, they _____ to have children now.

3. Eduardo and Hannah don't want children yet. Eduardo's parents' pressure bothers them.
   If they _____ children soon, his parents' pressure _____ them.

4. They live in Australia. They feel some pressure to have children.
   If they _____ in Peru, they _____ even more pressure to have children.

5. Hannah wants to have a career. She doesn't want to have children now.
   If she _____ to have a career, she _____ to have children.

(Continued on the next page)

6. They aren't living close to their families. They don't have family to help them take care of a baby.

   If they _____ close to their families, they _____ family to help them take care of a baby.

7. Eduardo works very hard. He doesn't have time to spend with children.

   If he _____ so hard, he _____ more time for children.

8. Hannah and Eduardo may decide not to have children. His parents will be terribly disappointed.

   If his parents _____ him to have children, they _____ so disappointed.

3 UNREAL CONDITIONS: PAST

Change the past tense in the *if*-clause to the **past perfect form** to show that an action was not true in the past.	(a) If she **had had** financial freedom, she probably **wouldn't have gotten** married. (*But she didn't have financial freedom.*)
The result clause usually has ***would + have** + past participle* in it.	(b) If they **had communicated** better, they **wouldn't have fought** so much. (*But they didn't communicate well.*)
It may also be in the continuous form: ***would + have** + past participle + ing* form of the verb.	(c) If they **had been communicating** better, they **wouldn't have been fighting** so much.
Might and ***could*** are also possible in the result clause.	(d) If she **had found** a job in her own country, she **might not have moved** to the United States.
(*See Box 6 for more about modals in conditionals.*)	(e) If she **had found** a job in her own country, she **could have stayed** there.

3.1 Get in Motion: Unreal Past Conditionals

Complete the sentences.

EXAMPLE
I was very happy there, so I wanted to stay.
If I *hadn't been* happy there, I wouldn't have wanted to stay.

Situation A

1. Fahad decided to marry his American girlfriend, Terry, instead of Leyla.

   If Fahad _____ to marry Terry, he would have married Leyla.

2. Fahad's parents were angry because they had arranged for him to marry Leyla.

   Fahad's parents might not have been so angry if they _____ for him to marry Leyla.

308 UNIT 14 *Alternatives*

3. Fahad could have decided to marry Leyla even though he didn't feel as strongly about her as he did about Terry.

   If he _____ to marry Leyla, he might have been unhappy.

4. Fahad's family felt embarrassed because Fahad and Terry moved back to Kuwait.

   If Fahad _____ to Kuwait with Terry, Fahad's family might not have been as embarrassed around Leyla's family.

5. In my opinion, Fahad did the (right / wrong) thing because if he _____,

   he _____.

Situation B

1. Kathleen and Roberto met at graduate school in the States. Kathleen wasn't sure about marrying Roberto, but he was going to go back to Venezuela and he could not take her if they didn't get married.
   If Roberto _____ back to Venezuela, Kathleen might not have married him.

2. After having three children, Kathleen and Roberto started arguing a lot. She felt very homesick. Kathleen might not have felt so homesick if she and Roberto _____ so much.

3. She wanted to go back to the States, but Roberto didn't want to lose his children.
   If they _____ children, Roberto might not have minded Kathleen's going back to the States.

4. Kathleen needed Roberto's permission to leave the country, so she pretended that she was just going on vacation with the children.
   If Kathleen _____ Roberto what she was planning, he wouldn't have let her leave.

5. Roberto never saw his children again. Kathleen took them to a place where Roberto could not find them.
   If Kathleen _____ the children, Roberto would have been able to continue to see them.

6. In my opinion, Kathleen did the (right / wrong) thing because if _____,
   _____.

UNIT 14 Conditionals

3.2 Unreal Conditionals

Complete the sentences.

EXAMPLE
Unver decided to go to the United States to study for an advanced degree in computer science.
If a university in Turkey had offered the program he wanted, he ___would not have gone___ to the States.

1. Unver met Jeanette when he was studying for an advanced degree at Ohio University.
   If he hadn't come to Ohio University, he _____ Jeanette.

2. Although he had planned to return to Turkey when he finished his degree, Jeanette would not leave the United States. He decided to marry her and to stay in the States.
   If Jeanette had been willing, Unver _____ to Turkey.

3. His family and his girlfriend, Yesim, in Istanbul were very unhappy about this news.
   If he hadn't met Jeanette, he _____ Yesim.

4. His company, which had paid for his studies in the United States, had hoped he would return to work for them again.
   If Unver had returned to Turkey, he _____ with his company.

5. Unver did not regret his decision. He had a very good job, a nice home, and a lovely family. However, he felt sad that his children weren't able to understand Turkish and he often missed his family and friends in Istanbul.
   If Unver had gone back to Turkey, his children _____ Turkish.

6. If I had been Unver, I would probably have made (the same / a different) decision because I _____ if I _____.

7. Rattikorn came to the United States to get a job because her aunt and uncle told her she would have more opportunities in the States.
   If she had had more opportunities to find a job in Thailand, she _____ to the United States.

8. She got a job with an international company and made a good salary. However, she missed her family.
   If she hadn't left Thailand, she _____ her family, but she also _____ such a good job.

9. She sent money to her family each month and they lived better because of this.
   If she _____ money to her family, they _____ so well.

10. Rattikorn wanted to go back to Thailand, but her job provided economic security for her family.
    If I _____ Rattikorn, I _____ (the same thing / something different) because _____.

310 UNIT 14 Alternatives

3.3 Present, Future, and Past Conditionals: Real and Unreal

Complete the sentences with an appropriate form of the verb in parentheses. Change the verbs to the negative if you want to.

1. It is hard when you marry someone from a different culture. If I _____ (fall) in love with someone from another country, I _____ (marry) that person. My family _____ (mind) if I _____ that.

2. Experts say that communication is the key to a successful marriage, but sometimes language difficulties make that very challenging. If you _____ (not, speak) the same language as your spouse, it _____ (be) harder to communicate clearly.

3. If you _____ (grow) up within one culture, you _____ (not, think) about the fact that your behavior may be different from behavior in another culture.

4. Cara moved to her husband's country. She took her in-laws a gift. Her husband was very embarrassed because the gift was not appropriate. If she _____ (tell) her husband what gift she _____ (plan) to give his parents, he _____ (explain) to her that was not a good idea. She _____ (not, give) them that if she _____ (know) that it was inappropriate.

5. However, problems with communication are not common only with mixed-culture marriages. Some people think that men and women have such different communication styles that miscommunication is inevitable. If men and women _____ (understand) each other better, there _____ (not, be) so many problems in marriages.

6. For example, Margo often wants to talk to her husband about the problems of her day. But if she _____ (tell) him any problems, she knows he _____ (try) to solve them. Men often think that if a woman _____ (share) a problem, they must do something about it.

7. Can marriage counselors really help couples communicate better? If I ever _____ (have) problems in my marriage, I _____ (go / not, go) to see a marriage counselor. I _____ (think / not, think) a marriage counselor is a good option for couples to consider.

4 CONDITION AND CONSEQUENCE EXPRESSIONS

Whether or not has these options for word order:	(a) **Whether** she wants to **or not**, she will have to go back to work. (b) **Whether or not** she wants to, she will have to go back to work.
Even if expresses a condition and emphasizes a contrast between the condition and the result.	(c) **Even if** women go back to work, they remain the primary caregivers in their families. (d) **Even if** I wanted to work, I'm not sure I could find a job.
Only if limits the condition to certain circumstances.	(e) I'll go back to work **only if** my husband insists.
Unless means "only if . . . not."	(f) I won't go back to work **unless** my husband insists.
These transition words also express conditions and results *if so* *regardless* *otherwise* *that being the case* Transition words require strong punctuation.	(g) She might return to work after the baby is born. **If so**, she will have to find day care. (h) They need more money. **Regardless**, she is not going back to work. (i) She will have to go back to work. **Otherwise**, they will not have enough money. (j) They are worried about their finances. **That being the case**, they have decided to wait to start a family.
Otherwise, or else, and ***if not*** are transitions which introduce a negative consequence.	(k) She needs to get a job; **otherwise / or else / if not**, they won't have enough money.
See Appendix F for more condition expressions.	

4.1 Get in Motion: Listening

A. Listen to three people describe their family situation. Match the families with the situations in the illustrations.

A.   B.   C.

B. Now listen again. Complete these sentences with the correct information.

Family 1:

1. Why have a baby _____ you want to bring it up?

2. If I _____ back to work, we'd _____ afford a bigger apartment and we _____ go out to dinner a few more times.

Family 2:

3. If I _____ work, I _____ happy.

4. Even if we _____ late getting home, we _____ worry.

Family 3:

5. If I _____ find another job right away, I probably _____ back to work, too.

6. Unless I _____ a job offer that _____ about a million dollars, I think I'll stay home until they _____ both in school.

UNIT 14 Conditionals   313

4.2 Restating with *Unless*

Restate the following sentences using *unless*.

EXAMPLE
If you don't come by 6:00, we won't make it to the movie.
Unless you come by 6:00, we won't make it to the movie.

1. Why have a baby if you don't want to bring it up?
2. We couldn't afford this house if my wife hadn't gone back to work.
3. If I didn't work, I wouldn't be happy.
4. If I'm not happy, the rest of the family won't be either.
5. If we can't find good day care, one of us won't go back to work.
6. We'll continue to have a nanny as long as we can afford it.
7. If my husband hadn't lost his job, he wouldn't have experienced being a house-husband.
8. If he doesn't find a job, he may get depressed staying at home.
9. If she gets a good job offer, she'll go back to work when her daughter is one year old.
10. If they don't have more children, they'll be able to afford to buy a house.

4.3 Condition / Consequence Expressions

A friend, Greg, is asking advice about child-care options. Decide which response fits your opinion. Then discuss this with a classmate. If your response is not there, add it to the choices.

1. GREG: "We have a very limited income and had planned to work a few years before having children, but now Lana is pregnant."
    (a) Even if he doesn't have much money, Lana should quit working after the baby is born. The most important thing is for a child to be with his / her mother in the early years.
    (b) Lana should continue to work. If not, they will have a lot of money problems and this will put more pressure on their family life.

2. GREG: "Lana could probably work part-time."
    (a) Lana should work part-time because that would help them out financially and still give time with the baby. Otherwise, she should get a full-time job.
    (b) Lana shouldn't work part-time unless they can find a really good day-care center or baby-sitter.

3. GREG: "Lana's salary is two times my salary."
    (a) He should stay home and let Lana return to work after the baby is born. Otherwise, they are going to have even less money to live on than they do now.
    (b) Regardless of who makes the most money, Lana should stay home. Otherwise, the baby will not have the love that a mother can give.

4. GREG: "I have more experience with children than Lana does."
    (a) Whether or not Greg has more experience, Lana should stay home with the baby.
    (b) Regardless of the fact that Greg is a man, he should stay home with the baby because he has more experience.

5. GREG: "A lot of our friends put their children in day care and both go back to work."

   (a) Unless you can find someone good to come to your home, both of you should not go back to work.
   (b) Whether you put the baby into an institutional day care or a private home day care, you should both go back to work. It is good for a child to be with other children during the day.

6. GREG: "Lana's mother has offered to move here to take care of the baby."

   (a) Even if it is a little inconvenient for you, you should have Lana's mother move in. It is always best to have family care for family.
   (b) Unless you get along really well with your mother-in-law, don't have her move in.

4.4 Talk It Over and Optional Writing

Do you agree or disagree with the following statements? Discuss them with a group of classmates. Then choose one statement and write your opinion in a paragraph.

1. Men and women are not naturally better at certain roles. If men could have babies, they would be nurturing just like women are now.

2. If both the husband and wife work, they should share household chores.

3. When a child becomes sick and both parents work, the person who is closest to the child should take time off from work to be with the child.

4. Caring for children at day-care centers is no different from caring for them at home.

5 MIXED PAST AND PRESENT CONDITIONALS

Depending on the situation, sentences may contain a mixture of past and present unreal conditionals.	(a) If I **had married** him, I **would be** a wealthy woman today. 　　　past unreal　　　　present unreal (I didn't marry him; thus, I am not wealthy.) (b) If I **were married**, I **wouldn't have had** money to go on that trip. 　　present unreal　　　　past unreal (I'm not married; therefore, I had enough money for the trip.)

UNIT 14 Conditionals

5.1 Mixed Time Conditions

Read the statement and then complete the mixed time sentence.

EXAMPLE
I got married young.
If I _hadn't gotten married_ young, I _would be_ more advanced in my career today.

1. I ate seafood in a restaurant last night.
   If I _____ seafood, I wouldn't _____ sick today.

2. I didn't go to see a doctor when I first got sick.
   If I _____ to see a doctor, I _____ better right now.

3. I shouldn't have ordered the seafood.
   If I _____ steak, I _____ fine today.

4. I love seafood.
   I _____ seafood last night if I _____ it so much.

5. I ate seafood and now I feel sick.
   If I _____ seafood, I _____ sick.

6. I grew up in small town.
   I _____ uneasy living in a big city if I _____ in a small town.

7. Patty grew up in a large family.
   If she _____ in such a large family, she _____ so comfortable having so many people visit her.

8. My parents divorced when I was young.
   I _____ so uneasy about getting married if my parents _____ when I was young.

9. I didn't have children.
   If I _____ them, we _____ probably _____ grandparents today.

10. I lived in a foreign country when I was in my twenties.
    I _____ so interested in international news today if I _____ abroad when I was young.

5.2 Listening: A Big Wedding?

A. Listen to the discussion and write T (true) or F (false) next to each statement.

_____ 1. Sylvia's mother wants her to have a big wedding.

_____ 2. They are not rich.

_____ 3. Sylvia's parents are going to pay for the whole wedding.

_____ 4. Sylvia's parents are divorced.

_____ 5. Gary had a large wedding.

_____ 6. Gary and his wife did not leave on their honeymoon right away.

_____ 7. Sylvia wants a small wedding.

_____ 8. Gary didn't enjoy himself at his wedding.

B. Complete these sentences with your opinions.

1. If Sylvia weren't the only daughter, . . .
2. If her parents were rich, . . .
3. If Sylvia's parents were paying for the whole wedding, . . .
4. If Sylvia's parents had not gotten divorced, . . .
5. If Sylvia's father had not remarried, . . .
6. If Gary had not had a large wedding, . . .
7. If Gary had not left on his honeymoon right away, . . .

UNIT 14 *Conditionals*

6 MODALS IN CONDITIONAL CLAUSES

Use **will / would** in the *if*-clause to show willingness.	(a) If you'**ll** help me, I'll be able to finish this very soon. (b) I'd appreciate it if you **would** give me a hand.
Use **can, could, be able to** to express ability or opportunity in the condition.	(c) If I **can** contact her today, I'll telephone you. (d) If I **could** type better, I could get a job. (e) If I **could** talk to her, she might change her mind. (f) If I **were able** to see her, I know I could make a difference.
We often express possibility or ability in the result clause with **can, could, may, might,** or **might have**.	(g) If your car isn't working, I **can** give you a ride. *(ability)* (h) If your car isn't working, I **could** give you a ride. *(possibility)* (i) If we had talked earlier, we **might** not **have had** this problem.
Conditions are weakened by using **were to, should, happen to,** and **should happen to**. They indicate that the speaker doesn't expect the condition to be met.	(j) If they **asked** my opinion, I would tell them. *(They might ask.)* (k) If they **were to / should** ask my opinion, I would tell them. *(It's a possibility that they will ask.)* (l) If they **happen to** ask my opinion, I would tell them. *(It's unlikely they will ask.)* (m) If they **should happen to** ask my opinion, I would tell them. *(It's highly unlikely they will ask.)*

6.1 Get in Motion

Read the situations and underline the correct form of the verbs in parentheses.

EXAMPLE

I was adopted. I wish I knew my birth parents.
If I (<u>could locate</u> / locate) my birth parents, I (wanted / <u>would want</u>) to meet them.

1. Kay's father left her family when she was a baby, so she has no memory of him.
   If she (were / had been) older when he left, maybe she (would have been able to remember / can remember) him.

2. Her mother never remarried. There was no step-father to be her father.
   If her mother (remarried / had remarried), Kay's step-father (can adopt / could have adopted) her since her father had disappeared.

318   UNIT 14 *Alternatives*

3. Now that she is grown and a mother herself, Kay sometimes wonders about her birth father. She thinks he still lives in their city.

   She wonders what (happens / would happen) if she (can / could) find her birth father or if she (were to / had) run into him by accident one day. If he (looked / had looked) like her, she (might be able to recognize / might have recognized) him. However, she's not sure.

4. She is also worried about her mother's feelings. How (would / could) her mother react if she (could find / had found) her birth father?

5. She also doesn't know how her birth father would feel about seeing her. If he (has felt / feels) guilty all these years, he (should not want / might not want) to have any contact with her.

6. Then she (might feel / were to feel) rejected if her birth father (didn't want / would not want) to know her.

6.2 Modals in Conditions

A. Read the situations, and complete the sentences with the correct form of the verb and a modal when indicated.

1. Margaret had a baby boy when she was in her early twenties. Since she was unable to support the child, she gave him up for adoption.

   If Margaret _____ (*modal*, support) her child, she

   _____ (not, give) him up for adoption.

2. A few years later she married a man and had three lovely children—another boy and two younger girls. Over the years she often thought about her first child, the one she had given away. She was never able to forget her first child, but she never told her husband about him.

   If she _____ (*modal*, talk) to her husband about it,

   she _____ (*modal*, feel) better.

3. If she _____ (*modal*, forget) her first child,

   she _____ (not, feel) so guilty for all those years.

4. She wondered how his life had been. However, she did not search for that boy out of respect for her husband. When her husband died, she finally began to look for her son.

   If she _____ (respect) her husband's feelings so much,

   she _____ (*modal*, begin) to look for her first son earlier.

5. When she finally found him, a successful grown man with a family of his own, they began a mother–son relationship.

   If he _____ (not, want) to, they _____

   (*modal*, not, develop) a successful mother–son relationship.

(*Continued on the next page*)

6. Margaret's two daughters had no problem accepting a new brother into the family, but her second son was very jealous of the "new" son. Although Margaret had gained her lost son, her relationship with her other son suffered greatly.

   If Margaret _____ (never, contact) her first son, her second son _____ (modal, experience) these unhappy feelings of jealousy.

7. If one of your parents suddenly _____ (tell) you about another brother or sister, how _____ you _____ (feel)? _____ you _____ (modal, accept) this new member of your family?

B. Discuss this situation with your classmates.

1. What should / could each person have done differently?
2. What should happen now? Whose rights are more important — the child's or those of the birth parents?

6.3 Modals in Conditions

In pairs, discuss what the result could be for these *if*-clauses.

1. If I couldn't have children, I might . . .
2. If I couldn't adopt a baby, I might . . .
3. I know a couple who couldn't have children. If they could have adopted a child, they might have . . .
4. My neighbors are having trouble finding a baby to adopt. If they can't find a baby in their own country to adopt, they . . .
5. They . . . if another country would let them adopt a baby.
6. If they . . . be away from work for six weeks, they won't be able to meet the residency requirement to adopt in some Latin American countries.
7. If they . . . a baby from another country, that baby . . .
8. If they . . . a baby from another country, they should . . .
9. If the birth mother will provide information about her medical history, they will be able to . . .
10. If the birth mother should want her name to remain a secret, the adopted child may . . .
11. If the adopted child should want to find her birth mother some day, . . .

6.4 Talk It Over and Optional Writing

Discuss these questions with a group of classmates. Then write a paragraph about your group's opinion.

1. What are the advantages and disadvantages of allowing childless couples to adopt babies from another country or culture?
2. Are adopted children treated differently from birth children in your country?

7 REDUCED AND IMPLIED CONDITIONAL CLAUSES

If the subject of the conditional clause and the main clause are the same, you may reduce the clause by using *if*, *whether*, or *unless* + an adjective or past participle.	(a) **Whether a single parent is divorced or never married**, she will have a difficult time raising a child. (b) **Whether divorced or never married**, a single parent will have a difficult time raising a child. (c) **Unless they were married**, they could not travel together in that country. (d) **Unless married**, they could not travel together in that country.
If the subject in the conditional clause is the false subject *it*, you may also reduce it.	(e) **If it is possible**, they want to hire a woman to come to the house to take care of the baby. (f) **If possible**, they want to hire a woman to come to the house to take care of the baby.
For emphasis, you may replace the *if* in *if*-clauses with *should*, *had*, and *were* and then change the word order.	(g) **If she should call**, tell her I'll be back in an hour. (h) **Should she call**, tell her I'll be back in an hour. (i) **If she had known** the truth, she would have told us. (j) **Had she known** the truth, she would have told us. (k) **If she were here**, she could tell us. (l) **Were she here**, she could tell us.
Some conditions are implied, that is, not directly stated, with an *if*- and a result-clause.	(m) She would have stayed home to take care of the children, but they needed two incomes. *(If they hadn't needed two incomes, she would have stayed home to take care of the children.)* (n) She wouldn't have worked otherwise. *(If she didn't have to work, she wouldn't have.)*

7.1 Reduced Clauses

Underline the reduced clauses in these sentences.

EXAMPLE

<u>Had I known they were in town</u>, I would have invited them to dinner.

1. Were you to ask him, I'm sure he'd tell you honestly if you could get a raise.
2. I know he'd have given you one, had it been possible.
3. Had you asked him before the holidays, he would have been more receptive.
4. Whether married or single, you have to take care of your parents when they get old.
5. Everyone, unless sick, has to attend this meeting.
6. We really need the money. If not, I wouldn't think of asking him.
7. Whether possible or not, I at least have to try.
8. Proceed as normal, unless advised otherwise.

7.2 Implied Clauses

Circle the letter of the best conditional sentence to explain the implied condition.

1. I know he'd give you a ride, but he didn't drive.
    a. If he drives, he'll give you a ride.
    b. If he had driven, he would give you a ride.
    c. If he had driven, he would have given you a ride.

2. You have no alternative. You have to speak to him.
    a. If you didn't have an alternative, you would have to speak to him.
    b. If you had an alternative, you wouldn't have to speak to him.
    c. If you had an alternative, you wouldn't have had to speak to him.

3. I would have asked him a couple of weeks ago, but I didn't have the nerve.
    a. If I had had the nerve, I would have asked him.
    b. If I had the nerve, I would ask him.
    c. If I have the nerve, I would ask him.

4. It's late. Otherwise, we wouldn't have to go.
    a. If it had been late, we would have had to go.
    b. If it weren't late, we wouldn't have to go.
    c. If it were late, we would have to go.

5. We didn't have the picnic because of the rain.
    a. If it hadn't rained, we would have had the picnic.
    b. If it had rained, we wouldn't have had the picnic.
    c. If it rained, we wouldn't have had the picnic.

6. But for the expense, we would take that cruise to Alaska.
    a. If it weren't so expensive, we wouldn't have taken the cruise to Alaska.
    b. If it weren't so expensive, we would take the cruise to Alaska.
    c. If it hadn't been so expensive, we would have taken the cruise to Alaska.

8 AS IF / AS THOUGH

As if / as though introduce adverb clauses of manner. These clauses are often in sentences with **look, seem, act,** or **behave.**

If there is a possibility that the statement is **true**, use the **real conditional**.	(a) They look **as if** they **are** happily married. *(I think they are.)*
If the statement is **not true**, use the **unreal conditional**.	(b) They act **as if** they **were** happily married. *(But they aren't happily married.)* (c) The newlyweds acted **as though** they **had been** married for years. *(But they hadn't been married for years.)*
You may reduce these clauses to *as if / as though* + an adjective, prepositional phrase, or infinitive.	(d) He lived his married life **as though he were single.** (e) He lived his married life **as though single.** (f) **As if they were in a fog**, the relationship continued with no clear direction. (g) **As if in a fog**, the relationship continued with no clear direction. (h) **As if she wanted to forget** the past, she changed her name after the divorce. (i) **As if to forget** the past, she changed her name after the divorce.
In conversation, *like* is commonly used to mean *as if*.	(j) He looked **like he had seen a ghost.** (k) They acted **like everything was OK.**

8.1 Get in Motion

Complete the sentences with the correct form of the verb in parentheses. How would you complete these sentences in your language?

1. He ate as though he _____ (be) a bear.
2. They were so happy that they acted as if they _____ (be) crazy.
3. After three years, we talked as though we _____ (never, be) separated.
4. She moved across the room as though she _____ (walk) on air.
5. She waited on her husband as if he _____ (be) a king.
6. The house felt empty, as if someone _____ (die).
7. When he came out of the boss's office, he smiled as if he _____ (swallow) a goldfish.
8. After that stressful experience, he felt like he _____ (be) through the wringer.

UNIT 14 Conditionals

8.2 Condition and Manner Expressions

A. Circle the best choice for each sentence.

(1) (If / As if) you have to make a tough decision, it can be hard to choose between two very attractive alternatives. Remember that you have control over the decision-making process, but (2) (if / though) you think you can control the results of your decision, you will be very frustrated. Therefore, don't approach the decision (3) (if / as if) you were going to control the results. In the same way, don't be surprised (4) (as if / if) you do feel frustrated.

To begin, write down what your needs are (5) (even if / if) they seem to be contradictory. Then rank your needs. (6) (As if / If) they seem contradictory, choose the most attractive one. For example, (7) (if / as if) you are looking for a new job, would you prefer a higher salary or more control over your work hours? Would you prefer a more interesting job (8) (unless / if) it meant moving from your present location?

Next, get a lot of information (9) (as if / if) possible to help you make the decision. If you choose path A, what are the advantages and disadvantages? If you feel (10) (if / as if) you are reacting emotionally to the decision, try to step back and be as objective as possible. Determine which risks you are willing to take. (11) (Unless / As if) you are willing to take them, consider what the safest alternative is. Choose the one which has the best chances for success. (12) (Or else / Unless) choose the risky alternative which may result in failure, but a failure that you can live with. Finally, picture how you would deal with negative consequences.[1]

B. Discuss this question with a group of classmates. Then write a paragraph about a decision you made.

What is a difficult decision you had to make? Describe the process you went through to make the decision. Did you use any of the suggestions in A? Be sure to explain what would have happened if you had chosen a different alternative.

---

[1] Adapted from: *Communication Briefings: Ideas That Work,* Volume XII, Number III, p. 8.

9 TROUBLE SPOTS: WISHES AND HOPES

Use the **conditional to express wishes** since the wish is for something which is not true.	(a) We don't have children, but we wish we **did**. *(present)* (b) We can't have children, but we wish we **could**. *(present)* (c) I can't see you tonight. I wish I **could**. *(future)* (d) They won't go to the reception, but I wish they **would**. *(future)* (e) We couldn't have more children. We wish we **could have had** two more. *(past)*
Use **were** for the verb **to be** in present tense wishes no matter what the subject is.	(f) I am not married, but I wish I **were** married. (g) She's still dating him but she wishes she **weren't**.
In contrast, use **hope** for something that is true or possible.	(h) I hope this **isn't** too difficult. (i) I hope they **will be** happy together. (j) I hoped they **would be** happy together, but they weren't.

9.1 Get in Motion: Expressing Wishes

Circle the letter of the best choice.

1. I like to read about famous people in the news. I wish the newspaper _____ more stories about famous people.

    a. have   b. had   c. had had

2. I envy the writer who gets to interview famous people. I hope I _____ a job like that some day.

    a. had   b. get   c. have

3. A friend of mine went to a wedding and a prince from Saudi Arabia was there. I wish I _____ there.

    a. were   b. had been   c. went

4. Movie stars have such exciting lives. I wish my life _____ more exciting.

    a. is   b. be   c. were

5. They never have to worry about money. I really wish I never _____ to!

    a. have   b. had   c. having

(Continued on the next page)

6. Of course, I bet famous people wish they _____ walk down the street without being recognized.
   a. would b. can c. could

7. I'm sure they sometimes wish that photographers _____ follow them around all the time.
   a. wouldn't b. hadn't c. can

8. Sometimes they probably wish they _____ famous at all.
   a. aren't b. weren't c. could be

9. Do you ever wish you _____ be someone different?
   a. may b. would c. could

10. My grandfather used to say that he wished he _____ 50 years later.
    a. could be born b. were born c. could have been born

9.2 Talk It Over

Discuss these questions with a classmate.

1. Do you ever wish you were someone else? Did you when you were younger?
2. Do you ever wish your life were different?

9.3 Wishes about the Weather

4-Day Forecast

Day 1: Tomorrow fog in morning, afternoon sun, high in the 70s

Day 2: Friday, chance of thunderstorms, high in the 70s

Day 3: Saturday, cloudy, afternoon sun, high in the high to low 80s

Day 4: Sunday, sunny all day, high in the low 80s

A. Complete the sentences with wishes. Base your ideas on the weather information above.

1. It's going to be _____ tomorrow afternoon. I wish I
   (weather)
   _____ to be inside working all day.

2. They are expecting _____ on Friday. I wish it
   (weather)
   _____ sunny so that we could have our baseball game.

3. It's going to be _____ on Saturday morning. I wish it
   (weather)
   _____ sunny. We could get up early and go bicycling.

4. Sunday sounds like it's going to be a great day to be outside because it's going to be
   _____. I hope I _____.
   (weather)

326   UNIT 14 *Alternatives*

International Temperatures

C = Cloudy   R = Rain   S = Sunny
W = Windy   T = Thunderstorm   Sh = Showers

	Yesterday			Tomorrow		
	Hi	Lo	Weather	Hi	Lo	Weather
Athens	92	69	S	91	70	S
Beijing	76	55	S	74	55	C
Copenhagen	63	54	R	61	57	Sh
Helsinki	56	46	W	58	49	Sh
Riyadh	106	78	S	100	65	S
Winnipeg	64	41	R	78	59	T

B. Complete the sentences. Base your ideas on the information in the weather chart above.

1. It was so cold here. I wish I _____ in Riyadh yesterday. It was 106 there and _____.
   (weather)

2. I wish I _____ fly to Athens, but I don't have the money.
   (modal)
   Tomorrow they are going to have a high of _____ degrees.

3. We were in Winnipeg yesterday. It was _____ all day. I wish we
   (weather)
   _____ somewhere else.

4. I wish it _____ so _____ in Helsinki yesterday.
   (weather)
   We wanted to walk around and see more of the city, but we ended up staying in our hotel most of the day.

5. It's going to be _____ in Beijing tomorrow. I wish it
   (weather)
   _____ clear.

6. A: What does the paper say about the weather tomorrow in Copenhagen? We have to fly in there en route to Germany.
   B: They're expecting _____.
   (weather)
   A: I wish it _____ to rain. I wanted to do some sightseeing between flights.

C. Where is the weather better than where you are? Complete these sentences. Write the correct form of the verb in parentheses and give your ideas.

1. I wish I _____ (be) in _____ yesterday because it was cooler / warmer than here.

2. I wish I _____ (fly) to _____ tomorrow because it is going to be _____.

3. I'm glad I _____ (be) not in _____ because it's . . .

4. I hope the weather tomorrow _____ (be) . . .

UNIT 14 Conditionals

10 PREPOSITIONS AND PHRASAL VERBS

for	indicates a relationship to a goal, a distance, length of time, or exchange	**for** a college degree, **for** 10 miles, **for** 2 hours, exchange X **for** Y
like / as	indicates comparison	**like** a rock, **like** mad, **as** a modern family
on	indicates manner	**on** sale, **on** credit, **on** a loan, **on** a whim
Adjectives + Prepositions	(a) He's **famous for** being **prepared for** a test long before the rest of them. (b) I was **ready for** the worst. I knew I wasn't really **qualified for** the job. (c) **Good for** you. Your work is more than **sufficient for** this class. (d) Do you think this exercise is **suitable for** intermediate level students?	
Phrasal Verbs	(e) Did anyone **call for** me? *(telephone)* (f) The protesters **called for** change. *(demand)* (g) She **fell for** that excuse in a minute. *(believe)* (h) I don't think I'm **cut out for** this line of work. *(be appropriate for)* (i) The bald eagle **stands for** the United States. *(represent)* (j) Did you **ask for** help? *(request)* (k) How can you **account for** your good fortune? *(explain)* (l) I've been **looking for** you for two hours. *(search)*	

See Appendix D for more phrasal verbs.

10.1 Preposition Practice

With a partner, complete these sentences. Use *for*, *like*, *as*, or *on*.

1. We worked _____ mad to finish the project
   (very fast)
   _____ time.

2. It's really cold _____ this time of year.

3. I see you have your work clothes _____. You look ready
   _____ action.

4. He shot out of here _____ a house on fire.
   (fast and forceful)

328   UNIT 14 *Alternatives*

5. Whatever problems they faced _____ parents, they worked _____ them _____ one.
(united)

6. When she walked into the art gallery opening, she felt _____ a fish out of water. She'd never been around artists before.
(awkward)

7. He can do it _____ his own. He's very independent for a seven-year-old.

8. I've been _____ edge all day. I always get nervous before I speak in front of a crowd. _____ the other hand, my mother is always very relaxed doing public speaking.

9. Isn't that just _____ him? It's so typical of him to arrive an hour late. When have you known him to be _____ time?

10. A: What are we having _____ dinner?

    B: As a matter of fact, I've fixed something special.

    A: Good. Let's relax and talk _____ a while before we eat.

11. _____ a rule, we always rent a video _____ Friday night entertainment.

12. She talks _____ miles on end. No one gets a word in edgewise.
(endlessly)

13. _____ a last resort, we booked a ski holiday in Colorado. We didn't know how the skiing would be around here.

14. They treat him _____ one of the family since he is a close friend of their son's.
(very familiarly)

15. A: Are they in town or away _____ vacation?

    B: They went to Toronto. You can get a good hotel there _____ $60 a night right now.

16. A: Are you _____ good terms with your brother-in-law these days?

    B: _____ a matter of fact, we are getting _____ very well at present.

17. _____ luck would have it, I found a good resource _____ line. So I don't need to go to the library after all.
(By chance)
(on the computer)

UNIT 14 Conditionals

10.2 Practice with Phrasal Verbs

Ask your partner the following questions. Answer in complete sentences.

1. What does the design on your national flag stand for?
2. What foods are not good for you?
3. What do you think your used books would sell for?
4. Who will care for you when you are old?
5. What kind of studying does that class call for?
6. Are you prepared for the next test?
7. What will it take to get qualified for the career you want?
8. What are you not cut out for?
9. What is your hometown famous for?
10. What are you looking for at this time in your life?

LISTENING TEST

Circle the letter of the sentence which best describes what you hear.

1. a. I invited my uncle.
   b. I didn't want to invite my uncle.
   c. My uncle was out of town.

2. a. You weren't planning to go.
   b. You didn't call.
   c. You called.

3. a. What were the plans in case of bad weather?
   b. What went wrong?
   c. What was the weather?

4. a. I'm going no matter what you decide.
   b. I won't go if you don't go.
   c. I'm not going.

5. a. We were able to help you.
   b. It is possible that we could have helped you.
   c. You might not have told us.

6. a. You might see him.
   b. You are definitely going to see him.
   c. You need to talk to him.

7. a. If I help you, will you tell me?
   b. I'm too busy.
   c. I am willing to help you.

8. a. We will not invite them if they are divorced.
   b. We will invite them no matter what.
   c. We might not have to invite both of them.

9. a. If she didn't need the money, she wouldn't work.
   b. We can't understand why she works.
   c. She wants to work no matter what.

10. a. They are not married.
    b. They have been married for four years.
    c. They have not been married for years.

UNIT 14 Conditionals

QUIZ YOURSELF

Circle the letter of the error in each of the following sentences.

1. If a woman (a) was unable to become pregnant, she (b) can have another woman give birth to her husband's child. The other woman (c) is called a surrogate mother.

2. (a) Unless a couple will have about $30,000, it (b) will be hard to find a woman to be the surrogate mother. This money (c) covers the medical and insurance expenses of the pregnant woman and a $10,000 fee.

3. About 600 babies (a) have been born in the United States through surrogate mothers since 1976. This trend will probably grow (b) if the practice (c) will remain legal.

4. (a) Were you to live in England, you (b) would not be able to hire a surrogate. In the same way, some states have banned the practice of surrogates because it is a very controversial topic (c) as if you consider the many legal and social problems.

5. (a) What if a woman in the same family agrees to be the surrogate? A woman in South Africa gave birth to triplets for her daughter, who could not become pregnant. (b) If this happens, is the child's mother legally its mother or its grandmother? What other problems (c) maybe happen, if this continues?

6. (a) Had one woman considered the difficulty of giving up her child, she (b) might not have become a surrogate. She was the mother in the famous "Baby M" case in the 1980s. This surrogate mother refused to give up the baby and broke the contract with the parents. If the parents had had any idea that this would happen, they never (c) would do it.

7. This was an upsetting case for everyone involved. Some people feel (a) even if there (b) had been better guidelines, it still (c) will have been a difficult situation.

8. At first, the courts reacted (a) as if the surrogate mother (b) has no rights since she (c) had signed a contract to give the child up.

9. Later, the Supreme Court said that the surrogate mother (a) could keep the child. (b) As if courts have upheld the contracts, they (c) have allowed surrogate mothers to visit their children.

10. Some people wish that these matters (a) will be dealt with privately and that the state (b) would not ban surrogate mother contracts. (c) If legal, would you support the rights of couples to hire surrogate mothers?

APPENDIX A

NON-CONTINUOUS VERBS

Non-continuous or **stative** verbs may not be used in any of the continuous tenses, except when they have an active meaning.

1 Verbs of Perception or Physical Sensation:
hear, notice, overhear, see, smell, sound, taste

Exceptions:
(a) Are you **hearing** from her? (*getting communication*)
(b) I **am seeing** a lot of him lately. (*meeting with*)
(c) She **is smelling** the roses in the garden. (*action of smelling*)
(d) They **are sounding** the dinner bell. Let's go! (*causing a sound*)
(e) She's **tasting** the soup for more salt. (*trying*)

2 Verbs of Mental Perception:
believe, desire, doubt, feel, find, forget, forgive, know, mean, please, prove, recognize, remember, suppose, think, trust, understand

Exceptions:
(f) He's **feeling** each apple to get the best ones. (*touching*)
(g) We've been **meaning** to get together for months. (*intending*)
(h) Are you **thinking** about taking that job? (*considering*)
(i) She **isn't remembering** things correctly. Is something wrong? (*recalling*)

3 Verbs of Condition:
apply to, be, belong, concern, consist of, contain, cost, depend on, deserve, equal, fit, have, include, involve, lack, matter, owe, own, possess, remain, require, resemble, result, tend, weigh

Exceptions:
(j) He's **applying** the rules to this set of data. (*using*)
(k) He **is being** very difficult today. (*behaving*)
(l) They **are depending** on you to tutor them. (*trusting*)
(m) We're **having** trouble with the television. (*experiencing*)
(n) They **are fitting** me for new glasses. (*causing to fit*)
(o) They **are** always **involving** me in their problems. (*causing to be included*)
(p) Are you **weighing** your fruit before you buy it? (*putting on a scale*)

4 Verbs of Attitudes and Emotions:
adore, agree, appear, appreciate, care, differ, disagree, dislike, distrust, doubt, guess, hate, hope, imagine, impress, like, love, mind, need, prefer, seem, trust, want, wish

Exceptions:
(q) My favorite actor **is appearing** in that film. (*performing*)
(r) I **am guessing** that it will take 4 hours to prepare for that test. (*estimating*)
(s) He's **imagining** relaxing on a beach in Mexico. (*picturing in his mind*)
(t) She's **minding** the front desk while Marie takes a break. (*taking care of*)
(u) Money **is not wanting** in that family. (*lacking*)

APPENDIX B

SPELLING RULES FOR VERBS

RULE 1

If a verb ends in -e, drop the e.

	Present Participle	Present Tense 3rd Person Singular	Regular Past Tense
	Add -ing	add -s	add -ed
Examples: hope	hoping	hopes	hoped
live	living	lives	lived
refuse	refusing	refuses	refused

RULE 2

If a verb ends in -o, -(t)ch, -s, -sh, -x, or -z, add -es to the 3rd person singular.

	Present Tense 3rd Person Singular
Examples: go	goes
do	does
punch	punches
watch	watches
pass	passes
wish	wishes
box	boxes
buzz	buzzes

RULE 3

If a verb ends in a -y and there is a consonant before the -y, change the -y to -i and add -es in the 3rd person singular and past tense.

	Present Participle	Present Tense 3rd Person Singular	Regular Past Tense
Examples: copy	copying	copies	copied
carry	carrying	carries	carried
study	studying	studies	studied

RULE 4

If a verb ends in a vowel and a single consonant and it has one syllable or an accented last syllable double the consonant in the present participle and the past tense.

	Present Participle	Present Tense 3rd Person Singular	Regular Past Tense
Examples: stop	stopping	stops	stopped
beg	begging	begs	begged
omit	omitting	omits	omitted
prefer	preferring	prefers	preferred

APPENDIX C

IRREGULAR VERBS

Base	Simple Past	Past Participle	Base	Simple Past	Past Participle
awake	awoke	awoken	fall	fell	fallen
			feed	fed	fed
bear	born	born	feel	felt	felt
beat	beat	beaten	fight	fought	fought
become	became	become	find	found	found
begin	began	begun	fit	fit	fit
bend	bent	bent	fly	flew	flown
bet	bet	bet	forbid	forbad / forbade	forbidden / forbid
bid	bid	bid			
bite	bit	bitten	forget	forgot	forgotten
bleed	bled	bled	forgive	forgave	forgiven
blow	blew	blown	freeze	froze	frozen
break	broke	broken			
bring	brought	brought	get	got	gotten (got [British])
build	built	built			
burn	burnt / burned	burnt / burned	give	gave	given
			go	went	gone
burst	burst	burst	grind	ground	ground
buy	bought	bought	grow	grew	grown
cast	cast	cast			
catch	caught	caught	hang	hung	hung
choose	chose	chosen	have	had	had
come	came	come	hear	heard	heard
cost	cost	cost	hide	hid	hidden / hid
creep	crept	crept			
cut	cut	cut	hit	hit	hit
			hold	held	held
deal	dealt	dealt	hurt	hurt	hurt
dig	dug	dug			
dive	dove (dived [British])	dived (dived [British])	keep	kept	kept
			knit	knit	knit
			know	knew	known
do	did	done			
draw	drew	drawn	lead	led	led
dream	dreamt / dreamed	dreamt / dreamed	leave	left	left
			lend	lent	lent
drink	drank	drunk	let	let	let
drive	drove	driven	lie	lay	lain
			light	lit / lighted	lit / lit
eat	ate	eaten	lost	lost	lost

Base	Simple Past	Past Participle	Base	Simple Past	Past Participle
make	made	made	slit	slit	slit
mean	meant	meant	speak	spoke	spoken
meet	met	met	spend	spent	spent
			spin	spun	spun
put	put	put	split	split	split
prove	proved	proven	spread	spread	spread
			spring	sprang	sprung
quit	quit	quit	stand	stood	stood
			steal	stole	stolen
read	read	read	stick	stuck	stuck
rid	rid	rid	sting	stung	stung
ride	rode	ridden	strike	struck	struck
ring	rang	rung	swear	swore	sworn
rise	rose	risen	sweep	swept	swept
run	ran	run	swim	swam	swum
			swing	swung	swung
say	said	said			
see	saw	seen	take	took	taken
seek	sought	sought	teach	taught	taught
sell	sold	sold	tear	tore	torn
send	sent	sent	tell	told	told
set	set	set	think	thought	thought
shake	shook	shaken	throw	threw	thrown
shine	shone	shone			
shoot	shot	shot	wake	woke	woken
shrink	shrank	shrunk	wear	wore	worn
shut	shut	shut	wet	wet	wet
sing	sang	sung	win	won	won
sink	sank	sunk	wind	wound	wound
sit	sat	sat	withdraw	withdrew	withdrawn
sleep	slept	slept	write	wrote	written
slide	slid	slid			

APPENDIX D

PHRASAL VERBS

Phrasal verbs can be **separable** or **inseparable**. They are marked by (S) or (I) in the list that follows.

(I) INSEPARABLE (may not be separated by an object)

Example: call for   (I)   *demand*
The students protesters are calling for change. They have been **calling for it** with protests that are sometimes violent. (**NOT** *calling it for*)

(S) SEPARABLE (may be separated by an object; must be separated by a pronoun object)

Example: call off   (S)   *postpone*
The students **called off** the last demonstration.
They **called it off**. (**NOT** *called off it*)

List of Phrasal Verbs

account for	(I)	explain
ask about	(I)	inquire
ask for	(I)	request
back away (from)	(I)	retreat
back down	(I)	yield
back off	(I)	yield
back out (of)	(I)	fail to fulfill, break a commitment
back up	(S)	support; reverse (vehicle); make a copy (computers)
be about	(I)	concern
be against	(I)	oppose
be back	(I)	return
be cut out for	(I)	be appropriate for
be in on	(I)	participate in
be into	(I)	be interested in, like
be out of	(I)	not have any more
be through	(I)	be finished
bear down (on)	(I)	press
bear up	(I)	show strength
bear with	(I)	show patience
blow over	(I)	stop; go away (a problem; a storm)
blow up	(S)	explode
break away (from)	(I)	become independent

break down	(I)	stop working
break down	(S)	analyze
break in (on)	(I)	interrupt
break off	(S)	end
break out	(I)	start suddenly
break out of	(I)	escape
break through	(I)	penetrate
break up	(S)	end
break up (with)	(I)	end (relationship)
break with	(I)	end (relationship)
bring about	(S)	cause
bring around	(S)	persuade
bring back	(S)	cause to return
bring down	(S)	cause to fall
bring in	(S)	introduce; produce
bring in	(I)	catch (criminals)
bring on	(S)	cause
bring out	(S)	produce
bring up	(S)	introduce
burn down	(S)	destroy by fire (building)
burn up	(S)	destroy by fire (paper)
call about	(I)	inquire
call back	(S)	recall
call for	(I)	demand; telephone
call off	(S)	postpone
call on	(I)	visit; ask to do

call up	(S)	phone
care about	(I)	think important
care for	(I)	like
carry off	(S)	do successfully
carry on (with)	(I)	continue in spite of change
carry out	(S)	fulfill
carry through	(S)	help continue
catch on	(I)	understand; become popular
catch up (with)	(I)	get to the same level
catch up on	(I)	get the news
check back	(I)	recheck
check in	(I)	report
check in on	(I)	visit to make sure
check off	(S)	mark
check out (of)	(I)	officially leave
check up (on)	(I)	visit to make sure
clean off	(S)	wipe
clean up	(S)	tidy
clear away	(S)	remove
clear off	(S)	remove
clear up	(S)	put in order; become better
close down	(S)	stop operation
close in on	(I)	surround
close up	(S)	block
come about	(I)	happen
come across	(I)	find
come along	(I)	accompany; advance
come around	(I)	visit
come around to	(I)	accept
come away	(I)	leave
come back	(I)	return
come between	(I)	cause trouble
come by	(I)	get; drop by for a visit
come down	(I)	decline
come down with	(I)	get an illness
come from	(I)	originate
come in	(I)	enter
come into	(I)	inherit
come off	(I)	happen; unfasten
come on	(I)	start
come out	(I)	appear; finish
come over	(I)	visit informally
come through	(I)	fulfill expectations
come through with	(I)	provide
come to	(I)	total
come up	(I)	happen
come up with	(I)	think of
count in	(S)	include
count on	(I)	depend on
cry out	(I)	scream
cry out against	(I)	protest
cut across	(I)	take short way; touch different levels or groups
cut back	(I)	reduce
cut down (on)	(I)	reduce
cut in (on)	(I)	interrupt
cut off	(S)	discontinue
cut out	(S)	cease
cut through	(I)	penetrate
divide into	(S)	partition
do away with	(I)	end
do in	(S)	kill
do over	(S)	repeat
do up	(S)	fix nicely
do with	(I)	need
draw away from	(I)	retreat
draw back from	(I)	recoil
draw on	(I)	use
draw out	(S)	extend
draw up	(S)	write
drop in on	(I)	visit without making arrangements first
even out	(S)	balance
even up	(S)	balance
face up to	(I)	confront bravely
fall back on	(I)	rely on
fall behind	(I)	lag
fall for	(I)	believe; become infatuated with
fall through	(I)	not work out
figure out	(S)	understand
fill in	(S)	complete
fill out	(S)	complete
fill up	(S)	make full
find out	(S)	discover
get ahead	(I)	succeed
get across	(S)	communicate; transverse
get along	(I)	leave
get along with	(I)	be congenial
get around to	(I)	finally attend to
get around	(I)	avoid

(*Continued on the next page*)

Appendix D   A-7

get at	(I)	reach
get away	(I)	escape
get away with	(I)	do without being caught
get back	(S)	return
get behind	(I)	support; lag
get between	(I)	cause trouble
get by	(I)	continue
get down	(S)	swallow
get down to	(S)	reduce
get in	(S)	be admitted
get off	(S)	escape being punished
get on	(I)	continue; age
get on with	(I)	be congenial; continue
get out	(I)	leave
get out of	(I)	escape
get over	(I)	recover
get through	(I)	reach; communicate
get together	(S)	unite
get up	(I)	arise
give away	(S)	donate
give back	(S)	return
give in	(I)	surrender
give off	(I)	emit
give out	(I)	distribute
give up	(I)	stop
go about	(I)	do
go against	(I)	oppose
go after	(I)	seek
go ahead	(I)	begin
go along	(I)	continue
go along with	(I)	support
go at	(I)	attack
go away	(I)	leave
go back	(I)	return
go by	(I)	pass
go down	(I)	decrease
go for	(I)	try to win
go off	(I)	explode; ring (alarm)
go on	(I)	continue
go on in	(I)	enter
go over	(I)	review
go through with	(I)	complete with difficulty
go under	(I)	sink
go up	(I)	increase
grow away from	(I)	become distant (relationship)
grow into	(I)	become
grow on	(I)	become comfortable with an idea; get used to
grow out of	(I)	become too big for
grow up	(I)	become mature
hand back	(S)	return
hand down	(S)	leave to younger people
hand in	(S)	submit
hand out	(S)	distribute
hand over	(S)	relinquish
hold back	(S)	control
hold down	(S)	control
hold off	(I)	delay
hold on	(I)	wait; continue
hold over	(S)	continue to a later time
hold up	(S)	block; rob; last / endure; delay
jump at	(I)	be eager for
jump on	(I)	criticize
jump in	(I)	volunteer
keep at	(I)	continue
keep down	(S)	control
keep on	(I)	continue
keep up	(S)	maintain
keep up with	(I)	maintain level
leave behind	(S)	fail to bring; outdistance
leave off	(I)	stop
leave out (of)	(S)	exclude
let in	(S)	admit
let down	(I)	disappoint
let on	(I)	tell
let out	(S)	express; enlarge; finish (movie; class; school)
let up	(I)	decrease
light up	(S)	give light to; begin (a cigarette)
live by	(I)	live near; follow (a code of conduct)
live down	(S)	cause to be forgotten
live on	(I)	subsist
live through	(I)	experience
live up to	(I)	meet expectations
lock away	(S)	keep safe
lock up	(S)	secure
look ahead	(I)	plan
look after	(I)	take care of
look around	(I)	observe or examine your surroundings

look at	(I)	watch
look back (on)	(I)	remember
look down on	(I)	scorn
look for	(I)	search
look in (on)	(I)	check
look into	(I)	investigate; do informal research
look alike	(I)	resemble
look on	(I)	regard
look over	(I)	examine
look through	(I)	examine
look up	(S)	research
look up to	(I)	respect
make out	(S)	understand
make over	(S)	change
make up	(I)	fabricate
make up for	(I)	compensate
mix up	(S)	confuse
move out of	(I)	leave an area
pass away	(I)	die
pass down	(S)	leave to younger people
pass off	(S)	deceive as
pass over	(S)	disregard
pass on	(I)	die; transfer
pay back	(S)	pay something owed
pay off	(S)	pay all of the debt
pay up	(I)	pay all of the debt
pick over	(S)	examine to choose
pick up	(S)	collect
pick up on	(I)	notice, figure out
play around with	(I)	try in different ways
point out	(S)	indicate
pull away from	(I)	start to move
pull back	(I)	retract
pull in	(I)	arrive (vehicle)
pull out of	(I)	leave a speace or a place (vehicle)
pull through	(S)	succeed with difficulties
pull up	(I)	come to a stop
put across	(S)	explain
put away	(S)	store; save
put back	(S)	return
put down	(S)	defeat
put in	(I)	spend (time); contribute
put off	(S)	delay
put on	(S)	cover
put out	(S)	extinguish (fire)
put together	(S)	form
put through	(S)	connect
put up with	(I)	tolerate
round off	(S)	finish
round up	(S)	gather
run across	(I)	meet or find accidentally
run after	(I)	chase
run away (from)	(I)	escape
run down	(S)	disparage; knock over with a vehicle
run into	(I)	meet accidentally
run off	(I)	escape
run out of	(I)	deplete, use up
run over	(I)	overflow; knock over with a vehicle; go beyond the time
run through	(I)	practice; use up
run up	(S)	cause to go up
see about	(I)	arrange
see off	(S)	say good-bye to someone going on a trip
see through	(I)	recognize the truth; continue to support
see to	(I)	take care of
sell out	(I)	sell everything
send back	(S)	return (by mail)
send for	(I)	request
send in	(S)	submit (by mail)
send off	(S)	mail
set about	(I)	start
set back	(S)	delay
set off	(I)	begin (a trip)
set out	(I)	begin (a plan)
set up	(S)	arrange
shut away (from)	(S)	isolate
shut down	(S)	cause to no longer work
shut off	(S)	disconnect
shut up	(S)	be quiet
show around	(S)	give a tour
show off	(S)	boast
show up	(I)	arrive; appear
sing along	(I)	join in song
stand against	(I)	oppose
stand between	(I)	separate; cause problems
stand behind	(I)	support

(Continued on the next page)

stand by	(I)	support
stand for	(I)	represent
stand in	(I)	substitute
stand up	(I)	work in spite of use
stand up for	(I)	support
stay in	(I)	remain inside
stay on	(I)	remain
stay up	(I)	not go to bed; remain at a high level
take after	(I)	resemble
take back	(S)	withdraw
take care of	(I)	look after
take down	(S)	break into its parts
take in	(S)	provide a home for
take off	(I)	leave;
	(S)	remove
take on	(I)	accept responsibility for
take over	(S)	take control of
take out	(S)	remove
take part	(I)	participate
take up	(S)	occupy; begin
talk about	(I)	discuss
talk back	(I)	speak with no respect
talk down to	(I)	speak to someone as if they are lower
talk (someone) into	(S)	persuade
talk (someone) out of	(S)	dissuade
talk over	(S)	discuss
talk up	(S)	make it sound good
think about	(I)	consider
think ahead	(I)	plan
think back on	(I)	remember
think over	(I)	consider
throw away	(S)	discard
throw in	(S)	supply extra
throw out	(S)	discard
throw up	(S)	vomit
try on	(S)	test the fit
try out	(S)	test
try out for	(I)	compete for
tune in on	(I)	get a broadcast
tune out	(S)	stop listening to
turn against	(I)	become opposed to
turn away	(S)	refuse
turn back	(I)	refuse; lessen volume / intensity
turn in	(S)	submit
turn on	(S)	start the power
turn out for	(I)	gather for a meeting / event
turn over	(S)	give possession of
turn to	(I)	ask
turn up	(I)	find
walk away (with)	(I)	steal
walk off (with)	(I)	steal
walk out of	(I)	leave
walk out on	(I)	desert
wear away	(I)	disappear
wear down	(S)	lessen the quality or strength
wear out	(S)	become useless
wind down	(S)	work slowly
wind up	(S)	conclude
wipe out	(S)	destroy
wipe up	(S)	remove with a cloth
work way (at)	(I)	continuously make an effort
work off	(S)	remove through work or exercise
work out	(S)	solve; exercise
work up	(I)	excite; develop

A-10   Appendix D

APPENDIX E

VERBS WITH GERUNDS OR INFINITIVES

afford	I **can't afford to buy** that.	believe	How could they **believe him to be** a dishonest person?
admit	He **admitted forgetting** it was their anniversary.	bother	Don't **bother to call** first. Just drop in.
advise	She **advised me to get** the application in early.	care	He didn't **care to talk** about it.
	She **advised getting** the application in early.	cause	The earthquake **caused them to lose** their home.
	Did she **advise them to apply** for work study?		The disease **causes shaking** and **sweating**.
agree	I **agreed to go** to an early movie.	choose	The students **chose to have** a farewell party.
aim	We **aim to please**.		We **chose her to represent** the class.
allow	Her parents don't **allow her to date**.	claim	He **claimed to be** a qualified doctor.
	They don't **allow smoking** in their house.	come	They **came** here **to learn** English.
appear	It **appears to be** a bird's egg.	complete	Have you **completed filling out** the application?
appoint	The government **appointed him to be** an ambassador.	consent	Her parents would not **consent to her living** in an apartment by herself.
appreciate	I don't **appreciate receiving** calls late at night.	consider	Did they **consider him to do** the job?
	She really **appreciated his doing** the laundry.		They are **considering hiring** her for the job.
arrange	Let's **arrange to see** that movie next week.	continue	If you **continue to do** that, you'll be in trouble.
ask	He **asked to borrow** the car.		If you **continue doing** that, you'll be in trouble.
	He **asked his mother to lend** him some money.	control	Can he **control losing** his temper?
attempt	Did they **attempt to reach** their parents by phone?		She **controls her eating** by drinking lots of water.
	Could they even **attempt climbing** the mountain in that weather?	convince	I can't **convince him to go** dancing.
avoid	I **avoided doing** the work until the last moment.	coerce	Could they **coerce her to marry** him?
			She was **coerced to leave** her job.
be	He**'s to get** married in August.	dare	Do you **dare to go** parachuting?
bear	I **can't bear to do** housework.		The older boy **dared the younger ones to steal** apples.
	They **couldn't bear his practicing** the drums.		I don't **dare eat** raw onions.
beg	He **begged to have** his own car.	decide	We **decided to go out** for dinner.
	He **begged his parents to buy** him a car.	declare	The company **declared itself to be** bankrupt.
begin	Did he **begin to understand** the problem between them?		
	Did she **begin learning** yoga?		

(Continued on the next page)

Appendix E

decline	She **declined to marry** him.	enable	My parents **enabled me to go** to college.
decrease	They **decreased hiring** until new orders came in.	encourage	They **encouraged me to work** hard.
	She **decreased her smoking** to one pack a day.	endeavor	They **endeavored to give** me a good education.
defer	They **deferred paying** tuition until the check arrived from home.	endure	We **endured testing**.
			We **endured their singing**.
	The school **deferred her taking** the exam due to the airlines strike.	enjoy	Did you **enjoy singing**?
			Did you **enjoy his singing**?
defy	Her attitude **defies understanding**.	entitle	The degree **entitled her to teach**.
	She **defied her parents to make** her stay home.	escape	We nearly **escaped crashing** into the wall.
delay	Should we **delay fixing** breakfast until she wakes up?	excuse	Can you **excuse arriving** so late?
			Can you **excuse our arriving** so late?
	His parents **delayed his entering** school until he was six years old.	expect	She **expected to be** a working mother.
demand	They **demanded to get** their test results.		They **expect me to be** there by 6:00
deny	He **denied** ever **having met** her.	fail	He **failed to win** the election.
describe	She **described studying** in a foreign country very accurately.	favor	I **favor going out** for dinner.
			Who **favors my fixing** dinner?
	Could you **describe getting** a visa and **taking** the TOEFL?	fear	We **fear dying**.
			We **feared his dying**.
deserve	After all that work, he **deserved to get** a raise.	feel	I **felt him to be** the best choice.
		find	They **found him to be** inadequate for the job.
	After all that work, he **deserved getting** a raise.	finish	Did you **finish studying**?
desire	She **desired to move** into a comfortable old home.		Did she **finish her studying**?
despise	I **despise eating** liver!	forbid	They **forbid her to dance**.
determine	We **determined not to stay** in expensive hotels.		Can they **force you to do** it?
detest	I **detest waiting** in long lines!	forget	I **forgot meeting** him
			I **forgot to meet** him an hour early.
	She **detested his playing** loud music and smoking a cigar.	get	Let's **get going**!
direct	The receptionist **directed them to wait** in the lobby.	give up	She'll never **give up jogging**.
		go	Shall we **go swimming**?
	The therapist **directed her exercising** after the operation.		We **went to get** the new car.
		guess	She **guessed him to be** the manager.
discover	He was **discovered to be** stealing from the company.	happen	I just **happen to have** the right amount.
dislike	I **dislike arguing**.	hate	I **hate to miss** my bus.
	I **dislike his arguing**.		She **hates his smoking**.
dread	I **dread riding** in his car.	hesitate	I **hesitated to interrupt** their conversation.
	I **dread his driving**.	hire	We **hired her to clean** the house weekly.
drive	She **drove him to meet** her parents.		
educate	They **educated him to respect** older people.	hope	I **hope to finish** this by Friday.
empower	She **empowered us to administer** her property.		

imagine	**Imagine not hearing** from them in 10 years.	manage	I **managed to finish** it on time.
	I can't **imagine his saying** that.	mean	Did you **mean to say** that?
	We **imagined him to be** married by now.		I **meant him to get** that money.
			The traffic detour **meant going around** the construction.
implore	They **implored him to be** more serious about his school work.	mind	Do you **mind clearing off** the table?
incite	The mob **incited rioting**.	miss	**I really miss talking** to her.
	A few **incited the audience to demand** more.	motivate	Is he **motivated enough to learn**?
			It **motivated me to get** my work done.
increase	They **increased ads to reach** a bigger market.	need	I **need to talk** to you right away.
	We **increased spending**.		Do you **need me to do** anything?
	We **increased our spending**.		It really **needs cleaning**.
induce	They **induced him to commit** the crime.	neglect	How did you **neglect to tell** me that?
			How did you **neglect telling** me that?
intend	I **intended to write** you months ago.	notify	They **notified us to appear** in court.
	The company **intended her to be** the new president.	object to	I don't **object to doing** it.
			We **objected to his leaving** so early in the evening.
instruct	They **instructed us to keep** our doors locked.	oblige	I felt **obliged to tell** her the turth.
investigate	The police **investigated his leaving** the accident.	offer	Did you **offer to take** them to dinner?
invite	We always **invite them to eat** here on holidays.	omit	They never **omit visiting** her on Sundays.
			They **omitted his having given** a donation in their program.
judge	It was **judged to be** the best.	order	She **ordered the children to clean up** their rooms.
keep	**Keep working** on it. You'll succeed.		
keep from	Don't let me **keep you from doing** your work.	permit	Don't **permit them to leave** without taking some food.
know	I **know it to be** the best hotel in town.		They **permitted dancing** on the gym floor but with shoes off.
lead	She **led him to believe** she was in love with him.	persuade	Can you **persuade them to stay** a few more days?
learn	You can **learn to use** computers there.	plan	I **plan to have** dinner ready by 6:00
		pledge	We **pledge to come up with** the money in six months.
let	**Let me do** it.		
like	I don't **like to do** dishes.	postpone	They **postponed marrying** until December.
	I don't **like doing** all of the housework.		They **postponed her marrying** until she was 21.
	I **like his doing** the housework.	put off	Don't **put off going** to the doctor.
long	He **longed to see** her again.		They **put off their leaving**.
love	He **loved to eat** at her place.	prefer	I **prefer to eat out** tonight.
	He **loved her cooking**.		I'd **prefer you to call** for the pizza.
	She **loved cooking** for him.		I'd **prefer not having** onions on the pizza.
make	Don't **make me do** it.		

(Continued on the next page)

Appendix E A-13

prepare	I'd **prefer your going** to pick it up. Are you **prepared to hear** the truth? They were **preparing him to take** over the company.	return	The kids **returned to get** some different toys. I **returned the shirt** to get my money back.
pretend	She **pretended not to understand**.	risk	Don't **risk losing** all your money gambling. Don't **risk his getting** lost in such a crowd. Stay home.
proceed	She **proceeded to tell** us all of the details.		
promise	I **promise to be** good. I **promised them to be** home by 11:00.	rule	The judge **ruled to give** the boy to his mother.
propose	Do you **propose doing** it by yourself?	save	His hard work **saved hiring** another employee. His hard work **saved their hiring** another employee.
prove	It **proved to be** a very entertaining evening.	say	It **says to soak** the beans in water overnight.
quit	I **quit to see** more of my children. Why did you **quit seeing** him?	see	We **saw him do** it. I can't **see buying** another. Can you **see my doing** it?
recall	I don't **recall having met** him before.	seem	They **seem to be** happy.
refuse	I **refused to do** it.	seek	I never **sought to have** that job.
regret	I will never **regret going** to visit her.	select	They **selected him to represent** them.
remember	Did you **remember to turn off** the lights? Do you **remember him to have been** there? I don't **remember meeting** her that night. I **remember his being** the life of the party.	send	**Send him to do** the job.
		stand	I can't **stand washing** windows. How can you **stand his playing** the music so loud?
		start	It has **started to rain**. It has **started raining**. He has **started his practicing** already.
remind	Please **remind me to send** her that money.	state	They **stated it to be** their best model.
report	We **reported him to have** him arrested.	stimulate	It **stimulated the economy to grow**.
		stop	He **stopped to smoke**. He **stopped smoking**. He **stopped their smoking** in the bedroom.
request	They **requested her to teach** them.		
require	The school **required them to wear** uniforms. They **require wearing** uniforms.	strive	We always **strive to offer** the best service.
resent	I **resent having** to listen to them arguing. I **resented their arguing** in front of us.	struggle	They have **struggled to get by** all their lives.
		swear	Do you **swear to tell** the truth?
		suggest	What do you **suggest doing**? What do you **suggest her doing**?
resist	I couldn't **resist buying** some chocolate. We **resisted their treating** us to dinner.	suppose	It's **supposed to be** the best in town.
		teach	He **taught us to work** hard.
resolve	We **resolved never to eat** there again.	tell	They **told him to pick up** some milk on the way home.
resume	Can we **resume studying** this in the morning? He **resumed his studying** after a dinner break.	tempt	We **tempted her to go out** for the evening with us.
		tend	I **tend to forget**.

think	I always **thought him to be** the best choice.	undertake	They **undertook to build** a house on their own.
train	We **trained the dog to get** the newspaper.	urge	We **urge you to give** money to that cause.
threaten	It has **threatened to rain** all day.		
trust	You can **trust me to be** honest with you.	wait	We **waited to hear** from them late into the night.
try	I've been **trying to reach** you all day.	want	Do you **want to have** some more cake?
	I've **tried reaching** them at various times.		Do you **want me to pick you up** tonight?
		warn	They **warned us to get** home before dark.
understand	It was **understood to be** the last time.	wish	I don't **wish to be** a burden on you.
	I **understand their wanting** to be there.		I **wish him to get** the prize.

APPENDIX F

CONNECTING WORDS

(SC) **Subordinate conjunctions** connect dependent clauses with independent clauses. If the dependent clause comes first, it must have a comma.

Because it's hot, they turned on the fan.
They turned on the fan *because it's hot.*

(P) **Prepositions** are followed by pronouns or noun phrases. If the prepositional phrase comes first, it usually has a comma.

Because of the heat, they turned on the fan.
They turned on the fan *because of the heat.*

(AT) **Adverbial transitions** are words that act as signposts. They show relationships between complete sentences and other parts of the text. They need strong punctuation to set them off.

It was hot. *Consequently,* they turned on the fan.
It was hot; *consequently,* they turned on the fan.
It was hot; they turned on the fan, *consequently.*
It was hot. They, *consequently,* turned on the fan.

Time and Place

Sequential Time	SC	before, up to the time that, by the time that, until (till), once, since, ever since, from the time that	(a) **Before she got married,** she lived at home. (b) She lived at home **up to the time that she got married.** (c) **Until (till) she got married,** she lived at home. (d) **Once she got married,** she moved out of her parents' home.
	P	before, prior to, previous to, until, once, after, since	(e) She traveled a great deal **prior to getting married.** (f) **Previous to her marriage,** she traveled a great deal. (g) **Until marrying,** she traveled a great deal.

Sequential Time	AT	*before*	in the past, formerly, before that, earlier, beforehand	(h)	**In the past,** he enjoyed his life as a single man.
		now	presently, at present, at this point, at this time, nowadays	(i)	He is a happily married man **presently.**
		after	after that, afterward, later, later on, in the future	(j)	He got married; **after that,** his life settled down.
		listing	first, then, next, with that out of the way, eventually, finally, last	(k)	**First,** they found a nice apartment to live in.
		length of time	before long, immediately (thereafter), soon after that	(l)	**Before long,** they decided to start a family.
		change of events	by the / that time, subsequently, thereafter, from then on, following that, since then, previously	(m) (n)	He lost his job. **By that time,** she was ready to return to work. He lost his job. **Subsequently,** she had to support them.
Simultaneous Time	SC		when, whenever, as, while, during the time that, each / every time (that), so long as, as long as	(o)	**When he was at college,** he lived in a dorm.
	P		during, when, whenever, while	(p) (q)	**Whenever he was at college,** he did his own laundry. He lived away from home **during his college years.**
	AT		meanwhile, in the meantime, concurrently, simultaneously, at the same time	(r)	He attended college. He lived in a dorm **meanwhile.**
Place	SC		where, wherever, everywhere	(s)	**Where she looked,** there were no part-time jobs.
	P		where, wherever	(t)	She got part-time work **where possible.**

(Continued on the next page)

Appendix F

Contrast

Direct Opposition	SC	while, whereas	(a) **While she was working,** she was not making much money.
	P	while	(b) **While working hard,** she was not making much money.
	AT	but, and yet, however, in contrast, by way of contrast, by / in comparison, in fact, conversely, on the contrary, on the other hand, when in fact	(c) She was working hard, **but** she was not making much money.
Concession	SC	although, though, even though, while, in spite of the fact that, regardless of the fact that	(d) **Although** it was raining, we still had the picnic.
	P	despite, in spite of, regardless of, although, though, even though, while	(e) We still had the picnic **despite** the rain. (f) **Although** raining, we still had the picnic.
	AT	even so, for all that, granted (this), be that as it may, just the same, nevertheless, nonetheless, regardless, after all, anyhow, anyway	(g) It was wet. **Be that as it may,** we still had fun.
Dismissal and Replacement	P	instead of, rather than	(h) **Instead of** cooking, let's eat out.
	AT	either way, whatever happens, in either case / event, all / just the same, in any case / event, at any rate, no matter how / what, whatever, instead, at least, rather	(i) **Either way,** we'll have Chinese food, OK?

Cause and Effect / Result

Reason	SC	because, as, since, as / so long as, considering that, in that, seeing that, now that, whereas, in view of / due to / because of / owing to / on account of the fact that	(a) He's absent **because** he's sick.
	P	because of, due to, owing to, on account of, in view of, since	(b) **Because of** his illness, he is missing lots of school.

Purpose	SC	so that, so, in order that, in the hope that	(c) He's studying **so that** he can graduate in June.
	AT	with this in mind, with this intention	(d) **With this in mind**, he's been studying hard.
	Other	so as, in order to (followed by an infinitive)	(e) He is studying **so as** to pass the TOEFL.
Result	SC	so . . . that, such a(n) . . . that	(f) He wrote **so** powerfully **that** readers were deeply touched. (g) He wrote **such an** interesting book **that** she couldn't put it down.
	P	as a result of	(h) **As a result of** his writing, many people experienced his homeland.
	AT	consequently, as a result of, thus, in / as a consequence, accordingly, for this reason, so, therefore	(i) **Consequently**, he made a lot of money on the book.

Condition and Consequence

Condition	SC	if, whether (or not), in case that / provided that, on condition that, in the event that, given that, granted that, as / so long as, supposing that, considering that, assuming that, admitting that, presuming that, even if, only if, unless	(a) **If** we don't leave soon, we'll be late. (b) We'll be late **even if** we leave now. (c) **Unless** we leave immediately, we'll miss the bus.
Consequence	AT	in that case, if so, that being the case, under those circumstances, then, otherwise, or else, if not	(d) It may rain. **In that case**, we'll cancel the picnic.

Appendix F

Manner and Comparison

Manner	SC	as if, as though, like, as, to the extent that	(a) They act **as if** they were children. (b) They fought **as** siblings often do.
	P	as	(c) **As** children they lived in England.
	AT	in much the same way, likewise, by the same token, in like manner, similarly, equally	(d) **In much the same way**, they had to start life over again.
Comparison	SC	as . . . as, -er . . . than, more . . . than, the . . . the . . .	(e) They were friendl**ier than** most siblings. (f) **The** more children they had, **the** happier they were.

APPENDIX G

FILES

File 1

Cue Words	Enrico Caruso	Auguste Rodin	Sir Isaac Newton	Sir Winston Churchill
who / be		sculptor		prime minister
when / live	late 19th–early 20th century			late 19th–mid-20th century
where / work		France		
what problem / experience / in school			did poorly in grade school	

File 2

A. Leo Tolstoy
B. Louis Pasteur
C. Napoleon Bonaparte
D. Ludwig van Beethoven
E. Albert Einstein

File 3

Who	Where	What	What
President Kennedy		ride / a motorcade	
Monica Seles	Germany		
Queen Elizabeth	Buckingham Palace		
John Lennon		enter / his apartment building	shoot
Prince Charles			

(Continued on the next page)

Appendix G A-21

File 4

You are an admissions director:

You want to find the applicant who has these qualities:
    loves music, but has a balanced life
    has experience working with other people
    has played an instrument for a long time
    is a good student

Write some questions that you can ask in your interview to find out which student has these qualities. Try not to be too direct, so that the students will answer honestly.

File 5

Ask your partner questions with these cues.

Jackie Kennedy <u>was</u> 31 when she became first lady.
<u>Had there been</u> a First Lady as young as Jackie Kennedy before?

The Kennedy family (be) Roman Catholic

_____ a Roman Catholic ever (be) President?

The Vice-President (take over) when Kennedy died.

_____ a Vice-President ever (take over) before?

Jackie Kennedy (have) a college education.

_____ First Lady (have) a college education?

Answer your partner's questions with these cues.

Someone (shoot) President Abraham Lincoln in 1865.
People (never, see) an assassination on TV before Kennedy's assassination.
No one (ever, have) such young children in the White House before.
A president's widow (never, remarry) before Jackie Kennedy.

File 6

You are applying for admission to this famous college.

These are some of the things to mention about yourself in your interview. You can mention other things, too (that you make up), but be sure to mention these.
    listen to every rock song ever recorded
    go to every concert that comes to your city (you work for the concert hall)
    teach yourself to play guitar and drums

File 7

Find out the answers to these questions:

    Did Raymond North need money?

    Who owned the murder weapon?

You know these facts:

    Mr. North was shot.

    Mrs. North was at the bank.

File 8

You are applying for admission to this famous college.

These are some of the things to mention about yourself in your interview. You can mention other things, too (that you make up), but be sure to mention these.

> write music for the classical guitar
> think about a career as a music teacher for children
> sing in the church choir all your life

File 9

Find out the answers to these questions:

> Did Mr. North leave all his money to Mrs. North?
>
> Where was Angel North at the time of the murder?

You know these facts:

> The Norths had two sons, Raymond and Angel.
>
> Raymond North's business is about to go bankrupt because it owes $1.5 million to the bank and cannot pay.

File 10

1. Canada (*Canadian*)
2. China (*Chinese*)
3. Colombia (*Colombian*)
4. Japan (*Japanese*)
5. Russia (*Russian*)
6. France (*French*)
7. Switzerland (*Swiss*)
8. Spain (*Spanish*)
9. Sweden (*Swedish*)
10. Mexico (*Mexican*)
11. Brazil (*Brazilian*)
12. Italy (*Italian*)
13. England (*English*)
14. the United States (*American*)

File 11

Find out the answers to these questions:

> Where was Mrs. North at the time of the murder?
>
> Did the Norths have any children?

You know this fact:

> Mrs. North is independently wealthy.

File 12

Ask your partner questions with these cues.

Someone (shoot) John Kennedy.

_____ anyone (ever, shoot) a U.S. president before?

People (watch) the assassination on TV.

_____ people (watch) an assassination of a President?

The Kennedys (have) two small children.

_____ (be) small children in the White House?

Jackie Kennedy (remarry).

_____ a President's widow (ever, remary)?

Answer your partner's questions with these cues.

No First Lady (be) younger than 31 before Jackie Kennedy.
No President (ever, be) Roman Catholic before Kennedy.
A Vice-President (take over) when other presidents (die) in office.
Several First Ladies (have) a college education before Jackie Kennedy.

File 13

You are applying for admission to this famous college.
These are some of the things to mention about yourself in your interview. You can mention other things, too (that you make up), but be sure to mention these.

play the trumpet in the school orchestra since you were 11 years old
consider a career as a doctor, but decide to be a musician
be class president for the last three years

File 14

	Tuesday	Wednesday
9:00		
12:00		
2:00	arrive at the San Regis Hotel	attend a presentation on food aid
3:30	register for the conference	
4:30	meet with the Planning Committee	go through the exhibits
7:00	speech–Director of World Relief	

File 15

	Saturday	Sunday
morning		study
afternoon	go shopping?	
evening		dinner with friends

Partner B: Make suggestions and invitations for these three activities: play tennis
go out for dinner
go to the beach

Use these expressions: *Maybe we could . . .*
Why don't we . . .
Would you like to . . .

Figure out where you will meet, who will drive, etc.

File 16

Partner A: Invite your partner for these activities: walk around to see the city
have dinner

File 17

Find out the answer to these questions:

Where was Raymond North at the time of the murder?

Did Mrs. North need money?

You know these facts:

Angel North is a gambler who owes almost $1 million dollars to the Mafia.

In his will, Mr. North divided his $3 billion equally between the members of his family.

File 18

Partner B: Invite your partner for these activities: get some coffee
have lunch

Appendix G

File 19

	Saturday	**Sunday**
morning	do the laundry clean the apartment	have brunch with friends
afternoon	tennis	
evening	study?	study

Partner A: Make suggestions and invitations for these three activities: go for a hike
go out for coffee
go to see a movie

Use these expressions: *Maybe we could . . .*
Do you want to . . .
How about . . .

Figure out where you will meet, who will drive, etc.

File 20

Find out the answers to these questions:

How was Mr. North murdered?

Did Angel North need money?

You know these facts:

Raymond North was at work at the time of the murder.

Mrs. North owned the murder weapon.

File 21

1. Nelson Mandela of South Africa
2. Ayrton Senna of Brazil
3. Kevin Costner
4. Arnold Schwarzenegger
5. Princess Stephanie of Monaco
6. *Mona Lisa*
7. Sherpas
8. Apple Computer

File 22

Invention	the elevator	Velcro	
When		1954	1843
Who	Elisha Otis		
Where		Switzerland	

File 23

Year	Number of Home Computers
1982	
	5,100,000
1989	
	6,400,000
Year	Percent of Household with Computers
1990	
	33%

File 24

	Monday	Tuesday	Wednesday
9:00		register for the conference	breakfast with Frieda and Karl
12:00		meet with Alex	lunch with Carl and Suzanne
2:00		attend a presentation on family planning	attend a presentation on food aid
2:30	arrive in Paris Hotel Napoleon		
3:30		attend a presentation on farmer education	
4:30		go through the exhibits	
7:00		speech–Director of World Relief	

INDEX

A, an, 133
A number of / the number of, 24
Ability, 128, 169
    be able to, 128
    can, 128
    could, 129
Academic writing, 140
Act, 323
Action
    began in the past, 36
    completed in the past, 40
    continued, see Continuous tenses
    finished, 15
    happening now, 2, 32, 36
    incomplete, 32
    intended in the past, 68
    interrupted, 21, 45
    length, 160
    non-action, see Non-continuous verbs
    not completed in the past, 32
    relevant to another, 40, 160
    repeated, 15, 45, 62, 132
    temporary, 62
Active voice, 140
    active participial adjectives, 150
Adjective clauses, see Clauses
Adjectives, 49, 179, 321, 323, 328
    + to + present participle, 116
    active participial, 150
    passive participial, 150
    with false subject it, 198
    with too, enough, 197
Adverb clauses, see Clauses
Adverbial transitions, 276, 278, 285, 289, 297, 312
    after that vs. after, 299
    anyway, anyhow, after all, 286
    if not, 312
    on the contrary, 286
    on the other hand, 286
    or else, 312
    otherwise, 312
    when in fact, 297
Adverbs, 49, 262
    frequency, 5
        always, 5
        every time, 5
        never, 5
        occasionally, 5
        often, 5
        once a week / day, 6
        rarely, 5
        seldom, 5
        sometimes, 6
    in comparatives, superlatives, 26, 49
    negative adverbs, 5
        never, 5
        position in sentence, 5
        rarely, 5
        relative, 233
        seldom, 5
        with too, enough, 197
Advice, 81, 168, 264
    had better, 78
    ought to, 78
    should, 78
    should have, 81
Advise, 265
After, 41, 274
    vs. after that, 297
Ago, 15
Agree, 9
Agreement
    subject-verb 5, 24, 96, 242
All, whole, 242
All right, 123
Already, 33, 41
Always, 5
Another, 49
Anyway, anyhow, after all, 286
Appear, 12
Arrive, 59
Articles, 13, 96, 114, 133, 153, 177, 198, 218
As, 21
As if / as though, 323
As soon as, 274
Ask, 265
Aspect, 160
Attempt, 207

Bad / badly, worse, the worst, 26
Barely, 41
Be, 2, 5, 9, 15, 62, 107, 140, 142, 240, 295, 305, 325
Be able to, 128, 318
Be going to, 55, 62
Be supposed to, 90
Be to, 90
Be used to, 133

Because, 289
Because of, 289
Been, 36, 45, 65
Before, 41, 274, 276
Behave, 323
Believe, 12
Belong, 12
By the time (that), 41, 65

Can, 128, 254
Can't have, 110
Causatives, 148, 189
Cause-result clauses, see Clauses, adverb clauses
Clauses
    adjective clauses, 224
        either of which / whom, neither of which / whom, 238
        expressions of quantity, 238
        fronting preposition, 229
        object of preposition, 229
        omitting relative pronouns, 226, 229, 235
        one of the, the only one, 242
        possession, 231
        reducing, 240
        relative adverbs, 233
        relative pronouns, 224, 226, 229, 231
        replacing object, 226
        replacing subject, 224
        restrictive, 235
    adverb clauses, 274
        after, 274
        as soon as, 274
        because, 289
        before, 274
        cause-result clauses, 289
        concession clauses, 285
        contrast clauses, 285
        everywhere, 281
        in order that / to, 290
        now that, 289
        once, 274
        place clauses, 281
        reduced adverb clauses, 295

Index   I-1

sequential time clauses,
      54, 274
   simultaneous time
      clauses, 278
   since, 274, 289
   so . . . that, 289
   so / as long as, 278
   so that, 290
   such (a) . . . that, 289
   until, 274
   when, 278
   whenever, 278
   where, 281
   whereas, 285
   wherever, 281
   while, 278, 285
  conditional clauses, 302
   even if, 312
   implied conditionals, 321
   mixed time conditionals,
      315
   modals in conditionals, 318
   only if, 312
   real conditionals, 302, 323
   reduced conditionals, 321
   tense in, 59
   unless, 312
   unreal conditionals, 305,
      308, 315, 323
   whether or not, 312
   wishes, 325
  manner clauses, 323
   as if / as though, 323
  noun clauses, 248
   -ever words, 258
   expressions of urgency, 264
   reducing, 254
   reported speech, 261
   that clauses, 249
   the fact that, 249
   wh- question clauses, 254
   whether / if clauses, 251
Come, 59
Command, 265
Comparatives, 26
Complement of a verb, 182, 184, 204
Concession clauses, *see Clauses, adverb clauses*
Condition, 125
Conditional clauses, *see Clauses, conditional clauses*
Conjunctions, *see Subordinate conjunctions*
Consider, 248
Continuous tenses, 2, 21, 36, 45, 62, 64, 142, 160, 165

Contrast clauses, *see Clauses, adverb clauses*
Conversational, spoken, or informal English, 28, 54, 83, 105, 125, 148, 215, 226, 242, 261, 265, 286
Cost, 9
Could, 102, 110, 120, 123, 128, 254, 261, 290, 318
Could have, 131
Count nouns, 26, 114, 133
Custom, 4

Definitions, 4
Demand, 265
Depart, 59
Desire, 265
Determination, 54
Did, 15
Direct object, *see Object*
Distancers
  Do, does, 5
  Doubt, 9
  Do vs. make, 177
  Do you think, 121, 123
  Due to, 289
  During, 278
  in permission, 123
  in requests, 20

Each, every, each of the, 24
Each other, 49
Either of which / whom, 238
Enough, 197
Even if, 312
-Ever words, 258
Ever, 41
Every time, 5
Everywhere, 281
Expectation, 90, 168
  be supposed to, 90
  be to, 90
  had better have, 92
  was / were supposed to (have), 92
Explain, 248
Expressions of quantity, 242
  in adjective clauses, 238
Expressions of urgency, 264

False subject *it*, 182, 190, 198, 249
Far, farther, the farthest, 26
Feel, 9, 189
Few vs. a few, 71
Fewer, the fewest, 26
Find, 12

Fly, 59
For, 45, 65, 190
Forget, 209, 248
Formal or written English, 54, 83, 90, 105, 125, 209, 215, 226, 229, 231, 261, 285
From . . . to . . ., 15
Future tenses
  future continuous, 62
  future in the past, 68
  future perfect, 64
  future perfect continuous, 64
  in conditional clauses, 59
  in time clauses, 59
  passive, 142
  present tenses as, 59
  simple future, 54
  with transition verbs, 59

General fact or truth, 4, 125, 249, 261
Gerunds, 182
  as complements, 204, 207, 209
  as nouns, 212
  as objects of prepositions, 212
  forms, 216
  have exressions + gerund, 218
  objects of, 215
  modifying, 215
  possessive form, 215
  to + gerund, 218
  verbs that take infinitive or, 207
  verbs that take infinitives but change in meaning, 209
Get, 148
Get used to, 133
Go, 59
Good / well, better, best, 26

Habit, 4
Had, 41, 45
Had better, 78
Had better have, 92
Happen to, 318
Have, 9, 32, 36, 65, 148, 189
Have got to, 83
Have to, 83
Head, 59
Hear, 12, 189
Help, 189
Hope, 9
  vs. wishes, 325
How
  wh- question noun clauses, 254
How about, 102, 105
However, 258

If, 248, 251, 302, 305, 308, 312, 318
If not, 312
Imagine, 248
Imperatives
   directions, orders, warnings, 20
   obligation, 83
Include, 12
Indirect object, *see* Object
Indirect speech, *see* Reported speech
Infinitives, 125, 182, 265, 323,
   as reduced noun clauses, 254
   forms, 193
   noun phrase + infinitive, 187
   of, for with infinitives, 198
   reduced, 198
   verbs which take, 184, 187
   with *too, enough,* 197
   without *to,* 189
In order that / to, 290
In the . . . 's, 17
In the past week, month, year, 33
Inform, 248
Instead vs. *instead of,* 297
Intend, 207
Interested in, 105
Invitations, 55, 105, 168
It as a false subject, 182, 191, 198, 249

Just, 36, 41

Kind, sort, type, 96
Know, 9

Last week / month / year, 15
Lately, 33
Less, the least, 26
Let, 189
Let's, 102, 105
Like, 218
Like better than, 125
Listen to, 189
Little vs. *a little,* 71
Logical conclusions
   can't have, 110
   must, 107
   must have, 110
Look, 323
Look at, 189

Maintain, 248
Make, 189
   vs. *do,* 177
Matter, 12
May, 107, 261, 290, 318

May have, 110
Maybe, 110
Mean, 209
Might, 102, 107, 128, 261, 290, 318
Might have, 110, 318
Modals
   be able to, 128
   can, 128
   can't have, 110
   could, 102, 107, 120, 123, 129, 290
   could have, 110, 131
   had better, 78
   had better have, 92
   have got to, 83
   have to, 83
   in conditionals, 318
   in reported speech, 261
   may, 107, 290
   may have, 110
   might, 102, 107, 290
   might have, 110, 318
   must, 83, 107
   must have, 110
   ought to, 79
   ought to have, 81
   passive, 142, 165
   review of modals, 168
   shall, 103
   should, 78, 102, 290
   should have, 81
   would, 105, 120
More, the most, 26
Most vs. *almost, the most, most of,* 49
Must, 84, 107
Must have, 110

Necessity, 83, 168
Need, 9
Negative adverbs, *see* Adverbs, negative adverbs
Negatives, 5
Neither of which / whom, 238
Never, 5, 41
Non-continuous verbs, 8, 12, 36, 45, 62, 160
Non-count nouns, 26, 71, 133, 153
Non-restrictive clauses, 235, 238
None of the, 24
Notice, 189
Noun clauses, *see* Clauses, noun clauses
Noun phrase, 105, 276
   preposition +, 276, 278, 289, 297
   verb + NP + infinitive, 187
   verbs of perception + NP +

   gerund / base form, 189
Nouns
   Count, *see* Count nouns
   gerunds as, 212
   in comparatives and superlatives, 26
   mass, *see* Non-count nouns
   non-count, *see* Non-count nouns
   proper, 235
   with *too, enough,* 197
Now, 3
Now that, 289
Number of, 24
Numbers and numerical expressions, 153

Object, 140, 148
Obligation, 83, 168
   don't / doesn't have to, 86
   has / have to, 83
   have got to, 83
   imperatives as, 83
   must, 83
   must not, 86
Observe, 189
Occasionally, 5
Often, 5
Omit *being,* 295
On the contrary, 286
On the other hand, 286
Once, 274
Once a week / day / year, 5
One another, 49
One of the, the only one, 242
Only if, 312
Opinion, 78, 168
Opportunity, 129
Opposition, 285
Or else, 312
Or not, 251
Orders, 264
Other(s), the others, another, each other, one another, 49
Otherwise, 312
Ought to, 78
Ought to have, 81

Parallel form, 218
Participle
   past, 32, 41, 65, 81, 105, 110, 140
   present, 2, 21, 36, 45, 62, 65, 105, 107, 240
Passive voice, 140, 148, 187
   forms, 142, 165
   gerunds, 216
   have, get as passives, 148

Index I-3

infinitives, 193
passive participial adjectives, 150
review of passive, 165
Past habit, 132, 169
   be used to, 133
   used to, 133
   would, 132
Past tenses
   passive, 142, 165
   past continuous, 21
   past perfect, 41
   past perfect continuous, 45
   simple past, 15
Percentages, 153
Perfect tenses, 32, 36, 40, 45, 64, 142, 160, 165, 302, 308
Permission, 123, 169
   all right, 123
   can, 123
   could, 123
   do you think, 123
   may, 123
   would, 123
Phrasal adjectives, *see* Phrasal expressions
Phrasal expressions with
   about, 97
   about, on, by, 298
   after, between, behind, ahead, back, 243
   at, 74
   away from, away, out of, out, 269
   down, 200
   for, 328
   from, 116
   in(to), 28
   of, 178
   on, 50
   through, across, along, 220
   to, 116, 218
   up, 136, 157
Phrasal verbs, *see* Phrasal expressions
Plan, 207
Plans and intentions, 54
Please, 120
Politeness, 102, 105, 120, 123
Possibility, 107, 110, 168, 318
   could, 107
   could have, 131
   may, 107
   may have, 110
   might, 107
   might have, 110
Possibly, 123
Prediction, 54
Preferences, 125, 169

prefer, 125, 265
prefer it if, 125
prefer that, 125
would prefer, 125
would rather, 125
Preposition + noun phrases, 276
   because of, 289
   despite, 285
   due to, 289
   during, 278
   in spite of, 285
   instead of, 297
   regardless of, 297
Prepositional phrases, 323
Prepositions
   about, 97, 298
   above, 97
   across, 220
   after, 243
   against, 298
   ahead, 243
   along, alongside, 220
   among, 243
   around, 97, 298
   as, 328
   at, 27, 74
   away from, 269
   back, 243
   because of, 289
   before, 243
   behind, 243
   below, 97
   beneath, 97
   beyond, 243, 298
   by, 140, 178, 298
   despite, 285
   down, 200
   due to, 289
   during, 278
   except, 178
   for, 33, 45, 65, 191, 198, 328
   from, 116, 269
   from . . . to, 116
   fronting, 229, 233
   in spite of, 285
   in(to), 27, 28, 74, 298
   instead of, 297
   like, 323, 328
   near, 298
   of, 178, 198, 238
   of location, 27
   on, 27, 50, 74, 298, 328
   out of, 269
   over, 97
   regardless of, 297
   since, 33, 45, 65
   than, 125

through, throughout, 220
to, 116, 125, 184, 198, 218
towards, 116
under, underneath, 97
up, upon, 136, 157
with, 178
with adjectives, 97, 116
without, 178
Present tenses
   in conditional clauses, 302
   in time clauses, 274
   passive, 142, 165
   present continuous, 2
   present perfect, 33, 274
   present perfect continuous, 36
   simple present, 4
Pretend, 248
Probability, 107, 168
   could, 107
   may, 107
   might, 107
Probably, 107, 110
Promise, 54
Pronouns
   in reported speech, 262
   relative pronouns, 224
Prove, 12
Punctuation, 235, 274, 276, 278, 285, 290, 312
Purpose, 289

Questions, 2, 15
Quite a few / a little, 71

Rarely, 5
Rather than, 297
Recently, in recent years, 33, 41
Recommend, 265
Reductions
   adjective clauses, 240
   adverb clauses, 295
   conditional clauses, 321
   noun clauses, 254
Refusal, 54
Regardless of, 297
Regret, 209
Relative adverbs, 233
Relative pronouns, 224
Remember, 12, 209, 218, 248
Remind, 218
Reply, 248
Reported speech, 261
Requests, 54, 123, 169, 264
   responses to, 123
Require, 12, 265
Restrictive, non-restrictive clauses, 235

Sail, 59
Say, 248, 267
Scarcely, 41
See, 9, 189
Seem, 323
Seldom, 5
Sequence of events, 41
Sequence of tenses, 261
Shall, 103
Should happen to, 318
Should, 78, 102, 128, 254, 318
Should have, 81
Simple tenses 4, 15, 142, 160, 165
Since, 33, 45, 65, 274, 289
Smell, 12
So / as long as, 278
So far, 33
So that, 290
So . . . that, 289
Sometimes, 5
Sound, 9
Start, 59
State, 248
Stop, 209
Spelling rules
    comparatives, superlatives, 26
    present continuous, 2
    simple past, 15
Stative verbs, *see Non-continuous verbs*
Still, 41
Subordinate conjunctions
    after, 41, 274
    as if / as though, 323
    as soon as, 274
    because, 289
    before, 41, 274
    by the time (that), 41, 65
    even if, 312
    everywhere, 281
    if, 251
    in order that / to, 290
    now that, 289
    omitting, 295
    once, 274
    only if, 312
    since, 274, 289
    so / as long as, 278
    so that, 290
    so . . . that, 289
    such (a) . . . that, 289
    unless, 312
    until, 274
    when, 278
    whenever, 278
    where, 281
    whereas, 285
    wherever, 281
    whether, 251
    whether or not, 312
    while, 278, 285
Such (a) . . . that, 289
Suggestions, 102, 168, 264
    could, 102
    how about, 102
    let's, 102
    might, 102
    shall, 103
    should, 103
    why don't, 102, 105
Superlatives, 26, 49
Suppose, 12
    vs. be supposed to, 96

Taste, 12
Tell, 248
    vs. say, 267
Tenses
    changing in clauses, 249
    formal sequence of, 261
    future
        continuous, 62
        in conditional clauses, 59
        in the past, 68
        in time clauses, 59
        passive, 142, 165
        perfect, 64
        perfect continuous, 64
        present tenses as, 59
        simple, 54
        with transition verbs, 59
    past
        continuous, 21
        passive, 142, 165
        perfect, 40, 308
        perfect continuous, 45
        simple, 15, 305
    present
        continuous, 2
        passive, 142, 165
        perfect, 33, 302
        perfect continuous, 36
        simple, 4, 302
    review of tenses, 160
Than, 125
That, 224, 226, 229, 235, 240
    that clauses, 248, 249, 267
The, 73, 96, 114, 153, 177, 198, 218
The more, the . . . -er, 26
The only one, one of the, 242
Think, 12, 248
Time
    specific, 15, 21, 125, 129
    unspecified, 32
Time clauses, *see Clauses, adverb clauses*
Time expressions,
    after, 41
    ago, 15
    already, 33, 41
    as, 21
    at present / this moment, 3
    barely, 41
    before, 41
    by the time (that), 41, 65
    currently, 3
    ever, 41
    for, 33, 45
    from . . . to . . . , 15
    in the . . . 's, 15
    in the past week, month, year, 33
    just, 36, 41
    last week / month / year, 15
    lately, 33
    never, 41
    now, 32
    recently, in recent years, 33, 41
    right now, 2
    scarcely, 41
    since, 33, 45
    so far, 33
    still, 41
    these days, 3
    this month, year, 3
    today, 3
    up until now, 33
    while, 21
    yet, 33, 41
To + grrund, 116
Too with infinitives, 197
Transitions, adverbial, *see Adverbial transitions*
Transitive verbs, 148
Trust, 12
Try, 209
Two-word verbs, *see Phrasal expressions*

Understand, 9, 248
Unfulfilled potential / possibility, 131, 169
    could have, 131
Unless, 312, 321
Until, 274
Up until now, 33
Urge, 265
Urgency, *see Expressions of urgency*
Used to, 132, 133

Verbs
  attitudes, 9, 12
  causatives, 148, 189
  condition, 9, 12
  emotions, 9, 12
  irregular, 15
  mental perception, 9, 12
  non-continuous, *see* Non-continuous verbs
  perception, 9, 12, 189
  physical sensation, 9, 12
  possession, 9, 12
  reporting and mental activity, 248
  phrasal, *see* Phrasal expressions
  stative, *see* Non-continuous verbs
  transition, 59
  transitive, 148
  urgency, 265

Want, 9
Was / were, 15, 21
was / were going to, 68
Was / were (to) / (about to), 68
Watch, 189

Were, 305, 325
Were about to, were to, 68
Wh- question clauses, 248, 254
What, 5, 15, 254
Whatever, 258
When
  relative adverb, 233
  subordinate conjunction, 278
  wh- question noun clauses, 254
When in fact, 297
Whenever, 258, 278
Where
  conjunctive adverb, 281
  relative adverb, 233
  wh- question noun clauses, 254
Whereas, 285
Wherever, 258, 281
Whether or not, 312
Whether / if clauses, 248, 251, 321
Which, 5, 224, 226, 229, 233, 240
  noun + *of which*, 231
  wh- question noun clauses, 254
Whichever, 258
While
  contrast, 285
  time, 278

time word, 3, 21
Who, 5, 15, 224, 226, 240, 254
Whoever, 258
Whole, all, 242
Whom, 226, 229, 254, 267
Whomever, 258
Whose, 231, 254
Why
  relative adverb, 233
  wh- question noun clauses, 254
Why don't, 102, 105
Will
  future, 55, 62, 65, 128
  request, 120
  willingness, 54, 120, 318
Willingness, 54, 120, 318
Wishes, 325,
  vs. hopes, 325
Word order, 5, 248
Would, 68, 105, 120, 125, 132, 305
Would prefer, would rather, 125
Would you mind, 120, 123

Yes / no questions, 251
Yet, 33, 41